W9-BIT-636

From Discussion to Writing

Instructional Resources for Teaching

America Now

Short Readings from Recent Periodicals

From Discussion to Writing

Instructional Resources for Teaching

America Now

Short Readings from Recent Periodicals

Ninth Edition

Edited by

Robert Atwan
Emerson College

Prepared by

Valerie Duff-Strautmann

Jeffrey Ousborne
Suffolk University

Gregory Atwan

Bedford/St. Martin's   Boston ♦ New York

Copyright © 2011, 2009, 2007, 2005 by Bedford/St. Martin's

All rights reserved.

Instructors who have adopted *America Now: Short Readings from Recent Periodicals*, Ninth Edition, as a textbook for a course are authorized to duplicate portions of this manual for their students.

Manufactured in the United States of America.

6 5 4 3 2 1
f e d c b a

For information, write: Bedford/St. Martin's, 75 Arlington Street, Boston, MA 02116 (617-399-4000)

ISBN: 978-0-312-60265-9

Contents

Preface xiii

Introduction: Writing and the Art of Discussion
  by Robert Atwan xv

Forming Forums: Student Presentations to
Encourage Research, Discussion, and Better Writing
  by Liz deBeer xxv

1. What's in a Name? 1

2. Happiness: Can It Be Defined? 16

3. Is There an Ethics of Eating? 27

4. Photography: Can We Believe What We See? 38

5. What Do We Fear? 50

6. How Is Today's Media Altering Our Language? 61

7. Gender Roles: Should Women Act More Like Men? 73

8. Does Our Need for Security Threaten Our Right to Privacy? 89

9. Barack Obama: What Does His Election Mean to America? 105

10. Social Networking—How Is It Transforming Behavior? 118

11. Saving the Planet: Is It Too Late? 130

12. Immigration: Who Is an American? 141

A Rhetorical
Table of Contents

America Now includes numerous examples of rhetorical strategies that aid us in expressing ourselves clearly, cogently, and convincingly. Listed below are eight of the most common rhetorical categories with a brief account of how they are generally used in both verbal and visual texts. Nearly every selection in the book relies on more than one category, so you will find that several selections appear multiple times. The selections listed are those that most effectively demonstrate—either in whole or in their various segments—a particular strategy. Page numbers refer to the textbook.

R. A.

1 *NARRATION* Some uses: telling a story; reporting or summarizing a sequence of events; constructing a historical chronology; recounting a biography or autobiography; detailing how something is done or comes about; breaking down a process into a sequence of events.

Adriana Barton *If You're Happy and You Know It, You're in Third*, 83
Ira Berlin *Migrations Forced and Free*, 356
Liz Breslin *Does a Family Need to Share a Surname? (Yes)*, 65
Mary Katharine Ham *We Shall Overshare*, 280
Tom Hewitt *Learning from Tison (student essay)*, 91
Vicente Martinez *The Crossing*, 336
Diane McKinney-Whetstone *The First Family*, 251
Luis J. Rodríguez *Slurring Spanish*, 345
Jeffrey Rosen *Nude Awakening*, 227
Clay Shirky *A Rant about Women*, 201
Brian Jay Stanley *Confessions of a Carnivore*, 109
Elizabeth Stone *Grief in the Age of Facebook*, 291
Elyse Toplin *Uniting Families (student essay)*, 350
Garry Trudeau *Hi, Dad*, 277
Erica Zucco *Quit Living in Swine Fear (student essay)*, 161

2   *DESCRIPTION*   Some uses: creating a picture in word or image; making information more clear or vivid; reporting objective details.

Chris Clarke   *How to Write an Incendiary Blog Post*, 190
Jeff Goodell   *Warming Gets Worse*, 309
Tom Jacobs   *Romance Novel Titles Reveal Readers' Desires*, 221
Vicente Martinez   *The Crossing*, 336
Diane McKinney-Whetstone   *The First Family*, 251
Patrick Olsen   *Does Your Pickup Truck Have a Nickname?*, 49
John Edgar Wideman   *Street Corner Dreamers*, 256
Pearl Wong   *Obama—President for All (student essay)*, 261

3   *EXEMPLIFICATION*   Some uses: providing a "for instance" or "for example"; illustrating ideas; making something abstract more concrete; representing a larger concept or event by a single incident or image.

Liz Breslin   *Does a Family Need to Share a Surname? (Yes)*, 65
Kim Elsesser   *And the Gender-Neutral Oscar Goes To . . .* , 211
Daniel Gilbert   *What You Don't Know Makes You Nervous*, 79
Jay Griffiths   *The Tips of Your Fingers*, 241
Mary Katharine Ham   *We Shall Overshare*, 280
Christopher Hedges   *Celebrity Culture and the Obama Brand*, 266
Tom Jacobs   *Romance Novel Titles Reveal Readers' Desires*, 221
Tamar Jacoby   *Does Immigration Increase the Virtues of Hard Work and Fortitude in the United States? (Yes)*, 330
Steven D. Levitt and Stephen J. Dubner   *What Should You Worry About?*, 151
Yevgeniya Lomakina   *"Going Green" Misses the Point (student essay)*, 317
Erin McKean   *Redefining Definition*, 179
Bill McKibben   *Waste Not Want Not*, 301
Rebecca Mead   *What Do You Call It?*, 30
Shannon Morgan   *Defending Camelot: Chivalry Is Not Dead (student essay)*, 215
Luis J. Rodríguez   *Slurring Spanish*, 345
Warwick Sabin   *The Rich Get Thinner, the Poor Get Fatter*, 101
Irwin Savodnik   *All Crisis, All the Time*, 156
Clay Shirky   *A Rant about Women*, 201
Elizabeth Stone   *Grief in the Age of Facebook*, 291
Cal Thomas   *Sinking "Climate Change,"* 313
Clive Thompson   *The New Literacy*, 173

Garry Trudeau   *Hi, Dad,* 277
John Edgar Wideman   *Street Corner Dreamers,* 256
Laura Williamson   *Does a Family Need to Share a Surname? (No),* 69

4   DEFINITION   Some uses: clarifying key terms; reflecting on the significance of a word; enlarging or restricting a term's meaning; eliminating confusion or ambiguity; challenging conventional meanings and euphemisms.

Brent Baughman   *Growing Older in the Digital Age: An Exercise in Egotism (student essay),* 285
Ira Berlin   *Migrations Forced and Free,* 356
Ann Friedman   *Swagger Like Us,* 207
Rob Haggart   *This Photo Is Lying to You,* 127
Tom Jacobs   *Romance Novel Titles Reveal Readers' Desires,* 221
Rebecca Mead   *What Do You Call It?,* 53
Shannon Morgan   *Defending Camelot: Chivalry Is Not Dead (student essay),* 215
Jed Perl   *Picture Imperfect,* 134
Irwin Savodnik   *All Crisis, All the Time,* 156

5   CLASSIFICATION AND DIVISION   Some uses: dividing a subject into several key parts; organizing material into categories; making distinctions; constructing outlines; arranging ideas in the most appropriate order; viewing an issue from its various sides.

Brent Baughman   *Growing Older in the Digital Age: An Exercise in Egotism (student essay),* 285
Ira Berlin   *Migrations Forced and Free,* 356
Chris Clarke   *How to Write an Incendiary Blog Post,* 190
Ann Friedman   *Swagger Like Us,* 207
Mary Katharine Ham   *We Shall Overshare,* 280
Christopher Hedges   *Celebrity Culture and the Obama Brand,* 266
Tom Jacobs   *Romance Novel Titles Reveal Readers' Desires,* 221
Mark Krikorian   *Does Immigration Increase the Virtues of Hard Work and Fortitude in the United States? (No),* 333
Shannon Morgan   *Defending Camelot: Chivalry Is Not Dead (student essay),* 215
Patrick Olsen   *Does Your Pickup Truck Have a Nickname?,* 49
Jed Perl   *Picture Imperfect,* 134
Clay Shirky   *A Rant about Women,* 201

Elizabeth Stone   *Grief in the Age of Facebook*, 291
Elizabeth Svokos   *Head to Head—Print Photographs (student essay)*, 141
Elyse Toplin   *Uniting Families (student essay)*, 350
Pearl Wong   *Obama—President for All (student essay)*, 261

6   *COMPARISON AND CONTRAST*   Some uses: finding
similarities among different things or ideas; finding differences
among similar things or ideas; organizing material through point-
by-point resemblance or disparity; forming analogies; expressing
a preference for one thing or position over another.

Brent Baughman   *Growing Older in the Digital Age: An Exercise
    in Egotism (student essay)*, 285
Ira Berlin   *Migrations Forced and Free*, 356
Ann Friedman   *Swagger Like Us*, 207
Jeff Goodell   *Warming Gets Worse*, 309
Mary Katharine Ham   *We Shall Overshare*, 280
Mark Krikorian   *Does Immigration Increase the Virtues of Hard Work and
    Fortitude in the United States? (No)*, 333
Rebecca Rosen   *This Is Your Brain on the Web*, 177
Irwin Savodnik   *All Crisis, All the Time*, 156
Clay Shirky   *A Rant about Women*, 201
Elizabeth Stone   *Grief in the Age of Facebook*, 291
Elizabeth Svokos   *Head to Head—Print Photographs (student essay)*, 141

7   *CAUSE AND EFFECT*   Some uses: identifying the cause
of an event or trend; examining how one thing has influenced
another; looking at the consequences of an action or idea;
assigning credit, blame, or responsibility.

Ira Berlin   *Migrations Forced and Free*, 356
Kim Elsesser   *And the Gender-Neutral Oscar Goes To . . .*, 211
Ann Friedman   *Swagger Like Us*, 207
Rob Haggart   *This Photo Is Lying to You*, 127
Steven D. Levitt and Stephen J. Dubner   *What Should You Worry
    About?*, 151
Walter Mosley   *Get Happy*, 86
Jed Perl   *Picture Imperfect*, 134
Irwin Savodnik   *All Crisis, All the Time*, 156
Clay Shirky   *A Rant about Women*, 201
Elizabeth Svokos   *Head to Head—Print Photographs (student essay)*, 141
Erica Zucco   *Quit Living in Swine Fear (student essay)*, 161

8   *ARGUMENT AND PERSUASION*   Some uses: convincing someone that an opinion is correct; defending or refuting a position; gaining support for a course of action; making proposals; resolving conflicts to reach consent or consensus. (At the end of the following list, you will find a collection of the Debates in *America Now*.)

Adriana Barton   *If You're Happy and You Know It, You're in Third*, 83

Brittany Bergstrom   *The Fighting Sioux: The End of a Legacy? (student essay)*, 57

Ira Berlin   *Migrations Forced and Free*, 356

Liz Breslin   *Does a Family Need to Share a Surname? (Yes)*, 65

Amy Domini   *Why Investing in Fast Food May Be a Good Thing*, 105

Kim Elsesser   *And the Gender-Neutral Oscar Goes To . . .* , 211

Ann Friedman   *Swagger Like Us*, 207

Daniel Gilbert   *What You Don't Know Makes You Nervous*, 79

Jeff Goodell   *Warming Gets Worse*, 309

Jay Griffiths   *The Tips of Your Fingers*, 241

Rob Haggart   *This Photo Is Lying to You*, 127

Mary Katharine Ham   *We Shall Overshare*, 280

Aprille Hanson   *Stop Relying on Bloggers for News (student essay)*, 183

Christopher Hedges   *Celebrity Culture and the Obama Brand*, 266

Tamar Jacoby   *Does Immigration Increase the Virtues of Hard Work and Fortitude in the United States? (Yes)*, 330

Mohammed Khan   *The Need for Safety Is Paramount (student essay)*, 236

Mark Krikorian   *Does Immigration Increase the Virtues of Hard Work and Fortitude in the United States? (No)*, 333

Yevgeniya Lomakina   *"Going Green" Misses the Point (student essay)*, 317

Erin McKean   *Redefining Definition*, 179

Bill McKibben   *Waste Not Want Not*, 301

Diane McKinney-Whetstone   *The First Family*, 251

Shannon Morgan   *Defending Camelot: Chivalry Is Not Dead (student essay)*, 215

Walter Mosley   *Get Happy*, 86

Jed Perl   *Picture Imperfect*, 134

Luis J. Rodríguez   *Slurring Spanish*, 345

Jeffrey Rosen   *Nude Awakening*, 227

Warwick Sabin   *The Rich Get Thinner, the Poor Get Fatter*, 101

Irwin Savodnik   *All Crisis, All the Time*, 156

Connie Schultz   *New Airport Policy: Grin and Bare It*, 232

Clay Shirky   *A Rant about Women*, 201

Brian Jay Stanley   *Confessions of a Carnivore*, 109
Elizabeth Svokos   *Head to Head—Print Photographs (student essay)*, 141
Jacob Swede   *Remembering Johnny Appleseed (student essay)*, 117
Cal Thomas   *Sinking "Climate Change,"* 313
Clive Thompson   *The New Literacy*, 173
Elyse Toplin   *Uniting Families (student essay)*, 350
Garry Trudeau   *Hi, Dad*, 277
John Edgar Wideman   *Street Corner Dreamers*, 256
Laura Williamson   *Does a Family Need to Share a Surname? (No)*, 69
Pearl Wong   *Obama—President for All (student essay)*, 261

DEBATES

Debate: Does a Family Need to Share a Surname?
Liz Breslin   *Yes*, 65
Laura Williamson   *No*, 69

**Debate: Does Immigration Increase the Virtues of Hard Work
and Fortitude in the United States?**
Tamar Jacoby   *Yes*, 330
Mark Krikorian   *No*, 333

Preface

Using America Now *in Developmental and Composition Classes*

With its strong focus on current issues and its thought-provoking assignments, *America Now* is ideal for both developmental and composition classes. Many of the questions and writing assignments in the book will give students the practice they need to pass basic skills examinations. At the same time, these questions allow students to work within a real context, and all levels of writing classes might use them to practice writing skills, promote discussion, and prepare for take-home essay assignments. Though some questions and writing assignments in the book ask students to focus on just one selection, others require them to synthesize varying opinions and to come to their own conclusions about an issue, drawing on readings and their own observations for support. These more complex assignments might be more appropriate for composition classes or the latter part of developmental classes.

Because *America Now* presents readings on some of today's most important issues and provides all the help students need to understand, discuss, and write on the topics presented, it actively engages the interest of students from a range of courses and skill levels. This book is an excellent choice for developmental students, who need to know more than just where to put a comma or how to handle verb tenses. They need to read critically, to make connections among an author's various points, and to juxtapose these points with those of other authors. They also need to be able to engage in thoughtful classroom discussion and to express and support their own opinions in their writing. Most students can meet these challenges, and instructors report that developmental students effectively analyze texts far more complex than those found in many readers. Their students often say that they can think, but they need advice on how to write in a way that is accepted in academia. Often such students write best when they are asked to discuss topics meaningful to them, and *America Now* and this manual provide contexts for such meaningful expression.

Using This Instructor's Manual

The comments and suggestions that follow invite you to use the ninth edition of *America Now* to expand your students' reading and writing abilities. Each writing class is unique, and labels often do not adequately characterize the abilities, interests, and perspectives of a particular group of students. Therefore, the questions and activities in *America Now* and the suggestions provided here include a variety of options that may be adapted for students with a wide range of reading and writing experiences. We invite you to choose those that best suit your classes, those that best fit your particular teaching style, and those that work best within the curriculum for the specific course you are teaching. We hope that these materials will encourage students to read and write more thoughtfully and critically, challenge them to think about reading and writing in increasingly sophisticated ways, and make planning and organizing classroom activities more manageable for instructors.

This manual is organized to parallel the structure of the student edition of *America Now*. Each chapter begins with a brief introduction to the themes and selections offered in that chapter. Following the introductory material are suggested answers to questions in the text. These suggested answers correspond to the question sets that follow each selection in the student edition—Vocabulary/Using a Dictionary; Responding to Words in Context; Discussing Main Point and Meaning; Examining Sentences, Paragraphs, and Organization; Thinking Critically; In-Class Writing Activities—and those that follow each chapter: Preparing for Class Discussion; From Discussion to Writing; and Topics for Cross-Cultural Discussion. These suggested answers are meant to anticipate possible student responses, to raise further questions for discussion and writing, and to help you better use *America Now* as a tool for classroom discussion and more effective student writing.

Obviously, few classes will be able to read and work with all of the selections in the text in one semester. You may want to focus on thematic groupings of units, or you may prefer to select units that are of particular interest to your students. Some instructors may allow students to choose selections; others will be more comfortable making these selections or taking turns with the class. As an alternative approach, you might ask a group of students to select a unit for the class to read; then the group of students in charge would be responsible for the discussion and the activities in which the class participates.

However you use this manual, we hope that it will help you and your students use the text fully and thoughtfully, think critically about the issues and readings, and consider how these readings fit within the larger context that is America now.

Introduction: Writing and the Art of Discussion

by Robert Atwan

> I enter into discussion and argument with great freedom and ease, inasmuch as opinion finds in me a bad soil to penetrate and take deep roots in. No propositions astonish me, no belief offends me, whatever contrast it offers with my own. There is no fancy so frivolous and so extravagant that it does not seem to me quite suitable to the production of the human mind.
>
> —Michel de Montaigne,
> *Of the Art of Discussion* (1588)

> However unwillingly a person who has a strong opinion may admit the possibility that his opinion may be false, he ought to be moved by the consideration that, however true it may be, if it is not fully, frequently, and fearlessly discussed, it will be held as a dead dogma, not a living truth.
>
> —John Stuart Mill,
> *Of the Liberty of Thought and Discussion* (1869)

Students often begin their college writing courses with a popular misconception. They think that writing is an isolating activity demanding extraordinary inner resources. They picture writers as sitting alone at their desks or computers anxiously staring at a blank page or screen until inspiration strikes. Indeed, this romanticized image of anxious solitude followed by a burst of creativity has for centuries served as a powerful model of how literature is produced. But for the average student, who has little understanding of how real writers work and has perhaps never observed people writing professionally, this popular image can lead to a distorted view of writing and the role writing plays in a person's intellectual development.

Most writers work within a lively social context, one in which issues and ideas are routinely discussed and debated. They often begin writing on topics that derive directly from specific professional situations: a journalist covers a murder trial; a professor prepares a paper for a conference; a social worker writes up a case study; an executive reports on a business meeting. Usually, the writer consults with friends and coworkers about the task and solicits their opinions and support, sometimes even asking them to comment on a draft of the work. If the work is to be published, the writer almost always receives additional advice and criticism in the form of editorial comment, copyediting, proofreading, and independent reviews. By the time the work appears, it has probably gone through numerous drafts (for some writers as many as ten or twelve) and has been subjected to a rigorous sequence of editorial support, from fact checking to stylistic fine tuning.

Nearly all the published work a student reads, with the possible exception of work published on the Internet, has gone through this process. Even the most ephemeral article in a magazine has probably been revised several times by several people before publication. But, of course, none of this is visible in the final product. Students have little knowledge of all the various levels of work and collaboration that have gone into a piece of writing—the author's often extensive reading and research; the time spent traveling, interviewing, and discussing; the organization of the information; the composing of several drafts; and the concerted effort of editors and publishers. Unlike a film, a piece of writing shows only the author's name and seldom everyone else who helped make the published work possible (though some books include an acknowledgments page).

The point about student writing should be clear: Students write in a much narrower professional environment than do experienced people whose writing is a significant part of their work. Too often, the student writes in an intellectual vacuum. He or she may feel only minimally engaged by an assigned topic —which may seem to have come out of nowhere—and may not know anyone with whom the topic may be seriously and intelligently discussed. Unlike the professional writer, the student usually sits down alone and tries to write with little intellectual provocation or encouragement. No wonder students find it so hard to begin a paper. Instead of knowing they are writing for a group of interested people, they often feel that their writing will be read by only one other person—the instructor, who will read it not for further discussion but for immediate evaluation.

America Now is designed to help writing students avoid the intellectual and emotional vacuum that confronts them when they begin to write. Two of the biggest problems in composition, finding something to say and getting started, are in large part due to the student's lack of a vital connection with what other people have to say about an issue or idea. The basis of many student writing problems, I believe, is not so much grammatical or rhetorical as social. At their worst, these problems are clearly reflected in the writing, in a disjunctive prose that sounds oddly cut off from most public discourse.

The art of writing and the art of discussion are closely linked. Experienced writers invariably write in a climate of discussion. Their writing is usually embedded in a context of others' ideas and opinions. Many writers, especially in the academic community, are directly responding to other writers—a scientist reexamining the experimental procedures of other scientists; a literary critic taking exception to a prevailing method of interpretation; a sociologist offering an alternative explanation of a colleague's data; a historian participating as a respondent at a conference. Such people are not writing in a vacuum. Their ideas often originate in discussion, their writing is a response to discussion, and their papers are designed to stimulate further discussion.

The Art of Discussion

Discussion is one of those commonly used words from speech and rhetoric—like *essay* and *style*—that remains difficult to define precisely. The word has a long and complex history. It derives from a Latin verb (*discutere*) meaning "to dash, scatter, or shake out," and it gradually came to take on the legal and, later, the rhetorical sense of "breaking" a case or a topic down into its various parts for investigation. Though the word is ordinarily used today to mean "to talk over" or "to consider carefully," it still retains a rhetorical sense of sifting a topic into separate parts for close examination.

It is easier to say what discussion is not: It is neither conversation nor debate. Unlike conversation, discussion is purposefully conducted around a given topic. Unlike debate, it is not formally organized into two competing points of view. Think of discussion as a speech activity that falls between the informalities of conversation and the formalities of debate. For the purpose of this book, discussion is defined as the free and open exploration of a specified topic by a small group of prepared people. The goal of such discussion is not to arrive at a group decision or a consensus, but to investigate as many sides of a topic as possible.

To keep discussion from rigidifying into a debate between two competing sides or from drifting into aimless conversation, a discussion leader or moderator is usually required. The discussion leader may adopt an active role in the discussion or may choose to remain neutral. But regardless of the extent of the leader's role, he or she will ordinarily introduce the topic, encourage participation, maintain an orderly sequence of responses, and ensure that the group sticks to the topic. With its regularly scheduled sessions, its diversified members, and its academic purpose, the typical college composition class of fifteen to twenty-five students makes an ideal discussion group.

It should be noted that there are many different kinds of discussion groups and techniques. Instructors who would like to read more about various discussion groups and methods may want to consult such standard texts as Ernest G. Bormann's *Discussion and Group Methods* or Mary A. Bany and Lois V. Johnson's *Classroom Group Behavior: Group Dynamics in Education*. These and similar texts on discussion can usually be found in the education and psychology sections of most college libraries.

Like writing, discussion is a learned activity. To be adept at group discussion requires the development of a variety of skills—in speaking, listening, thinking, and reading. By encouraging students to participate in group discussion, you can help them become more intellectually mature and better prepared for professional careers. Since participation in group discussion is almost always voluntary, your students can improve their discussion abilities by observing a few ground rules. They should (1) be willing to speak in public,

(2) be willing to listen, (3) be willing to examine all sides of a topic, (4) be willing to suspend judgment, and (5) be willing to prepare. These rules are explained further in the introduction for students, "The Persuasive Writer," on page 1 of *America Now.*

Generating Classroom Discussion

Many college teachers in the liberal arts feel that a particular class has gone well when they've been able to generate discussion. This is not surprising. Lively class discussion surely indicates a healthy level of student interest in the course; it also minimizes the burden and monotony of classroom lecturing. I find that even teachers who conduct large lecture courses are pleased when students ask questions and raise relevant points. Anyone who has ever given a public lecture knows how awkward it can be when the moderator invites questions and no hands are raised. Many people instinctively measure the success of a lecture or talk by the number of questions from the audience.

Yet my talks with college instructors in many disciplines indicate that, though they invite class discussion, they don't expect to generate much. "These kids have nothing to say. They just sit there," a professor complained of his introductory European history course. "I do get some students to discuss the reading," a literature teacher told me, "but it's always the same two or three talking every class. The rest are silent." "At the end of class," a writing teacher remarked, "I'll ask, 'Does anyone have any questions about the assignment?' No hands. As I dismiss class and prepare to leave, I notice five or six students gathered around my desk. Each one has a question about the assignment." These experiences, it appears, are quite typical.

Every year hundreds of thousands of college students walk into classrooms throughout America with little knowledge of how to participate in intelligent, informed discussion. One can only speculate about why this is so, but there are clearly several contributing factors: the average student's native shyness and lack of training in extemporaneous speech; an overreliance on lecturing in classrooms; the dismal models of discussion found in the media, especially on radio and television talk shows; and the decline of family conversation as people have less leisure time and as family life grows more fragmented.

One important obstacle to discussion has grown directly out of a seriously misguided educational trend. As schools concentrate more and more on the mastery of isolated and "testable" skills, they leave less and less room in the curriculum for the tentative and exploratory discussion of complex topics. This trend can easily be seen in the growing importance of college and graduate school entrance examinations, which reduce all educational achievement to the "question-answer" level. Such educational instruments not only eliminate discussion and exploration entirely; they foster a mental attitude that is directly opposed to the free and open discussion of ideas: Their rigid format implies that for every question there is always one and only one correct answer.

All of these factors add up to silent college classrooms. In composition courses, lack of discussion can be especially counterproductive to education, since most writing instructors expect their classes to respond to reading assignments and participate in workshop sessions. Few college courses, in fact, are more dependent on class discussion than first-year composition. This often puts a special strain on the instructor, who, in addition to handling a semester's worth of writing assignments, must normally engineer ways to stimulate the discussion of each class's reading material. In more than twenty years of speaking with writing teachers about their teaching, I've noticed how frequently they define a "good class" as one in which the students talk.

The ninth edition of *America Now*, like its predecessors, is specifically designed to get students talking in class. The apparatus following each unit makes it clear to students that the readings are *meant* to be discussed. More important, it gives them questions to consider and small preparatory writing tasks that will help you get class discussion started. The material in this manual is directly linked to the student exercises in the book. The possible "answers" provided here are intended to anticipate student responses to the questions following the selections, and to provide some suggestions for using *America Now* in your course. We hope they will also offer you several ideas for building on what students have prepared and for moving the class discussion of the topic toward the writing assignment.

The book and manual are so directed toward improving class discussion that I'd like to offer a few practical suggestions for generating discussion and using it as a basis for writing. These suggestions are based on the trial and error of my own experience, and on the observations of other instructors and their reports. But because class discussion is so often spontaneous and unpredictable —and is rarely the subject of systematic educational inquiry—I'd like to remind instructors that these suggestions are largely the result of impressions (mine and others') of what works and what doesn't in a classroom. I hope that this book and manual will stimulate the further study of discussion techniques in the field of composition.

Here are a few suggestions designed to generate class discussion and direct it toward the primary goal of the course—student writing:

1. *Emphasize the Importance of Discussion.* Inform students from the start of the course that class discussion is an essential ingredient of the program and that you will be counting on full participation. Remind students that both speaking well and writing well are important factors in anyone's career (it is difficult to think of any profession in which participating in discussion meetings is not essential). Remind students, too, that discussion is neither systematic debate nor aimless conversation but is the free and open exploration of an agreed-upon topic. Since most students are naturally shy, the exploratory nature of class discussion should be emphasized: Questions should be freely asked and points raised without anyone being made to feel stupid.

2. *Create a Climate of Discussion.* Free and open discussion cannot exist in a tense or anxious atmosphere. From the start, therefore, try to know who your students are (learn their names as quickly as possible) and help them become familiar with each other. You might ask your students to stand up and introduce

themselves one by one to the entire class and to say something about themselves (where they're from; their major; what they want to be, and so on). This procedure helps break the ice and gets students talking in class. Remember: Productive classroom discussion is not a matter of students talking only to their instructor; they must also talk to each other.

You may have students suggest questions that they believe would make an interesting interview—what they would like to know about a person. Then divide the class into pairs and have students use those questions as a framework for interviews with each other. The students should write down each other's responses (if a class doesn't pair off evenly, a student can do two interviews or two students can handle one). This interview is then read by the interviewer as a way to introduce the other student. Clearly, this method takes the burden off individuals who would feel shy about introducing themselves in front of the class; it also gets the students writing as they learn about each other.

To create a relaxed atmosphere for discussion, it is important to avoid an overbearing manner or a sarcastic tone. Many students are dreadfully afraid of appearing stupid in front of their peers, and an adversarial or sarcastic style of teaching—though it may appeal to a few "knowing" students—may easily lead diffident students to retreat into the safety of silence. A teacher who wants to maintain a lively atmosphere of discussion will also need at times to restrain the sarcasm of the other students toward irrelevant or "stupid" comments. This is easily done by reminding everyone of the exploratory nature of this discussion and the ground rule that no one need be afraid to say anything. I've found that many disarmingly blunt comments or "off-the-wall" questions that I tended to dismiss proved later to be quite good. Questions that sounded ill-informed were merely ill-formed. Many students have not yet learned the art of posing questions, and everything possible should be done to encourage them to do so.

3. *Beware of the Socratic Method.* So many instructors were themselves taught by this method that they often resort to it instinctively in their classrooms. If conducted in the proper dialogic spirit, the method is, of course, a superb tool for both instilling knowledge and creating intellectual drama. But too often it becomes a question-and-answer game in which instructors ask a series of questions for which they possess definite answers. Often, these questions are posed as though the instructor didn't know the answer, but it becomes evident as answer after answer is rejected that this is a pretense of inquiry, that the process is simply leading to the answer the instructor wants. The apparent inquiry is merely a disguised lecture. Students see through this game quickly. Many are put off by it and refuse to play; a few others, adept at reading the instructor's mind, soon become the class's dominant participants. One of the dangers of this type of Socratic method is that it leads to classes in which discussion is limited to the instructor and several "star" pupils.

Quite clearly, some question-and-answer procedures are necessary to generate and direct discussion. But instructors are encouraged to expand class participation by asking more open-ended questions that invite a variety of "right" answers. The topics and instructional apparatus of *America Now* contain many questions designed to elicit more than one answer.

4. *Set Up Collaborative Tasks and Small-Group Activities*. People like to work together—consider how many composition texts are coauthored and coedited. A good way to broaden class participation is to get students working together in small groups. Most composition classes have from fifteen to twenty-five students. Though groups of this size can accommodate lively general discussion, it is sometimes useful to divide the class into several subgroups (preferably four to five per group) to work on specific tasks. These smaller groups can work together to brainstorm ideas, to consider subdivisions of a topic, or to prepare in-class reports.

Another way to expand participation and to organize discussion is the use of panel sessions or forums. These can take a variety of forms, ranging from the delivery of finished papers to brief statements of positions. One of the most practical ways to conduct panel sessions in the classroom is to divide the class into several groups of four to five students to discuss the various subdivisions of a topic. Either in or outside class, each group collaborates on a written response to the topic or takes a position on it. Each group then selects one of its members to participate on a panel in which papers from all the groups are read for open discussion. Panels introduce students to more organized methods of discussion and expose the class to a wider range of viewpoints. Panel sessions —even very informal ones—take time, however. Instructors who use them should be sure to schedule assignments carefully; a well-constructed panel could take up as many as three class periods.

Though setting up formal debates involves procedures that are outside the scope of this book (and of most composition courses), class discussion can also be enlivened by informal debates. Many topics in *America Now* suggest provocative issues for opposing points of view. If a class is not too large (fifteen students or fewer), it can be divided into two groups for debating purposes; larger classes may need to form smaller groups that come together as teams. As in the panel sessions, each group should select a member to represent its position. If the topic is one students are quite conversant with, impromptu informal debate can be arranged in class. With less familiar topics, outside preparation should be scheduled.

Panels and debates often involve the practical problem of seating arrangements. The most efficient way to set up small groups is to have students cluster their desks together in tight circles. For panel formation and informal debates, several students can bring their desks to the front of the classroom. The average composition classroom, with its instructor's desk set imposingly in front, is perhaps better designed for lecturing than for open discussion. Instructors who want to broaden student participation and interaction may want to experiment with different seating styles. Some instructors, for example, feel that sitting with students at one of their desks facilitates discussion. Others may ask the students to form a large circle of seats and then sit among them. If a class is relatively small and a seminar table is available, its use will generally enhance discussion.

5. *Keep Discussion Linked to Writing*. Though lively group discussion can be an end in itself, the agenda of *America Now* is to use class discussion as a

basis for writing. This agenda works two ways: (1) it encourages students to get the composition started in the classroom, and (2) it encourages students to use class discussion as a stimulus and a context for writing.

As you direct class discussion, keep in mind how the discussion can bear directly on the writing assignment. You might want to point out ideas that contain the germ of interesting papers, a tactic that also helps student writers learn how to see ideas emerge. Another way is to periodically focus attention on specific writing strategies as the reading material is discussed. Students almost always want to discuss topics and subjects, rarely techniques and strategies. It is therefore a good idea to initiate discussion by focusing on topics and gradually turn to a consideration of how the writers handled these topics.

From Discussion to Writing

As they prepare to write for college courses, students often confront difficulties that have less to do with the routine tasks of composition—spelling, punctuation, correct grammar—than with the deeper problems of finding something to say and establishing a context in which to say it. It is not uncommon for beginning students to turn in papers that contain few serious errors yet lack intellectual substance and a clear orientation. Using group discussion as a basis for composition can help remedy these problems. Group discussion can serve as a stimulus for an individual's ideas and provide a meaningful context in which to express them. Furthermore, as we will see, the art of discussion can function in many ways as an important model for the art of writing.

Finding something to say about a topic always ranks high on lists of student writing problems. It is the main reason that the blank sheet of paper or computer screen so often triggers a set of anxious questions: "What can I say?" "Where do I begin?" For many, intellectual panic sets in as the page or screen remains blank, the mind remains blank, and the entire writing process suddenly seems to exist in a total vacuum.

Exploratory discussion offers a solution to this dilemma. Years ago, an advertising executive, Alexander F. Osborn, developed a group method of generating ideas that became enormously popular in many fields. With typical advertising savvy, Osborn gave his technique a memorable name—*brainstorming*. Osborn's goal was to stimulate creativity by presenting a small group of people with a problem topic and then encouraging them to toss off as many ideas about it in as short a time as possible. Speed, spontaneity, and free association were essential to his method. But the most important part of his brainstorming procedure was a complete absence of criticism. No one in the group was allowed to criticize or disagree with any idea, no matter how silly or farfetched it seemed. This absence of criticism, Osborn found, kept ideas flowing since people were not afraid to sound ill-informed or just plain stupid.

This brainstorming technique can clearly help students come up with ideas to write about. It could be done in the composition classroom for a brief period, or small groups of students could profitably conduct brainstorming sessions on their own. Moreover, most exploratory discussion—if it is free, open, and relaxed—will contain some degree of spontaneous brainstorming in which ideas can sprout and grow. Students who take note of these ideas will find that when they sit down to write, they will not be starting out in a vacuum but will have a context of discussion out of which their composition can take shape.

An alternative type of brainstorming can also help students move from class discussion to writing. In this type of brainstorming (sometimes referred to by communication researchers as *nominal* brainstorming), each person, instead of vocalizing ideas in a group, works alone, silently jotting down a brief list of ideas. Afterward, all the lists are compared, and after some culling and combining, individual ideas are listed on a blackboard. This brainstorming method is very useful at the start of a class session in opening up various avenues of discussion. The written list also serves as a tangible source of ideas for individuals to pursue later in their papers.

If exploratory discussion can help reduce the anxiety students face in trying to develop ideas for papers, it can also alleviate another major writing problem—the student's alienation. Thinking and writing alone, with little awareness of an actual audience or of a practical situation, the beginning student often composes papers that sound hollow, disembodied, and disengaged. Ideas seem to come out of nowhere; transitions and connections are missing; conclusions that should grow out of the development of an idea are instead little more than blunt, unearned assertions. Though such papers are common, instructors find it difficult to pinpoint precisely what is wrong with them, since the problems are vague, not easily isolated, and therefore hard to identify by the usual marking symbols. The real problem with such papers is not in the writing but in the orientation of the writer. It is not one of style, structure, or content, but of overall *context*.

Experienced writers, as mentioned earlier, invariably work with a clear sense of audience and occasion. For example, a literature or composition teacher working on a critical article is writing within a clearly definable context: He or she has a sense of who the audience will be, where the article could be published, and—most important—why it is being written. No matter what its subject or point of view, the article will be intellectually oriented to a community of readers presumed to be aware of the topic and attuned to the various points of view involved in its discussion. That so many academic papers are first prepared for delivery at professional conferences underscores the vital importance of a concrete audience and situation.

As students discover the connections between discussion and composition, they will also find their bearings as writers. Their writing—no matter what the topic—will be oriented toward response. Their writing will be not only a response to an assigned topic but, more important, a response made in the context of a continuing discussion of that topic. The student, in other words, writes as an active participant, responding, as she or he would in group discussion, to the actual or anticipated responses of others. This texture of mutual response is what so often gives professionally written essays and articles their mature tone and clear orientation. Instructors might further encourage this climate of response by inviting students to cite comments by other class members in their papers.

Once your students see writing as a form of response, they will become more conscious of their social and intellectual attitudes as writers. Are they closed off to other opinions? Are they overbearing in their attitudes? Do they try to see all sides of an issue? Are they patient with complexity? Do they over-simplify difficult problems? Do they skirt issues? Do they base too much on personal experience? These are all considerations learned in group discussion that directly carry over into composition.

As your students work through *America Now*, they will observe how participation in group discussion is relevant to all kinds of writing tasks. It is perhaps easy to see how an awareness of conflicting opinions can play an important part in critical, analytical, and argumentative writing. But personal essays can also profit from exploratory group discussion. By discussing their personal experiences, your students can begin to view them from a broader social perspective and to understand them within a context of divergent human experiences.

Composition that is closely linked to lively group discussion reminds students that they are writing not in a vacuum but as part of a group, part of a community. In a written work, as in discussion, someone is always speaking and someone (or some group) is always being addressed. *America Now* encourages your students to view their writing as an extension of group discussion, to see writing as public, not private, behavior, as a social act rather than a solitary one. To think of writing as an extension of discussion, however, students need to reimagine themselves as writers. When they sit down to write, they should do so not as isolated individuals anxiously awaiting inspiration but as active participants in a process of communication with others. Students then will not expect ideas for writing to "come out of the blue." Rather, they will expect to find their ideas where they are most likely to originate—out of their considered responses to the ideas of others.

Forming Forums: Student Presentations to Encourage Research, Discussion, and Better Writing

by Liz deBeer

"The forums give a chance for students to participate verbally and not just listen to the teacher."

"Forums enabled students to get to know each other as they worked in groups."

"Forums made people get up in front of class and talk who otherwise didn't talk during class discussion."

"The forums presented lots of good information that I think I would not have learned anywhere else. They provided lots of discussion, and I think that was the best part. The class got a chance to communicate about their cultures and share their experiences or anecdotes, which made the class a much better place to be at 8:30 in the morning."

"Forums: Keep doing this!"

As the student evaluations above reveal, many students seem to enjoy my classes and learn the most when they are asked to work in groups and share their ideas with their peers. Panel presentations or forums help give students authority in the classroom and motivation to write in steps. Perhaps just as important, forums motivate teachers like me to listen more to their students. Even students who feared forums because they didn't like the idea of talking in front of the class acknowledged that they benefited from them, as one student wrote: "I found the forums to be very informative and interesting even though I hated speaking in front of the class."

Forums require students, working in small groups, to research a topic, make presentations, and lead classroom discussion. Forums motivate students to explore topics by interviewing experts, preparing surveys, and analyzing trends, just as many of the writers whose essays appear in *America Now* did. This type of research allows students to observe the controversy implicit in most of the topics in the text and prepares them for writing papers that go beyond clichés. On the first day of class, I tell students that forums allow them to teach part of the class; this comment always gets their interest.

Why Bother? The Value of Forums

After my first few years of teaching composition, I realized that I was doing more research than my students to prepare for my classes. Exhausted and overwhelmed, I decided to create a course where the students were responsible for much of the research and, later, the presentation of it. Although several students balked at the idea of speaking in front of their peers, all followed through, which created the most successful composition classes I had ever taught. In fact, previous students accosted me in the hall demanding to know why we hadn't done forums when they took the course.

There is much research to support the use of collaborative work like forums. Lev Vygotsky's emphasis on collaboration has been well documented; he asserts that students learn from working with others: "With assistance, every child can do more than he can by himself. . . . What a child can do in cooperation today he can do alone tomorrow" (187–88). Douglas Barnes and Frankie Todd reflect on a thirteen-year-old who wonders why the teacher can't just write all the questions and answers on the board so that the students can memorize them. The authors comment that "such students need opportunities and challenges that will enable them to see learning as constructing an understanding, not as reflecting and repeating ready-made formulae whose implications they have not grasped" (14). Talk is the antidote, according to Barnes and Todd, particularly talk that is student-centered, where students can "try out new ways of thinking and reshape an idea midsentence, respond immediately to the hints and doubts of others, and collaborate in shaping meanings they could not hope to reach alone" (15). Forums provide students with time to talk about their projects, reconsider their ideas, and listen to new ideas; forums also hold students accountable for their talk, because the forums eventually involve presentations and term papers, both of which are graded.

Additionally, talk in forums is genuine, unlike much classroom "discussion" where the teacher is searching for someone who can "reproduce what the teacher has presented to them" (Barnes and Todd 15). Jeffrey Wilhelm, reflecting on his own practice and why so many students dislike reading, notes, "If we take the theoretical stance that reading is, in fact, producing meaning, then the way reading education is traditionally practiced in schools must be rethought. . . . [Teachers] must take responses beyond boilerplate questions and 'correct' answers" (10). Wilhelm uses drama and art to teach literature as an active enterprise between students and text; I suggest using forums as an active enterprise between students and *America Now*. Forums rarely disappoint me in my main goal, which is to learn something new—related to the curriculum—from each student, for forums often involve students researching areas beyond the teacher's own knowledge. For example, in past years, students have done forums on immigration and have interviewed people whom I had never met, presenting information that opened my eyes. Other students shared their own stories, such as one student who included an anecdote about how she traveled to the United States from Vietnam on a tiny fishing boat.

Forums also challenge teachers to look differently at the common complaint about lack of resources (Moll). Forums motivated me to embrace the community as a resource, a means to reach out of the classroom door and windows—which are usually shut in college classrooms—and connect student worlds to the texts. Luis Moll calls this "mobilizing funds of knowledge" (231). Although he is referring to a program where community members physically enter the classroom to teach their special skills, forums use students as facilitators of these "funds of knowledge" through their research, which often involves surveys and interviews. For example, in past years, forums on parenting resulted in students presenting research on parenting in other cultures, much of which was unfamiliar to me.

Research strongly suggests that group work can increase tolerance among groups of diverse students, assuming the group work has "highly valued goals that could not be obtained without cooperation" (Schofield 13). However, research also suggests that if group work is not well planned and valued by the teacher, students may not take the tasks seriously (Weinstein). In fact, many teachers suggest that they do not use group work for fear of losing order (Weinstein). I have never experienced difficulty with classroom management when using forums, mainly, I believe, because so many students preferred them to lectures. Moreover, since the group work led to graded work, students knew that if they were unproductive during group work, they might not have a successful forum or a strong paper.

Steps: Preparing Students

Because forums follow the philosophy behind process writing, there are several steps involved. Four major writing activities are involved throughout the semester. First, students brainstorm in small groups for ideas and strategies for researching and presenting information effectively, writing ideas on the sign-up sheet and in their notebooks. Then, they write a two-page paper that summarizes and analyzes the student's individual topic, which is handed in the day of the presentation and is summarized for the student's forum presentation. (Time limits may be necessary.) Each presenter should also prepare a discussion question on the subtopic being presented.

Students who are not presenting must hand in a one-page critical response to each forum other than their own, due the class following each forum. This should evaluate the effectiveness of each presentation — not summarize it. This is excellent practice for students to hone their listening skills and discern the most important aspects of a talk. Recently, I have also asked students to write a one-sentence positive response, telling the presenter what they liked best about the presentation. I do this to help the class feel more like a community; I have found students with eyes brimming upon hearing positive comments from their peers, some telling me that this is the first time they realized anyone was actually paying attention to what they had said in class.

Finally, students in composition classes must write a research paper based on the data gathered for their forum presentation. (Basic skills instructors may choose to eliminate this step.) This paper should involve more sources, more analysis, more detail, and better editing than the two-page paper. After the presentations are all completed, instructors can explain the traditional research paper and how the students' presentations can be revised into longer, more scholarly works.

A typical syllabus for my Composition 101 class, which meets for one semester, includes four or five forum topics, so that about five or six students are members of each group. I organize my syllabus by beginning with a few lectures in which I describe my goals and allow students time to research and prepare their projects. I spend several class periods preparing students for these forums at least two weeks before the first group's topic is due. We spend one class period working on interviewing skills, usually based on a topic from *America Now*. For example, using past editions of the text, I might begin the semester with "Are our news media reliable? Why or why not?" and ask students to conduct an interview of another person about his or her opinions on the objectivity and quality of journalism and television news. Then, I would have students write an essay using a few quotes from the subject of the interview, perhaps also using one essay from *America Now* as a supplement to the paper. Because many of the students interview an expert for their forum presentation, I like to assign one interviewing project well before the forum projects are due.

I schedule one week (or two class periods of eighty minutes each) for each forum topic. For the first class, students are asked to read the unit in *America Now* that covers the assigned topic, and we then analyze the articles and write on each topic in our notebooks. The second class is a student forum based on the same topic. The entire class period is devoted to presentations and discussion led by about five students who are in charge of that topic. I organize my syllabus so that students are working on their projects at the same time. I usually reserve a class period in the middle of the projects for an in-class exam. We spend the rest of the semester concentrating on peer reviews, punctuation, writing, reading and test-taking skills, and work on other small projects like the ones described in units of *America Now*. Usually, I reorganize the order of the table of contents to meet the needs of my syllabus.

I choose forum topics based on which issues I believe will most interest students and create the most compelling forum presentations. Since the material in *America Now* addresses current events, many students are already thinking about the issues they are being asked to write about. Instructors should capitalize on students' interests and concerns when choosing the broad topics for the forums. If students are concerned about obesity or consumerism, then these are good topics for forums. If the issues of social networking, the environment, immigration, or racial conflict have been debated regularly on the news or in the campus paper, then these topics will have special appeal. Much of this evaluation of topics depends on a school's geography and demographics. I rely on past students' essays and discussion to gauge popular topics. Although all topics in *America Now* will interest most students, the ideal forum topic is one that students will be compelled to spend more than one class period discussing. I also avoid topics that are too polarized, such as abortion, which people tend to view as either inherently wrong or right. The topic should be broad enough that several students can explore different angles and should be covered by accessible research sources.

At the beginning of the semester, I write on the board four or five forum topics chosen from issues addressed in *America Now* and ask that each student pick one. Through this process, the small groups are formed. For example, the students who pick the topic obesity will work together on a forum for that topic. Because groups should be approximately the same size to allow for different angles to be addressed on each issue, instructors should limit the number of students allowed to pick each topic.

When groups have been formed, I hand each one a sign-up sheet with the chosen topic written on top. Then, each group member picks a subtopic or angle that relates to the general topic and lists some possible sources that will be used to research it. Students should be reminded that their research may require them to alter the proposed topic or sources.

Although I encourage students to create their own ideas for topics and sources, I provide each small group with some ideas to model how to create a specific topic from a broad one as well as some sources that might be applicable to the general topic. I usually give each group a separate handout along with the sign-up sheet. Examples of my ideas for approaching topics appear at the end of this essay.

At this point, I dedicate a whole class period to reviewing forums so that students know what I expect. Although I have already defined forums briefly before they picked their topics and subtopics, I define them in more detail once students know what area they will be researching. I also make a model presentation to show students the kind of work I expect. I include a visual aid and speak, without reading in a monotone, from my notecards. I pick a topic that is relevant to *America Now*. For example, I once made a presentation on patriotism, for which I interviewed instructors from the political science and journalism departments about their views regarding the role of patriotism in relation to the government, the media, and the public in America today. Students then evaluated my presentation orally as I wrote my expectations on the board; the students themselves provided excellent tips for each other. My use of model presentations has helped my classes improve their presentations over years past. It also reminds me of all the steps students need to take to be prepared for their presentations.

Next, I review how students should prepare their research, presentations, and class discussion. I discuss the importance of asking questions that elicit thoughtful responses and of asking follow-up questions, both during their research and during presentations. I explain how I evaluate forums based on whether presentations — and written reports — are focused and informative, and I discuss the value of current sources. Since students have usually begun to work on their projects, they are encouraged to ask specific questions.

At the next class period, groups meet for the second time so that students can discuss their plans for research and their overall strategy. Instructors should visit each group to learn of individual concerns and should discuss wider concerns with the whole class. Often, group members discuss their fears of talking in front of others. I try to point out the value of speaking skills and sometimes encourage students to participate in later forums so that they can see other students do presentations before they take a turn. Given that many high schools require oral presentations as part of their graduation requirements, many students are already knowledgeable about the basics of preparing forums.

After their second group meeting, students must conduct their research and prepare their presentations. I ask that they write a two-page (typed, double-spaced) report on their forum topic that includes at least one source other than *America Now*. Those sources may include books, magazines, interviews, or even personal experience. If students use personal experience as a source, they must also use one other source. To document their sources, I require a typed "works cited" page. Students may read from their papers, but they may not read the whole paper or they will go over their allotted time. It is imperative to save time for class discussion. Remind students not to use names of people interviewed if the topic involves personal material, as might be the case in a presentation on stereotypes, for instance.

Letting Go: Letting Students Learn

Perhaps instructors' greatest challenge in working with forums is allowing students to research and explore topics on their own and to work in groups during class time. This doesn't *feel* like teaching, but it is. If we want students to actually say something meaningful, as Berthoff suggests in *The Making of Meaning*, we must leave them alone to make their own discoveries. As Bartholomae and Petrosky write in *Facts, Artifacts, and Counterfacts*, "A course in reading and writing whose goal is to empower students must begin with a silence, a silence the student must fill" (7). When students conduct interviews, research their forum topics, or lead class discussion, they are literally filling the silence. Forum projects allow students to think for themselves, to take risks. All this, of course, leads to better writing.

Usually, students ask for little help. Most of them are eager to interview people they know or to find their own sources. Occasionally, students panic and ask me to help with library research, particularly those with limited library experience. (I usually arrange an on-campus library tour before the forums begin.) However, once I have given them enough pointers to get started, I try to leave them alone. Often, during such periods of silence, I observe students working together. Such collaboration confirms my belief that students learn not only from me and from sources but also from each other.

Other experiences have reinforced my belief in the value of forums and have helped me get through the waiting and worrying period. One student, who appeared to be half asleep during much of the class time preceding the forums, became so involved and excited by interviewing his Vietnam-veteran uncle for a forum on the gun-control debate that he suddenly sparkled, waking up enough to complete and pass the course. Similarly, a student from a local subsidized housing development admitted to me later that he planned on dropping my class because of an overloaded schedule. Instead, he stuck it out, comparing and contrasting attitudes about guns from ten men from "the projects" who did not attend college and ten men who did attend college, drawing conclusions about guns and lack of hope. He admitted that the reason he stayed in the course was because he felt impelled to work on his forum project and felt his background and insights were valued in the class.

Teacher as Listener

I like to start with a forum on an accessible topic such as body image because it makes students think critically about something with which they are already familiar. Although (or because) students' experiences vary, these topics should prompt a lot of class discussion. Students who are in these forum groups may interview campus counselors or social workers. One student might survey two generations' attitudes about body image and compare results or split the survey into two social or cultural groups.

Some students may resent it if their group has to present first, but others actually like to "get it out of the way." Once, when a student in the first forum group was unable to finish his research, I moved him to a different topic that was due toward the end of the semester. However, I discourage such behavior by telling the class that I will give an F to students who do not perform on the due date, unless they can be excused because of an extreme circumstance. Only once did a student miss the deadline without an excuse; I allowed her to hand in her written paper, and I averaged the F for the presentation with the written project.

On the day of the presentation, I take attendance and sit in the back of the class. Then, the group presenting moves to the front of the room and presents its reports. At this point, the class asks questions only for clarification so that there is time for everyone to present. Students who are not presenting should be taking notes for their one-page written response to the forum. Instead of a simple summary, I ask students to follow a formula that includes what the main idea was, what they liked best about the presentation, and what they learned. (Students don't have to write such a paper on their own forum topic or on anyone else's in their group. When all the students have presented, I average all of the critical responses of each student to equal one paper grade. Usually everyone who hands in the written response gets a high grade; the only way to fail is to cut class and not hand in any of these papers.)

After all the students in the group have finished their presentations, the rest of the class may ask questions. Sometimes, presenters need to ask the class a question to prompt discussion. I prefer to keep quiet and let the presenters lead the discussion, but sometimes I'll intervene when I feel it's necessary. Often, I have to remind myself to let the students talk, to let them fill the silence. I usually learn from these discussions. In one class, a student from Nigeria responded to a parenting forum presentation about how divorced American men are fighting to get custody of their children. The Nigerian student commented that in his country it is the norm for divorced men to have custody of the children. This led to a discussion of cultural issues concerning gender roles.

Occasionally, students make poor presentations. In the weakest one I have seen, a bright woman simply chatted for a few minutes without presenting material from any source. Another student twisted data about rape so that it sounded like the violence was justified by the victim's flirtatious behavior. In both instances, the students learned from their peers' responses and my commentary on their short papers, and their final research papers reflected their understanding. Much of this learning process occurs during the discussion following the presentations. Even a blunt comment like "Why do you always call the rape victim 'she'?" can lead to discussion about improving writing.

It is common for students to present too much general information without specific examples, to make rough transitions, or to analyze data inadequately. These problems can also be remedied with helpful commentary from fellow students and the instructor. Because the forum project involves writing in steps, I rarely receive plagiarized or sloppy papers. Before I used the forums, students often had only one chance to write their final research papers and no time to learn from their mistakes. By presenting their ideas and research orally before writing a final research paper, students have time to think and rethink. They learn to value their audience by striving to be clear, concise, and original. Since the projects are staggered, I can spend more time on the two-page papers, offering advice about revising for the final research paper.

When students write critical responses to their peers' presentations, they learn to analyze. One student commented that "I tended to . . . learn more from the people who analyzed their information rather than the ones who dictated the information to the class." Another wrote that "when [presenters] read off a sheet of paper, they were boring. . . . I feel you must get the audience involved." These comments reveal that students were able to learn important writing lessons from the oral presentations.

Other students' comments revealed that they enjoyed the forums. One wrote: "Forums are an excellent learning device. . . . Students taught students about what they had researched." Another reported that "the forums . . . forced the speakers to really know their topics. . . . I feel that a majority of the people got really involved in their subjects, enabling them to learn more about it than if they just read it out of a book. Also, the forums showed that how you say your information is important. You must try to catch the interest of your audience."

These remarks show how eager students are to fill the silence of the classroom, as long as we instructors are willing to give up some of our control. If we empower our students, they can provide the classroom with much more knowledge than any one person alone can.

Works Cited

Barnes, Douglas, and Frankie Todd. *Communication and Learning Revisited: Making Meaning through Talk*. Portsmouth, NH: Boynton/Cook, 1995. Print.

Bartholomae, David, and Anthony Petrosky. *Facts, Artifacts, and Counter-facts: Theory and Method for a Reading and Writing Course*. Portsmouth, NH: Boynton/Cook, 1986. Print.

Berthoff, Ann E. *The Making of Meaning*. Upper Montclair, NJ: Boynton/Cook, 1981. Print.

Moll, Luis. "Literacy Research in Community and Classrooms: A Sociological Approach." *Theoretical Models and the Process of Reading*. 4th ed. Ed. R. B. Ruddell, M. R. Ruddell, and H. Singer. Newark, DE: IRA, 1994. 211–44. Print.

Schofield, Janet W. *Black & White in School: Trust, Tension or Tolerance?* New York: Teachers College Press, 1989. Print.

Vygotsky, Lev. *Thought and Language*. Cambridge, MA: MIT Press, 1987. Print.

Weinstein, Carol S. *Secondary Classroom Management: Lessons from Research and Practice*. New York: McGraw-Hill, 1996. Print.

Wilhelm, Jeffrey D. *"You Gotta Be the Book": Teaching Engaged and Reflective Reading with Adolescents*. Urbana, IL: NCTE, 1995. Print.

What's in a Name?

"What's in a name?" asks Juliet in Shakespeare's famous play, and as we know from the play's ending, much is at stake. So, too, the authors in this chapter agree that names matter. Names for all kinds of things must be decided upon: for children, for trucks, for sports teams, for time periods, for countries. Among other things, names create our identity, they affect self-esteem, and they help establish our place in the world.

With nods to Shakespeare in her essay as well, Rebecca Mead's "What Do You Call It?" raises the dilemma of naming to a new level. What do we do when a name doesn't fit? When we seem unable to encapsulate a time period with a name (in this case, the first decade of a new century)? Mead shows how, post-9/11, our history feels like it is spinning out in new directions and how the decade we've just passed through did not live up to what we might have expected, "since this turned out to be the decade in which there were no good answers."

Patrick Olsen's "Does Your Pickup Truck Have a Nickname?" offers a different tone, but examines the question of naming as well. Certain people feel even their trucks need a name, and the naming is no light matter. Brittany Bergstrom agrees, as she follows the debate over the proposed name change for the University of North Dakota's athletic teams and notes how passionately some argue for the sake of the name "Fighting Sioux" despite the controversy over keeping it. "The Fighting Sioux: The End of a Legacy?" is more of an examination of the love of a name than of the damage it might do as a stereotype.

Two essays about whether a family should share a surname (take a mother's or father's last name) come from Liz Breslin and Laura Williamson. Breslin argues for the cohesiveness of the family under one name and suggests that her argument is not antifeminist. Williamson follows her own family story, with a focus on another woman in the family who disagrees with her point of view—her mother-in-law—and makes the case that the "family is more than a single surname."

The chapter ends with "America Then . . . 1507: Who Named America?" It might be surprising to find out how America was "misnamed," and that the name that stuck was established not by an explorer but a mapmaker. The detail from the map included shows how names and places can change in the minds of those who help discover and shape them. Following the history of a name sheds light on just how complicated this naming process can be.

Patrick Olsen

Does Your Pickup Truck Have a Nickname?

[*Cars.com*, September 22, 2009]

Vocabulary/Using a Dictionary

1. A *survey* is a poll, and in this essay people are *surveyed* to get their opinions on their pickup trucks. *Survey* can also be used as a verb and means to appraise or inspect.

2. When something is *hauled* it is drawn or pulled by someone or something else. The body of a pickup truck is built for the carrying or *hauling* of materials.

3. A *percent* is also called a *per centum* (Latin), or one one-hundredth part. The abbreviation of *per centum* is "per cent," and the words have since been joined to form *percent*. A *percentage* is a proportion, and this article deals with surveys and the comparison of those surveys' numbers.

Responding to Words in Context

1. An *age gap* refers to a disparity in ages. In this case, it simply means that the owners who give their pickups names are not usually the same age as the ones who don't care to name them.

2. The *truck bed* is the open rear cargo area of the truck.

3. The data may affect or worry the automakers. In this instance, *concern* is being used as a verb. If the automakers were concerned, they would be troubled or anxious.

Discussing Main Point and Meaning

1. The article suggests that most pickup truck drivers claim to love their pickups as much as they love family members. An intimate relationship, perhaps seemingly odd to some outsiders, is established between owner and vehicle, marking it as a special piece of property—the owner bestows a name on the truck, sleeps in it, values it as highly as a spouse or a house.

2. According to the data collected here, younger truck drivers are not as loyal to U.S. brands as are older drivers. Younger drivers feel more completely identified with the truck as a reflection of their personality and are more likely to have slept in their truck beds.

3. The statistic about drivers in the West sleeping in their trucks suggests that owners from that part of the country are more likely to view their truck as an extension of their home. Or perhaps it just indicates something about the region and its vast spaces lending itself to the use of the truck as a makeshift abode, either due to travel or the desire to experience the "great outdoors."

Examining Sentences, Paragraphs, and Organization

1. Students may say that the article reads like an advertisement because throughout it presents the pickup as a highly desirable object. The poll is of pickup drivers only and suggests that they value their vehicles tremendously. The lack of negative presentation in the article (which stops just short of saying "Go out and buy a truck!") is very much in line with an advertisement for pickups.

2. Many people find themselves defined by their material possessions, where they live, or other external factors. It does not mean that their trucks are serious, funny, outgoing, or any other facet that one associates with individual personality. Owning a truck might be a reflection of one's eagerness to travel or a choice to live outside the confines of a city (where one is less likely to need to use a truck on a regular basis). *Personality* can refer to such visible qualities, as referenced in this article, or it could refer to one's psychology.

3. The numbered points clearly outline the importance of trucks to their owners, and highlighting them in this way adds to the surprise of the response (many said a spouse, house, or sex were less important than their pickup). Olsen gives the results of his surveys throughout the article, but setting these responses apart near the end of the article creates greater effect.

Thinking Critically

1. Students may or may not be surprised at how excited truck owners are by their vehicles. Depending on how students view physical possessions, they might not understand why drivers are so in love with them (it doesn't seem strictly about their utility) or they may have a similar feeling about something they own or drive.

2. A discussion of numbers may be helpful—Olsen reveals that 1,068 truck owners age eighteen and up were questioned about their trucks. Ask students if they would be more convinced if a wider poll had been taken. How would they view the information if the pool of interviewees were smaller? Students may have wanted more personal or anecdotal information in the article or they may say the statistics give a more concise view of how pickup drivers feel about their trucks.

3. Answers will vary based on what vehicles students gravitate toward or have experience with. The question can be considered by examining each point made in the article about naming a vehicle, choosing one that is U.S.- or foreign-made, how they use their vehicle, and its importance in their lives.

In-Class Writing Activities

1. Students should consider how this article might have differed (or stayed the same) if it had not been found in an advertising supplement. They should make note of how "informational" articles are similar to or different from articles that push certain brands (in this case, the pickup

truck). Students should note how the push or "plug" for an item is phrased in these supplements or where they lack objectivity.

2. Responses to this question will vary from student to student. Students may choose a car or something similar and describe why it is so important to them, or they may choose something more unique and personal. Students should consider the nature of a "relationship" with something other than a person and what that relationship consists of, given Olsen's findings about pickup truck owners.

3. Students' answers will vary based on their research. Specific details should be included about one brand vs. another and the advantages and disadvantages for various people. They may choose to look at the truck-owning population in terms of age or region as Olsen does, or they may choose a different way of categorizing their information. Students should feel free to speculate about the appeal of trucks in general based on what they discover about various types.

Rebecca Mead

What Do You Call It?

[*The New Yorker*, January 4, 2010]

Vocabulary/Using a Dictionary

1. When one is *overwrought*, he or she is excited to the point of agitation or distress. It is, in fact, the past participle of *overwork*. To be *wrought* is to be pushed into a certain shape. *Over* can mean excessive (as when one is *overly* excited about something).

2. *Sobriquet* is a French word. One might be familiar with similar words that come from the French language like *bouquet* or *tourniquet*. Its etymology may be apparent by its dictionary pronunciation. The word means "nickname."

3. Something *comprehensible* is understandable. The root comes from the verb *comprehend*. When one *comprehends*, one understands or knows something. Whatever one is trying to grasp is then *comprehensible*.

Responding to Words in Context

1. When one *infringes*, one violates or trespasses upon something (infringement of copyright, infringement of privacy). Civil *liberties* are one's rights as a citizen. *Civil* in this case has to do with citizenship, like the word *civic*. A *liberty* is a freedom.

2. *Intractable* means not easy to control, difficult to manage. *Irresolvable* means not solvable. Both adjectives suggest a certain amount of difficulty or an impossibility of resolution.

3. *Omniscience* refers to unlimited knowledge or perception; *omnipotence* means unlimited power. *Omni* comes from Latin, meaning "all." *Omniscience* means "all-knowing" and *omnipotence* means "all-powerful."

Discussing Main Point and Meaning

1. The decade is problematic because no one has been able to pin a name on it, and before Mead discusses the years 2000–2010, she mentions that it turned out to be "the decade in which there were no good answers." The events of the decade that are mentioned were often catastrophic (9/11, Katrina, the economic downturn) or at the very least unsettling to the status quo (the United States had its first African American president and things like Facebook drastically changed the way we share information with each other). The events are presented as negative or as unusual enough to disturb past perceptions of ourselves and our world. Mead suggests that because of this, perhaps we'd rather not name the decade after all.

2. *Aught* is a corruption of the archaic word *naught*, which means "nothing" or "zero." *Naught* makes sense given that these are the years beginning with zero. The actual definition of *aught* is "anything." *Naught* and *aught* both suggest a void, which is how Mead paints the decade and our general feelings about it.

3. Mead finds it fitting that no name has emerged, suggesting that we would rather set this period of time adrift nameless after all of its disappointments and chaos.

Examining Sentences, Paragraphs, and Organization

1. The inclusion of the "alternate decade of fantasy" in which Al Gore ("forever slim and with hairline intact") becomes president, ratifies Kyoto, and avoids September 11 provides a stark contrast to the way events really unfolded in history. It underscores her view of the decade as a terrible, possibly preventable, tragedy. By putting her imagined decade in parentheses, she downplays its importance—it is simply her wish for what might have happened—but it also calls attention to an alternative to what did in fact happen.

2. The first references are to the zeros that follow as the year changes from 1999 to 2000. "Zero" suggests nothing, leading to "the zips" and "the nadas" ("nothing" in Spanish). "The naughties" follow that, possibly referring to "naught" and/or suggesting disobedience or something "not nice." All names suggest the absence of something. Mead makes each name in the list a sentence fragment and uses question marks, highlighting the fact that no consensus exists on a name.

3. Mead begins with a look at the words under consideration for the decade and then examines the most likely candidate: the "aughts." She gives reasons why this name feels appropriate and examines the decade, event by disastrous event. She mentions the dramatic change that took place, possibly because of those earlier events, with the election of Barack Obama. She ends with some of the odder inventions that came about during that time.

Thinking Critically

1. 9/11 is the turning point, as Mead sees it, for the new century and new decade. One might argue that the change that took place in our under-

standing of terrorism and safety in this country was vast enough to mark the previous decade as "reassuring" or "comprehensible" in retrospect. The nineties were also years of conservatism that appeared to be placid and ordinary on some level although they may have led directly to events that followed.

2. The main defining event that she points to is September 11, 2001. One might argue that 9/11 was the defining event because one can look at the other political and economic events she mentions (Katrina, war, and the fluctuations in the marketplace) as coming about as a direct result of the events of and reactions to that day. (She does mention that she sees 9/11 as a direct result of the earlier election.)

3. Consider names that encapsulate a group of people or a time period (Generation X, the Roaring Twenties). Those names label a particular group or time, forever coloring one's view of them. Names provide people with a way of speaking about something based on a general perception (not everyone in Gen X was aimless or hopeless, and not everyone in the Roaring Twenties lived a fast life, yet those names ellicit certain assumptions based on them).

In-Class Writing Activities

1. Students may begin their essays with a defense of the "aughts" or they may side with Mead. If they disagree with her, they should include examples from the decades not mentioned in the article that show the time period in a more positive light. Or they may expand upon the rise of Barack Obama to the presidency, exploring the message of hope brought by his campaign. If they agree with her, they may discuss war or the general perception of the U.S. abroad at the turn of the century, changing of weather patterns due to the greenhouse effect, the discovery of lead in myriad toys manufactured in and imported from China, the identification of the H1N1 virus in Mexico and its global spread, or any other events not mentioned in the article.

2. Students may focus on the fact that Obama is the first African American president of the United States. They may discuss how his campaign and policies differ from the Bush administration's or from any of the other 2008 presidential candidates. They may focus on Mead's quotation from the Nobel acceptance speech or explore reasons why Obama might have been nominated for and then received such a prize.

3. Answers will vary depending on the student. Students should be able to compare their event and how it defines the time with examples from Mead's essay.

Brittany Bergstrom (student essay)

The Fighting Sioux: The End of a Legacy?

[*The Spectrum*, University of North Dakota, September 29, 2009]

Vocabulary/Using a Dictionary

1. A *logo* is a representation or trademark that often accompanies a brand name (or in this case, the name of a sports team). A *nickname* is substituted for a proper name. A *mascot* is also something that represents a group (in this case, the sports team is represented by a fighting Indian).

2. A *rival* is a competitor. Sometimes people romantically interested in the same person are called *rivals* for his or her affection. Students may also be familiar with the term *sibling rivalry*.

3. A *connotation* is a suggestion or association. A *denotation* is the explicit meaning of a word.

Responding to Words in Context

1. The words *divide* and *unify* are opposites. When something is divided, it is separated into parts. If things are unified, they are made into a single unit.

2. An *alumnus* is a graduate of a particular school, college, or university. It is a Latin masculine noun. It can change to other forms such as *alumna*, a female graduate of a particular school, college, or university, or *alumni*, the plural form of *alumnus*.

3. *Race* refers to classifications of people by common descent or heredity. Physical characteristics (such as skin color), common history, and genetic similarity help determine a person's race. *Ethnicity* relates to a group of people sharing a common and distinctive culture, religion, or language. Race and ethnicity share much in common; however, race often refers mostly to one's skin color and ethnicity has more to do with common shared culture.

Discussing Main Point and Meaning

1. Opponents of the name object to the name itself, apart from the school team's history. They object on racial/ethnic grounds and feel that the characterization of the "Fighting Sioux" reflects badly on Native Americans as a people.

2. The nickname might harm people of the Sioux tribe who feel it characterizes them as a violent people. The image of the "Fighting Sioux" that accompanies the logo may not reflect the modern Sioux people or it creates a negative impression of their ancestry.

3. The history she is referring to is not the history of the Sioux people. She is talking about the school's history of a vibrant, determined, successful sports team.

Examining Sentences, Paragraphs, and Organization

1. Bergstrom writes in a journalistic style, includes many quotations, and is not particularly arguing her personal "side." However, the quotes she includes are overwhelmingly on the side of keeping the name "Fighting Sioux," and she does not interview any of the Sioux representatives in the lawsuit, nor does she expound upon the "harmful" aspects of the name "Fighting Sioux." Her final quote suggests that problems will not immediately be solved if the nickname is removed ("a new nickname may not be implemented for some time, if at all").

2. Bergstrom interviews former and current UND and NDSU students and faculty. The article would have changed to show more of the opposition if she had included some quotations from the tribes in question.

3. The quotations give the article an objective feeling because it is not an article presented in the writer's voice trying to persuade. In her selection of quotations, Bergstrom seems to believe that the evidence supports the continuation of "Fighting Sioux" as a nickname—she does present some mild opposition or questioning of the name, but no one vehemently opposed is quoted.

Thinking Critically

1. It is difficult to discover the opposition to the name in this article, since no one demanding a name change is interviewed. However, the article alludes to the controversy and states that "critics view the nickname as racially offensive." The Sioux were subjugated and have experienced prejudice in this country. The name could affect (or be perceived as harmful by) those who do not attend UND.

2. Native American peoples lost a good deal of their freedoms in this country as settlers arrived and moved west across the United States. Ultimately, native peoples were placed on reservations as their lands were given to pioneers by the U.S. government. Today, they are achieving more of a voice as laws against discrimination are passed.

3. Sports are very important to the faculty and students of UND. The Fighting Sioux are a popular and successful athletic body. This information comes across in the overwhelmingly positive quotations from students very proud of their school's teams. The construction of the Engelstad Arena is a good example of this.

In-Class Writing Activities

1. The arena is a fabulous and expensive construction, and after it opened, attendance at Fighting Sioux hockey games skyrocketed. Engelstad was a goalie on the UND hockey team and played as a "Fighting Sioux." Students may discover other details about Ralph Engelstad that shed light on his relationship to the university and to the name "Fighting Sioux."

2. A legacy is something handed down from generation to generation. A legacy could be financial or it could be something less tangible—a sports

legacy, a political legacy, a unique family legacy. Students' answers will differ based on their personal experience.

3. It will be easy for students to research the history of Native Americans, and they will come to this question with preconceptions. They may discuss the Battle of Little Bighorn or Wounded Knee and examine the outcomes for the Sioux. They may discuss historical events like the Trail of Tears and the removal of Native Americans to reservations.

Liz Breslin

Debate: Does a Family Need to Share a Surname? Yes

[*Brain, Child,* Winter 2009]

Vocabulary/Using a Dictionary

1. A *feminist* is someone who advocates for women's rights. *Paternal* means "relating to the father." In this essay, Breslin is engaging in a debate over the traditional use of the man's surname by his family. One assumes a feminist would be interested in the right of the woman to give her child her surname instead of using the paternal surname.

2. *Exclusion* comes from the verb *exclude*, which means "to shut or keep out." Other words that share the root are *exclusive* and *exclusivity*. Students may have heard of an "exclusive" club, or they may be more familiar with the opposite word: *inclusion* (*inclusive*, etc.).

3. An *assumption* is something taken for granted. Assumptions are suppositions, whereas facts have proof behind them.

Responding to Words in Context

1. A *default setting* is the setting set by a manufacturer or user that a computer returns to. A mother could be seen as a default setting because she is the parent (or "setting") her children instinctively choose for comfort.

2. A family might be considered exclusive because they shut out others to a certain extent. It is inclusive because it is all-embracing within the family unit. A single surname would add to a family's exclusivity as well as its inclusivity.

3. *Double-barrelling* literally means having two barrels mounted side by side. One may have heard of a "double-barrelled shotgun." When someone double-barrels a name, he or she usually hyphenates a couple's surnames to make one name. The double barrels are the two names side by side.

Discussing Main Point and Meaning

1. Breslin identifies herself as a feminist, but her argument rests on the statement that a single name—and in keeping with her family's choice, her husband's name—is best for her family. Students may still note a

discrepancy between her being a feminist and the argument that her husband's name is the best for the family, but Breslin says she is less concerned with the feminist side of this question and more concerned with the unification of her family.

2. In Breslin's mind, there is no doubt of the strength of the bond between herself and her children because she is the mother. Because of this intangible but indestructible bond, she is happy to choose to give her kids her husband's surname.

3. The world has a preference, it seems, for the consistent use of a surname. Historically, that name has been the father's. For those who take the mother's name or a new name, it may be difficult to prove a link to one's family if there is a need to prove identity. Breslin cites schools, doctors' offices, and immigration offices as places where the use of a different surname could be problematic.

Examining Sentences, Paragraphs, and Organization

1. The use of questions throughout shows that Breslin has anticipated her audience's challenges to her position. It makes the essay feel more like an interview and less like an argument. The questions provide a structure for the essay, and as a device they allow her to have a conversation with the reader instead of simply hammering a point home.

2. Breslin's use of questions followed by answers shows that she has considered the other side of the argument. She mentions in the early paragraphs that she discussed surnames with her partner early in the pregnancy and that she may even have entertained the opposing position at one time (para. 4) before giving it a good deal of thought. Her thoughts are what follow in the essay.

3. The father's position on surnames is mentioned both early and late in the essay. Breslin notes his early objection to the possibility of not using his surname, which led her to look at the question more closely. She ends by mentioning his pride in sharing his name and reiterates that her decision was a choice made by both of them for the good of all family members. Students may feel the essay ends too abruptly on that note without much talk about how they "chose" this together, but most may say that bringing the father back into the discussion helps round out her argument about the experience of the family as a whole (not just her decision).

Thinking Critically

1. Answers will vary depending on students' experiences. They may refer to religious or cultural traditions, or they may have more unique family traditions. Reasons for accepting or rejecting certain traditions will also vary depending on personal, cultural, and familial values.

2. Students may believe Breslin is a feminist because she clearly considered the question of surnames before assuming her husband's name. They

may also note that she doesn't come from a traditional marriage, and that may have some reflection on her feelings about traditional roles and women's rights. There is a question at the end about whether Breslin "chose" to give herself and the kids her husband's name or if she "let" him do it because he didn't want to give them her name. The discussion at that point is very brief and some may not be convinced without more explanation of their mutual decision (he seemed distressed at the beginning that she might not take his name). What, for example, would it have meant, given her argument, if they had all taken her name (husband included)? Or if they had all legally changed to a "double-barrelled or blended" name?

3. Students' answers will vary depending on which side they take in the argument. Some may agree with the need for a shared name while others will question whether it's necessary for a unified family. Expect students to form their responses around specific points brought out in the essay when they take on or side with her argument. Other reasons for deciding for or against a shared name may have to do with the configuration of the family or particular beliefs grounded in more traditional expectations or a more feminist perspective.

In-Class Writing Activities

1. The history of taking the male surname is not the focus of Breslin's essay, so it may be helpful for students to research traditions and expectations of married couples either via the Internet or personal research involving their own families. Students might explore the legal aspects of marriage and how it affects the family and women's struggles for rights in the past. They should consider the traditional role of the man as the sole breadwinner, or head of household, and how that role has altered (or not) in recent history.

2. Names have been very important to identity—not just for individuals, but for identifying land, for identifying property, and for establishing a family's heritage. Scottish clans were made up of relatives within a family, and they were associated with particular areas of Scotland that they controlled. Today, people with certain names can try to identify the clan they have descended from and learn more about their particular genealogical history. People settling in certain areas (the "small-towners" referred to) gave names, often their names, to streets, rivers, mountains, and towns, in order to make their mark on the world. A family name could stretch through time that way.

3. Holiday traditions may first spring to mind when students approach this writing assignment. Or they may think about traditions around life events (births, weddings, deaths). Some may choose to write about traditions that spring from their ethnic or religious background. Answers will vary, but students may also discover traditions unique to their families as they consider the question.

Laura Williamson

Debate: Does a Family Need to Share a Surname? No

[*Brain, Child,* Winter 2009]

Vocabulary/Using a Dictionary

1. A *sucker punch* is a blow that comes without warning. (It's slang, and it's derived from the verb form of *sucker punch*.) The term is a phrase used in boxing.

2. Williamson questions the statement that the surname is the male's *prerogative*, or special right—she feels it makes no sense that men automatically control the child's last name.

3. Quite literally, to *underwrite* means to write under or at the end of something. Williamson, in this instance, means that one assumption directly follows another. Students may have heard of sponsors providing the *underwriting* for a project or a television show, but in that case the word has to do with the guarantee of financial support for that project or show.

Responding to Words in Context

1. At immigration checkpoints, people are stopped and documentation is checked to confirm identity and citizenship. Often these checkpoints are at a country's borders (for example, one might encounter an immigration checkpoint on the border between the United States and Mexico). A difference in surname within a family might cause some confusion because a common surname easily establishes connection between members of a family.

2. Williamson is referring to the confusion caused by the assumption that paternity is bound up with a shared surname. The "pressures" are not weighty burdens, but instead revolve around the difficulties of having to explain a family's decision about names.

3. The word *gnaw* has negative connotations (as opposed to neutral words like *chew* or *suck*). Pregnancy and breastfeeding are often viewed as wonderful and natural events without any consideration given to the mother's possible struggles and pains. Williamson wants to convey the difficulties (and painful nature) of breastfeeding that one might not have considered.

Discussing Main Point and Meaning

1. In Williamson's opinion, families are not about names alone. Families are about the memories and histories that are created together, and they are about love that goes beyond measure. She also understands that families exist in many configurations and are not simply made up of the traditional mother-father-child unit.

2. The mother-in-law explains the couple's decision to others as best she can and then goes on to discuss her grandchild without dwelling on the

decision about his name. Williamson says that love in families runs deep, and her mother-in-law loves her grandchild because he's her grandchild—not because of the name attached to him.

3. Williamson speaks about the discomforts of pregnancy, such as swollen ankles and the need to be careful about everything she puts in her body. She also talks about the deep connection between a woman and the fetus inside her and how unfair it seems that the intense connection seemingly disappears after birth. To her, the sharing of her name feels like a natural progression from the pregnancy.

Examining Sentences, Paragraphs, and Organization

1. The essay opens with the information that Williamson's mother-in-law's "first grandchild had been born." She keeps her child gender neutral at certain points in the essay. Other times, she refers to her son or the grandson. It might make a difference to some that the child is a boy (and should take his father's name), and perhaps she avoids such an immediate reaction from the reader by not naming gender. Also, the taking of a surname is a gender-charged issue, and she diffuses this somewhat by leaving the child's gender ambiguous.

2. The question about the husband is interjected because of course another person has a say in the naming of the child. The question shows that Williamson is considering the other side of the argument (not just reacting to it), and its use keeps the essay from sounding too defensive (as it might have if the next paragraph simply began "My husband agreed with me").

3. The anecdotal information about the mother-in-law creates an intimate tone. She relates the story with some humor, and it cushions the argument within a personal narrative. Williamson very carefully begins and ends her essay on that note and shows the evolution of her mother-in-law's opinion of her position as well.

Thinking Critically

1. People who go against majority opinion often encounter dissent or ridicule—even within their own families. They also must face obstacles presented by the world at large (Williamson mentions "the dentist's office, immigration checkpoints, and PTA meetings" [para. 9]). Williamson finds that many other women support her decision, although they may not feel up to following in her footsteps. She draws support from her family as well, mentioning her husband's understanding of her position and her mother-in-law's eventual acceptance. Different ways of being in the world can become more acceptable in society, but it often takes time for change to feel normal.

2. Students may agree that Williamson would respect her son's decisions about parenting out of love; similarly, she hopes her mother-in-law will respect her decisions. However, she may hope that her son shares her values, since families live by a shared set of values (para. 14). Students may

wonder what the essay would be like if Williamson's husband had dis-
agreed with her desire to use her surname, or they may speculate on
what might happen if her son wants his child to take his name.

3. The question of surnames is a charged one, since the norm is for the child
to take the father's name (based on a history that has seen women struggle for rights at home and in society). Students may fall on the pro-
woman or pro-man side of the question, or they may feel that families
have changed so much over the last century that the question is more
about how to define a family and less about a power struggle between
men and women.

In-Class Writing Activities

1. Both women discuss their relationships and their pregnancies, but they
take very different approaches. Breslin mentions the "growing, nurturing, breastfeeding times," the closeness to her children which makes her
feel that giving them her name would not create additional intimacy.
Williamson, however, feels that giving her child her name allows her to
maintain that intimacy now that he is through that stage, which was
often quite a bit of work for her alone. Students may bring in other examples from the essays to compare and contrast.

2. Students' answers about what constitutes a family will differ based on
their personal experiences and values. Their answers about what surname to give a child may vary depending on whether they have experienced only the typical family unit or one of the configurations
Williamson mentions.

3. Students will find that women have gained many rights regarding citizenship, their names, and even their own bodies over the last several decades.
Essays will be concerned with social and personal changes, and students
may remark on Williamson's position in light of their findings. The feminist movement has encountered opposition from its very beginnings, and
even today students may have experienced disagreement or backlash
against it in one form or another.

Discussing the Unit

Suggested Topic for Discussion

You may want to discuss with students the outcome of the Fighting Sioux battle and talk about their opinions on the lawsuit. Why does a name mean so
much, and why was it being challenged? Regarding Mead's piece, your students might have some ideas about what to name the decade in which they
primarily grew up—see if they agree with Mead's arguments about 9/11 and
its aftermath. It is possible that these students, many of whom remember very
little of life before 9/11, have an entirely different perspective on the decade
and therefore disagree with her conclusions.

Preparing for Class Discussion

1. Students can draw from Williamson's and Breslin's essays for the first question. They might consider Mead, Olsen, and Bergstrom for the second question. In all essays, students should note the sifting of evidence and examination from all sides that go into the choice of a name.

2. In "America Then . . . 1507," America is named by a European mapmaker, but it had a different name before that. In "What Do You Call It?" Mead offers a variety of names to choose from, all of which have some connection to the time, but none of which encapsulate the decade. Williamson discusses her mother-in-law's difficulties with her grandchild not having her son's name, but the child is more than the name (and perhaps legally the child is named Williamson, but in her heart, her mother-in-law thinks of him as whatever her son's surname might be). There are many ways in which a name changes, even as we fight so hard to make it one thing.

From Discussion to Writing

1. Students may look at the issue of gender that arises in the Breslin/Williamson essays. They could consider the power of public opinion and politicians in Mead's essay, or the roles of different people such as explorers and mapmakers in other times.

2. Comparisons in these essays will vary depending on which ones students decide to pair.

Topics for Cross-Cultural Discussion

1. Answers will vary, but students might consider essays like Bergstrom's or "America Then . . . 1507" or the ones about surnames (Breslin and Williamson). They might notice the lack of race/gender as a category in Olsen's essay. They could consider Mead's gender as the author of "What Do You Call It?" if they can make a case for it as an influence on the naming process. They might also consider Mead's references to Obama and consider whether his race influences the naming of the first decade of the twenty-first century.

2. Students might consider the danger of investing power in one particular group if only one is in charge of naming people and places and things. Examples from both essays can be discussed when thinking about the dangers or harm done by the dominant naming group. Examples of shifts include changes to schools and street names to represent a minority's choices, and holidays instituted to celebrate names previously uncelebrated in American history.

2

Happiness: Can It Be Defined?

Americans often seem to be on a track to find happiness, but what that happiness consists of is open for debate. Does happiness lie in the material world (can it be bought)? Is it an internal satisfaction or self-knowledge? Many people feel more familiar with its antithesis—unhappiness, anxiety, failure. But still, everyone strives to be happy.

Fear puts one of the greatest dampers on happiness. Daniel Gilbert writes about fear and uncertainty and its effect on feelings of happiness in his essay, "What You Don't Know Makes You Nervous." In it, he makes the bold statement that "people feel worse when something bad *might* occur than when something bad *will* occur," stressing that anxiety has a more pronounced effect on our happiness than does the reality of something awful happening. The uncertainty protracts unhappiness; those who know their bad circumstances can deal with it and move on—hopefully to a happier condition.

Even when success is achieved, people still struggle with happiness. Adriana Barton's "If You're Happy and you Know It, You're in Third" shows us that even successful athletes grapple with happiness. The triumph of a medal is diminished depending on expectations—a second-place winner is less likely to feel positively about his or her achievement than a third-place winner. Barton focuses on the contrasting reactions of skiers Shannon Bahrke and Jennifer Heil as they received their medals in the Vancouver Olympics.

Walter Mosley identifies the unhappiness of many Americans and then invokes the Declaration of Independence to assert our "right" to pursue happiness. In "Get Happy," he suggests that Americans may need to set up a government agency to safeguard that right. How else will they keep up with a mood "cultivated under a sophisticated understanding of a rapidly changing world" (para. 6)?

"Learning from Tison" by student Tom Hewitt compares the happiness of a young American with the happiness of a ten-year-old Indonesian burn victim. Somehow the privileged person from the technologically advanced country experiences less happiness than the burned child from the developing nation. Hewitt draws his lessons about happiness from this juxtaposition.

Daniel Gilbert
What You Don't Know Makes You Nervous
[*The New York Times,* May 21, 2009]
Vocabulary/Using a Dictionary
1. A *breadline* refers to a line of people waiting to receive free food from an agency or charity.

2. *Fin de siècle* literally translates from the French as "end of the century."

3. A *dearth* refers to a scarcity or lack, so someone experiencing a "dearth of dollars" would be in need of money.

Responding to Words in Context
1. A dais is a raised platform. An *inaugural dais* would be a platform used during an inauguration. One might guess what it is from context because Gilbert mentions that President Roosevelt "took to the inaugural dais" to make a speech.

2. Psychologists study the science of the mind and behavior, and economists study how people use their resources and how wealth and production of goods are manifested within countries. Both psychologists and economists would have an interest in how the happiness of people is affected by wealth.

3. *Unremitting* means incessant; it is an adjective.

Discussing Main Point and Meaning
1. FDR was president during the Great Depression and World War II, when times were tough and very little money was available for most Americans. One of Roosevelt's most famous quotations is "The only thing we have to fear is fear itself." Gilbert explores the effect of money on happiness. He acknowledges that having little money is a problem, but that the most important influence on happiness is "fear" or "uncertainty."

2. People who were certain to receive a shock experienced less anxiety than people who were unsure about what sort of shock they were to receive. This practical data supports Gilbert's claim that people fare better or are "happier" knowing that something bad will happen instead of wondering if it will.

3. Gilbert explains that when we know the worst will happen, we experience the pain, fear, or sorrow over whatever will happen, and then we cope as best we can with the knowledge. When we are living in uncertainty, we are unsure of what to prepare for and unable to go on with life. In effect, we are paralyzed by the uncertainty.

Examining Sentences, Paragraphs, and Organization
1. Gilbert is saying that those who don't believe "material" goods are important have never experienced hardship (such as experiencing a

scarcity of food). The play on words (the echo of the words *material* and *immaterial*) harkens back to the FDR quote, "The only thing we have to fear is fear itself."

2. Again, Gilbert is harkening back to the rhetorical devices of Roosevelt, repeating words for effect. One is used to hearing the phrase "insufficient funds" when referring to money. He creates an effect by referring to "insufficient certainty." We may think our problems and unhappiness stem from not having enough money, when in fact the problem is that we must deal with economic insecurity and other uncertainties that affect us more.

3. By referring to fundamental needs such as shelter, sustenance, and security as "quaint assets" that "enhance happiness" (para. 3), Gilbert is being sarcastic. It goes without saying that someone who has no food, no place to live, no feelings of being safe would be unhappy indeed. These needs go beyond quaint and useful qualities—they are the basis of fundamental happiness.

Thinking Critically

1. Some students may disagree that they would be happier in the long run knowing they will develop a disease like Huntington's. They may argue that there is greater happiness in uncertainty about something like that vs. uncertainty about something like shocks in an experiment or fluctuations in the stock market. Others will agree that there is a peace that comes with not having to worry about whether something even as grave as Huntington's would occur. Students may talk about what they would want to know about vs. what they would not.

2. Some of the issues Americans are concerned about are brought up in the article: economics, illness, etc. Since the age of the atomic bomb, we live in an increasingly uncertain society, and 9/11 has furthered that uncertainty for Americans. We are uncertain of the state of our planet with increasing global warming and overpopulation. We are uncertain of our marriages given the growing divorce rate. We are uncertain of our jobs, our homes, and our finances thanks to the recession and bank crisis.

3. Students may feel that there are things they want that would make them happy. They should consider the degree of happiness that those things would bring in light of other kinds of nonmaterial happiness.

In-Class Writing Activities

1. Answers will differ, but most of the symptoms raised in Gilbert's essay will be mentioned: increased heart rate, perspiration/clammy palms, stomach ache, sleeplessness, fear. Students should consider what sort of relief comes even with an unfavorable response to the uncertainty, and whether living with that answer is better than the anxiety of not knowing.

2. Students may look at the state of the world, wars Americans are/were engaged in, financial stability, the state of technology, and other issues that could affect one's general anxiety. Students may compare and

contrast the situations of Americans at the turn of the twentieth century vs. Americans at the turn of the twenty-first century. They should feel free to agree with or argue with Gilbert's statements.

3. Students will find that many people didn't cope during the Great Depression, or barely made it through the great hardship and anxiety of the time. They may find stories of those who managed their anxieties and flourished through such difficult times. One person to look at is FDR, who is mentioned in the essay, and who had to guide a country through the Great Depression.

Adriana Barton

If You're Happy and You Know It, You're in Third

[*The Globe and Mail*, February 18, 2010]

Vocabulary/Using a Dictionary

1. A *mogul* is a bump or mound of hard snow on a ski slope.

2. The root of the word *objectively* is *object*. An object is a visible thing. If something is objective (as opposed to subjective), it is more about the object than about the perception of the viewer. The word *objectively* is an adverb.

3. If you *disconnect* something, you sever or interrupt a connection. The word *disconnect* is used here as a noun and refers to a lack of connection.

Responding to Words in Context

1. To *counter* something is to oppose it. *Factual* refers to facts, or truths. If something is *counterfactual*, it goes against observable facts. Counterfactual thinking is thinking that runs contrary to the facts at hand.

2. If something is *controversial*, it often engages people in debate. A *controversy* is a dispute.

3. *Footage* refers to a length of film or videotape.

Discussing Main Point and Meaning

1. Barton says third-place winners are often simply happy to have a medal (they came very close to not having one), while people who come in second can only think that they came close to winning but did not.

2. Jennifer Heil is a Canadian in an Olympics held in Canada. Many had pinned their hopes on her to win the first gold medal for the Canadians in this Olympics.

3. Barton cites the pressures of sponsors, teammates, and fans as influences on how an athlete may feel at the end of a competition. Media attention and advertising can create certain expectations that are also upheld or let down depending on the outcome.

Examining Sentences, Paragraphs, and Organization

1. Barton writes about the day in Vancouver when the competition takes place. She mentions the weather conditions and adds that Bahrke was able to see not the "silver lining" (a phrase that refers to seeing the good in what's happening around you) but the "bronze lining" in reference to her positive outlook about winning the third-place bronze medal.

2. Students' answers will differ on this question. Most will see that the quotations add depth to the discussion of events. They offer direct insight or add weight to the data offered.

3. The fact that Ms. Bahrke is soon to marry a man named Happe ("happy") and that she sees herself as becoming "Mrs. Happy" sheds light on her personality and the way she perceives her athletic win. It provides some personal detail that doesn't directly affect the argument, but gives the reader a more complete picture of the person being discussed. It also refers directly back to Barton's title, "If You're Happy and You Know It, You're in Third."

Thinking Critically

1. Barton mentions that Bahrke was much younger when she won the silver and that she was not expected to win any medals in Vancouver. Student opinions may differ on the value of a bronze medal vs. a silver or gold, but they can look back at the many details about Bahrke's personality and her career as a skier to answer this question.

2. Athletes who win silver can have a variety of feelings, both positive and negative, but the overriding thought brought out in this article is a feeling that winning the silver is more about missing the gold. Coming closer to winning, but not quite making it, can make the silver medal seem somewhat disappointing.

3. Bahrke is described as "bubbly." Since she had not expected to win a medal at all, she says she is honored just by being on the podium. At the time of her third-place win, she was considering retiring from her sport in order to focus on marriage. Not much personal information is given about Heil, but the writer makes it clear she had been hoping for a gold medal and had experienced a good deal of pressure from outside sources to win first place. Her disappointment is felt throughout the article, as she is described as "crestfallen" and "blunt with reporters."

In-Class Writing Activities

1. Students' answers will differ based on what they focus on about the two athletes. Essays should compare and contrast Bahrke and Heil. The conclusion should incorporate the argument in Barton's article in some way.

2. Students may agree or disagree with Barton's argument as they reflect on their own experiences. When writing about this question, students should discuss material from the article and use examples from it in addition to exploring their own feelings and experiences.

3. Students may or may not have much experience watching the Olympics. They may believe the Olympics has changed based on modern advertising and corporate sponsorship. They may document changes in the experiences of early athletes vs. modern ones, or they may note that competition in sports remains in some ways very much the same.

Walter Mosley

Get Happy

[*The Nation*, October 5, 2009]

Vocabulary/Using a Dictionary

1. *Domination* is mastery or control. Students may be familiar with *dominate, dominion, dominatrix, domineer, predominate.*

2. *Codify* means to reduce to a code or systematize. *Codify* is a verb.

3. A *subset* is a division within a set. *Sub-* means under, beneath, or below. A *subset* is smaller and more specific than a larger *set.*

Responding to Words in Context

1. A *barren* landscape is a sterile landscape. The *tropics* is an area that's hot and humid, where tropical plants grow.

2. *Urban sprawl* is a way of describing the spread of urban development into surrounding areas. In this context, it refers to the cities and outlying regions that are filled with pollution from cars.

3. *Consensus* is general agreement. It is achieved when people come to an agreement or abide by the majority of opinion.

Discussing Main Point and Meaning

1. Americans, according to Mosley, are driven by an all-too-fast-moving technology, are insatiable consumers, have "untreated physical and psychological ailments" (perhaps due to lack of health care), and are hard-pressed to find meaning in their lives.

2. While Mosley acknowledges that happiness often has a connection to wealth, he believes that happiness is a state of mind affected by the pace and conditions of the world that surrounds one.

3. Our capitalistic, consumer society is well-identified as a source of our unhappiness. The constant and rapid change we are undergoing as our world changes is another source. But our unhappiness is as complex as our society, and our happiness seems to be as complex as well.

Examining Sentences, Paragraphs, and Organization

1. The passage from the Declaration frames the essay, giving us the "pursuit of happiness" as an unachieved goal and an elusive right. Mosley

can refer back to it throughout the essay, and it directs him to a government agency that would help secure that right for us.

2. The questions in paragraph 15 are some of the more fundamental requests that we as a people would ask for in order to secure happiness—food, health, help with childcare, education, land, and knowing that our government is concerned for our welfare. Most people feel they are on their own in securing these paths to happiness or they are at a loss as to how to secure them. Mosley explains these are large undertakings and they are as complicated as our current society.

3. In this essay, Mosley puts forth some strong opinions about the happiness and unhappiness of the American people. By nodding to those who may feel happy with their lot as Americans, he admits that some may disagree with him. He phrases it in such a way that it makes anyone who disagrees seem privileged and out of touch with most Americans, however ("I certainly do not wish to bring unhappiness to anyone who feels they fit into this world like a pampered foot into a sheepskin slipper" [para 8]), and in paragraph 9 he speaks of the "many of us" who are unhappy in the current state of society.

Thinking Critically

1. Mosley may or may not believe that any such agency can be formed; however, he begins by discussing the branches of government formed to uphold the rights established in the Declaration of Independence and the Constitution. By suggesting that we need such an agency, he underscores the fact that most Americans feel unable to hold on to their right to the "pursuit of happiness."

2. Mosley mentions that the "pursuit of happiness" usually refers to the pursuit of property or financial success. Despite that, he widens the definition of pursuit of happiness to a general happiness in society and happiness within the boundaries of an ever-changing world. Money, he says, can influence happiness, but it can't secure it.

3. The rapidity of changing technology, values, and experiences has an effect on how we experience the world around us. Mosley describes the speed of the changes as disorienting. He raises the pointed question, "How can a normal person be happy with herself in this world, when the definition of the world is changing almost hourly?" (para. 13).

In-Class Writing Activities

1. The executive, legislative, and judicial branches refer to the President, the Congress, and the Supreme Court. The three branches were established for checks and balances when our government was formed, so that no one branch held too much control. There are ways in which a government that equalizes itself in this way might lead to its citizens having more happiness. But Mosley makes the case that the pursuit of happiness is much more elusive as a right than the right to life and liberty. Answers may differ.

2. Students may agree with Mosley's idea for a central agency that helps citizens achieve and maintain happiness, or they may feel that there is no real way a government agency could be entrusted to handle a pursuit of something so unclear. Essays should address ways in which the government can help rectify or redirect problems that cause our unhappiness, or they should propose ways in which other specific methods or ideas could be implemented.

3. Answers will vary. Statements by Mosley include the blurring of truth in our society, our use of drugs even while we fight a "war on drugs," our poor lifestyle choices, our anxiety about health and money, our desire to get rich quickly, our love affair with things, our need to wage wars, and our dwindling integrity in our relationships.

Tom Hewitt (student essay)

Learning from Tison

[*The Sun Star*, University of Alaska Fairbanks, December 15, 2009]

Vocabulary/Using a Dictionary

1. A *documentary* is a film or broadcast of some kind that presents its subject in a factual and informative way.

2. *En route* comes from the French and means "on the way."

3. *Terrain* is land or earth. It comes from the word *terra*, which is Latin for "land" or "earth."

Responding to Words in Context

1. A clinic can refer to a group that meets to tackle a particular problem (for example, a speech clinic), but in general clinics are connected to hospitals and offer treatment to people on an outpatient basis. Hewitt mentions that Tison is a child and a burn victim, which indicates that he is receiving medical treatment (and is probably part of a burn clinic).

2. When something is reconstructed, it is rebuilt or re-created. Reconstructive surgery is sometimes called plastic surgery, which is a branch of surgery concerned with restoring the form or functionality to various parts of the body.

3. To measure something, you gather its dimensions or extent by comparing it to a standard (a standard measurement). You make a judgment by comparing one thing with something else. In paragraph 11, Hewitt is talking about measuring people by seeing how they respond to a given situation.

Discussing Main Point and Meaning

1. Tison is a ten-year-old Indonesian burn victim. Hewitt is filming him because Tison will be flown from Indonesia to Fairbanks, Alaska, for

reconstructive surgery. Hewitt's paper is based in Fairbanks, so the story has local resonance.

2. Hewitt lives in Alaska and writes for a paper. He describes his "stress level," which is high because he is missing school and has many papers to complete. The Indonesian villagers lack most of the privileges and opportunities Hewitt's life provides. They live in shacks and have to cross a local river on rafts in order to get to a field for a soccer game. The simple fare of cold water and baked bananas is a tremendous treat for the teams.

3. The lives of the people of the village are much harder than the lives of most Americans. A soccer game provides a diversion and a chance to relax and enjoy other people that most Indonesians don't get when they are working daily to survive in poverty. Perhaps their lifestyle allows them to view a soccer game as the opportunity that it is, while most Americans would be focused on competition and more material concerns.

Examining Sentences, Paragraphs, and Organization

1. Hewitt chooses to begin at the "end" of his story, mentioning that he's been in Jakarta and is preparing to return to Alaska. By beginning in this way, he grabs his readers' attention and creates a little suspense by then stopping ("Let me back up") and starting again with the details the reader needs to know about Tison and his project.

2. Students may wish they had more details about Tison. Hewitt makes the claims about his "cheery" personality, but the reader might want more of a picture of Tison—the sort of picture they would see in a documentary. Hewitt states that "life isn't fair" (para. 9) and then says, "The Indonesians know that, but it doesn't stop them from finding fulfillment" (para. 9). Students may want more information on how that fulfillment manifests itself (beyond the details of the soccer game), or they might want to see more of the contrast between the Indonesians' needs and life experience with Americans' needs and life experience (or, at least, Hewitt's).

3. The reader knows Hewitt is a journalist and that he's willing to travel great distances for his work. In paragraph 5, he mentions the stresses in his life, which provide clues to his personality. He also states in paragraph 10 that the burn victim, Tison, is "several times cheerier than I am in the best of times."

Thinking Critically

1. Hewitt focuses on the villagers' happiness in the face of their extreme poverty. He portrays their experience in paragraphs 6 through 8 and makes the statement that despite the hardships they endure, they still manage to find fulfillment in simple experiences and pleasures.

2. Tison's situation is described, but we don't get much of a picture of his daily life or the pain he experiences (although we know he has burns over 40 percent of his body). We gather he is able to play soccer and

even endure some travel to do so, but we don't know the circumstances of his injuries or how he is able to travel to Alaska for surgery. Students may wish to be "shown" how Tison is cheerier than Hewitt instead of being "told."

3. One might expect a person who isn't "spoiled" by the advantages of the modern world to be happier in his/her life because he/she has more of a connection to community and family or to the land he/she lives on. He/she may be less distracted by technology and more focused on simple human actions and happinesses. However, Tison isn't just poor—he is a burn victim. The reader may want to know how Tison has come to cope with his burns and have a better sense of what support network he has in his village in order to understand his happy outlook. Some may feel that the conditions of Tison's life might indicate he would be less happy or even unable to find happiness in his life.

In-Class Writing Activities

1. Answers will vary depending on the country chosen. Most students will identify the similarity of basic human needs and perhaps a similarity in what is needed to create a satisfying or fulfilling life. Differences will include the value of money or at least the prevalence of it, and the differences between life in a modern "technological" world vs. a developing country in which people must be self-sufficient without modern conveniences. Whether or not students find similarities or differences in models of family and community depends on the student and the country.

2. Soccer is a team sport, so there is a sense of bonding together with one's teammates at a game in addition to competition with the opposing team. Because teams have joined to play the same sport, there is an element of camaraderie overall. Students should do some research on soccer, a game that is played in many developed and developing countries, and consider why this sport brings so many people together. Teams are a source of great pride in many places.

3. There are times when a journalist might want to comment on the story being told, but most journalists are asked to present news objectively. Students may feel that reporters today show their biases in the work, and they should explore how this bias might come across in the writing. They might use examples from current news stories or they might explore the difference between an article about Tison and an article that comments on Tison.

Discussing the Unit

Suggested Topic for Discussion

Students may want to discuss the differences between some of the conclusions drawn in these articles. Does money affect happiness and, if so, to what extent? As many of the authors do, the students will want to relate this idea of happiness to personal experience—have they had a moment of realization akin to that of Hewitt or a sense of frustration for their current situation like Mosley? Discuss the factors they think lead to happiness that do not appear in any of these selections and see if it is possible for the class to come to some sort of consensus.

Preparing for Class Discussion

1. Consider Hewitt's essay, which compares his happiness with Tison's. Other essays compare degrees of happiness of others—those who think something bad might happen with those who know something bad will happen (Gilbert) and the winners of first, second, and third place in a sporting event (Barton). Mosley assumes he is a spokesperson for the happiness of Americans, so he is drawing from his experience in the essay. Some may trust the objective consideration of happiness over the subjective one, although they might find the use of personal definitions of happiness to be more persuasive.

2. Answers will vary. It is important for students to be able to articulate the argument in the essay they gravitate toward, and they should use examples from that essay to support their own position.

From Discussion to Writing

1. Tison's story is useful when considering this question, because Tison has had something bad happen to him and has plenty to fear, but he continues to be quite happy. Fear of failure or the fear in Barton's essay—of not winning—affects our happiness. Fear of an ever-changing modern world, or fear of a lack of definition of happiness (Mosley), is also a factor that keeps us from achieving happiness.

2. Students must isolate the thesis statement of two of the essays in this chapter in order to effectively tackle this assignment. Then they must present examples from both essays and compare and contrast them.

Topics for Cross-Cultural Discussion

1. Some of these essays deal exclusively with the happiness or unhappiness of Americans. The question of knowing or not knowing if something bad will happen (or simply accepting that something bad could happen) is more universal. The question of the American mindset might be explored, given what's presented in these essays. The one essay that clearly offers a cultural distinction is Hewitt's essay about Tison, the Indonesian boy.

2. Some discussion about what constitutes Jefferson's definition of "happiness" in the Declaration might be in order, in addition to a consideration of what rights were available (or not) to nonwhites and immigrants over the course of American history. Students should be able to compare that information with the argument and definition of happiness that Mosley offers (as well as his suggestion of how to safeguard a right to happiness).

3

Is There an Ethics of Eating?

Decisions we make about the food we eat are no longer simple. The days of finding healthy foods grown on the local farm are gone. Most of the food we find in the store is imported, and we wonder whether it is treated with pesticides. Our lives are made simpler by fast food, but our bodies suffer. All the essays in this chapter consider the choices we must make about what we eat and how we eat now that we are so far removed from where and how our food is grown.

In "The Rich Get Thinner, the Poor Get Fatter," Warwick Sabin examines why people from poorer regions of the country like the South struggle with obesity and food-related health issues more than people in other regions of the country. Regional cuisine may be a reason for the rates of obesity, but it is now extremely hard for people in the South to buy some of the healthier foods the region is known for. Sabin shows us how the production and distribution of food has changed in the South and elsewhere.

This change extends to how we eat at restaurants. As Amy Domini points out in "Why Investing in Fast Food May Be a Good Thing," "fast food is a way of life" (para. 3). The days of eating a slowly prepared meal made from fresh foods are a thing of the past. Instead of fighting the fast food movement, which has an effect on our general health much like the one Sabin writes about, Domini suggests that we change the industry from within. In this way, we can improve what fast food chains offer and reduce their negative impact on the environment.

Like Domini, Brian Jay Stanley does not call for an end to our consumption, since we are "consumers by essence." In his essay "Confessions of a Carnivore," he speaks of our ability to have a conscience about what we eat, but suggests that the answer is to "destroy with respect." Domini asks the fast food industry to maintain an awareness of its behavior, and Stanley asks that we as individuals stay aware of what we eat and of our subsequent effect on the earth.

Jacob Swede, in "Remembering Johnny Appleseed," reminds us of the legacy of Johnny Appleseed. Appleseed was very aware of both the growing of food and the conservation of the earth. Swede says that in forgetting Appleseed's legacy, we have also forgotten our connections to the earth and to food. Swede doesn't have the faith that Domini and Stanley have in the growers and purchasers of food—in his account, food ignorance has become a problem for consumers and producers alike.

Warwick Sabin

The Rich Get Thinner, the Poor Get Fatter

[*Oxford American*, #68, March 2010]

Vocabulary/Using a Dictionary

1. The root of *ensnared* is the word *snare*. *Snare* is both a noun and a verb. As a noun it refers to a trap. The verb form means "to entangle." The prefix *en* means "to confine" or "to cause to be in."

2. *Processed* foods are prepared in a certain way by machinery, while fresh foods are items like vegetables and fruit from a garden or meat that is directly from the farm (with no extra additives or other manipulation).

3. An *epidemic* is something that spreads rapidly and usually refers to disease. An "obesity epidemic" refers to the exponentially growing numbers of people who suffer from obesity—almost as if it were spreading like an illness.

Responding to Words in Context

1. An "obesity rate" is the percentage of people in a given area who are considered obese, or extremely overweight. It might also be called an obesity trend.

2. *Cuisine* is derived from the French word for "kitchen." A Southern cuisine refers to the style of cooking and ingredients used that one would find in the South. A regional cuisine refers to the style of cooking and ingredients that one would find used in any particular region.

3. The word *corporate* refers to an organization or body of employees created by a group of shareholders. Corporations are usually large institutions, and they would handle the creation and distribution of foods much differently from the local farms and grocery stores that used to provide food to the general public. A *homogenizing force* is one that makes things more alike—the variety of choices in our foods would disappear under such a force.

Discussing Main Point and Meaning

1. The South has been, traditionally, a poor region of this country. Foods grown and prepared there would have been intentionally high in calories because of scarcity or poor economic conditions. The calories would have served people well if they only were able to grow or purchase small amounts of food.

2. The poor people of a hundred years ago did not have the enormous corporate supermarkets that are found across the country today. They would not have been familiar with the fast food chains that offer cheap "meals." Today those supermarkets and fast food chains provide sustenance for many of the nation's poor in the form of high-calorie, high-fat, low-nutritional-value foods.

3. Because of how food is mass produced and distributed today, the food grown in local, rural areas might be shipped far away to other chains or have inflated prices because of demand in other areas.

Examining Sentences, Paragraphs, and Organization

1. The bulk of the essay is written in third person and feels objective; however, the essay begins and occasionally reverts to first-person plural (we). In the second paragraph, it changes to second person (you). Using *we* includes the reader in the general argument being made. Using *you* is noticeable because it directly involves the reader in the issue at hand. (Will you eat that fatty food or not? Why?)

2. Economics deals with financial considerations. If once-cheap foods are now mostly available to the wealthy, then the economic shift makes no sense—the general rules have been turned upside down.

3. The writer made a reference earlier to Marie Antoinette who famously said of the French poor: "Let them eat cake." This statement refers directly back to that allusion, but also highlights the insensitivity of an economy that dooms its poor to foods, like cake, that provide little nutrition but make them fat. "Little Debbie" is a brand name that would be familiar to anyone in the packaged desserts aisle of an ordinary supermarket.

Thinking Critically

1. Students might go further than Sabin and outline some of the types of jobs that are in place now (sedentary computer jobs and the effect of technology on our ability and desire to burn calories). They might mention the prevalence of fast food and advertising. They might look at their own consumption of sodas and candy bars that Sabin mentions later.

2. Answers to this question will differ based on where students are from and what sorts of markets they choose. Many students may never have noticed that most foods are "from" somewhere. Choices may be affected by background, financial and time considerations, or other factors.

3. Because small farms have been dwarfed by big chain suppliers and supermarkets, a local food movement might seem quite radical in some areas. Consider what it would take to get such a movement off the ground. Students may have some familiarity with Fair Trade and farmer's markets or other groups that provide local foods, and they can comment on whether these groups constitute a form of protest.

In-Class Writing Activities

1. The South has always been an agriculturally based area of the country; many of its people have experienced poverty (and still do). Students may look at the beginnings of agriculture and industry in the United States, or they may look at the Civil War and Reconstruction. They may look

at how the poorer states in the South are represented. Then they can look at the sort of foods Sabin mentions (and others based on research) and discuss why those foods are grown and eaten in the region.

2. Answers may vary depending on whether or not students believe that choices for the poor are as limited as Sabin claims. They may argue other reasons for the obesity epidemic in this country. Essays should include some of Sabin's examples as touchstones, whether they are agreed with or refuted.

3. Students may be aware of the CDC because of disease epidemics they've encountered in their lifetime. Going to the CDC Web site will familiarize students with the scope of the CDC's work and give them a better idea of whether obesity and food are worthy of the CDC's attention.

Amy Domini

Why Investing in Fast Food May Be a Good Thing

[*Ode Magazine,* March 2009]

Vocabulary/Using a Dictionary

1. An *advocate* is someone who supports something. When used as a verb, "to advocate" means to support or urge by argument.

2. *Ailment* and *illness* are often interchangeable terms, but an ailment often refers to an illness that is chronic in nature. In this essay, it refers to the chronic conditions of diabetes, high cholesterol, and high blood pressure.

3. To *eliminate* something is to remove it.

Responding to Words in Context

1. A *phenomenon* is an observable fact. A global phenomenon is an observable fact that is apparent across the globe. Fast food is a global phenomenon because it exists almost worldwide.

2. A *consumer* is a person who consumes (or uses) something. In this case, it refers to consumers of fast food, but it could refer to anything anyone purchases or eats or uses in modern society.

3. If paper is *diverted* from a landfill, it is rerouted. In this case it is diverted in order to be recycled.

Discussing Main Point and Meaning

1. Slow Food is a movement started in reaction to the proliferation of fast food. It attempts to support small family farms, crop diversity, and the idea that food can be prepared slowly and intentionally so as to promote health and environmental consciousness. Fast food refers to an industry that took off in post–World War II America. Most food found in fast food restaurants is precooked and packaged in such a way that it can be delivered to the consumer within minutes.

2. Most Americans eat fast food at some point. It exists almost everywhere and is available at a relatively low price. Fast food chains are very much a part of American culture.

3. Domini points out the health issues involved with fast food (fast food's connection with the rise of diabetes, high cholesterol, and high blood pressure, now found even in children) and the issue of packaging, which causes forest destruction and an increase in waste.

Examining Sentences, Paragraphs, and Organization

1. The inclusion of information on the Dogwood Alliance adds strength to Domini's argument and illustrates how some companies come to "move in the right direction and listen to their critics" (para. 2). Dogwood Alliance shows the reader that there are groups in place to help "guide" companies to make supportable decisions.

2. The bulleted points stand out and show very specifically how companies are taking steps to reduce the amount of paper waste they generate.

3. Domini establishes herself as a supporter of Slow Food, which is important because she is trying to sway an audience that might view fast food as an evil industry. By aligning herself with Slow Food, yet finding a way to support investing in fast food, she manages to create a connection with the readers she is hoping to convince. Including that information again at the end serves as a reminder to those readers.

Thinking Critically

1. Student answers will differ based on their feelings about fast food's connection to unhealthy eating and environmental issues. Some may share Domini's opinion that investing in the fast food industry will have an impact on health and environment, but others may believe investing in fast food perpetuates a destructive industry. And still others may not feel fast food companies are responsible for health or environmental problems.

2. The companies Domini would invest in have taken steps to become more health and environmentally conscious. They might be dogged by watchgroups that keep them in line with certain standards or they might be run by people who have decided that healthier, more environmentally sound choices help promote a better business. Students may agree or disagree with Domini's statement about there being no "perfect" companies.

3. The idea of a "movement" is brought up at the beginning of this essay. Students may look at different movements and organizations that have influenced the way companies run their businesses. As environmental and health issues become more noticeable, individuals begin to voice their opinions and groups begin to form to take a stand against company policies that affect their lives.

In-Class Writing Activities

1. Students can research Dogwood Alliance and other watchdog groups on the Web. They may know of smaller groups that have a more local influence on companies, or they may look at the effect of larger, more well-known groups (such as Greenpeace) and discuss how they protest company policies or effect change.

2. Answers will vary. Some students may recycle; some may not. Some may have participated in the process of recycling and know what happens to the materials that get carted away. Answers about what could be recycled that generally isn't may be creative and surprising.

3. Fast food has taken off in many nations, including some (Greece is mentioned in this article) that previously had no significant difficulties with obesity and food-related ailments but now do. Some countries continue to resist Americanization and the incorporation of fast food in daily life. If students want to write an essay that examines the influence of fast food in several countries, they may do so; if they wish to stick to one particular country (such as Greece, Japan, or France), that essay will work as well.

Brian Jay Stanley

Confessions of a Carnivore

[*The North American Review*, September/October 2009]

Vocabulary/Using a Dictionary

1. *Nonchalance* is cool indifference or lack of concern. It is derived from French.

2. A *smorgasbord* is a buffet meal made up of a variety of foods. It is a Swedish word that translates as "sandwich table."

3. A *quadruped* is an animal that has four legs (*quadru-* meaning "four" and *ped* meaning "feet" in Latin).

Responding to Words in Context

1. A *proboscis* is the protruding mouth part of an insect, which is sometimes called the beak. *Proboscis* also refers to an elephant's trunk and is sometimes used to refer to a human nose.

2. When something is *callused*, it is hardened. In this context, it refers to cattlemen and their outlook on life. *Callused* is an adjective. A *callus* (noun) is a hardened or thickened part on the skin.

3. One has doubts or second thoughts about eating meat if one has *misgivings* about it.

Discussing Main Point and Meaning

1. Insects and animals seem to accept that killing and being killed are natural processes, while humans have the reaction of horror, fearing death in

any form. It is impossible to know how animals "think" about these things, if they even do, but Stanley is reporting from observation.

2. Humans seem to have a hand in the deaths of animals either directly or indirectly, whether they eat meat or not. If they don't eat meat, they still use resources that affect the lives of animals and demand goods that may entail the death of an animal or the destruction of its habitat.

3. Stanley offers few solutions, since the problem seems to be one of simply being human. He does suggest being aware of one's actions and their effects as a way of being less insensitive to the world around one.

Examining Sentences, Paragraphs, and Organization

1. Stanley's confessions are infused with a semireligious feeling or at least an acknowledgment of a certain sacredness to existence. The writing in this sentence alludes to the story of Christ and raises the impact of eating meat by doing so. Much of Stanley's writing is hyperbolic in this way, exaggerating his experience of daily occurrences for effect.

2. Stanley's paragraphs are fairly long and often go on for half a page. His style is somewhat verbose, and the reader can tell he enjoys going deeply into each story. Long paragraphs accommodate this style of writing and allow him to include great detail and emotion.

3. Stanley lets meaning unfold from narration in this essay. He might have started with the statement, but it would change his style of "show, don't tell" that runs through the essay, because he would first tell and then follow up with the example.

Thinking Critically

1. Stanley was speaking of the arribada in Costa Rica in which most of the tiny sea turtle hatchlings are devoured by other creatures as they make their way to the sea. He asks the question, "What five-star chef ever went to such trouble preparing a meal?" (para. 5). By saying "death is the stock in the soup of life" (para. 5), he continues the metaphor — there is no separating death from the "soup" that is life. They exist in an inextricable cycle.

2. Humans consume everything — food to make their bodies go, water to keep from dying of thirst, resources to create their homes, and their possessions, and so on. Often people don't consider how much they are taking and using every day to keep themselves alive and happy and well.

3. While Stanley feels a good deal of guilt and shame over how much he affects the life of the planet, causing the death of animals that he eats, or removing vital resources from the earth for his daily life, he realizes that there isn't much for him to do besides acknowledge these feelings (or "confess" them). By living "appreciatively," he can be aware of the great impact he has on other creatures and the planet as a whole.

In-Class Writing Activities

1. Annie Dillard begins much of her stories and nonfiction with anecdotes from the natural world, just as Stanley does here. She has an appreciation of her impact on the world as well and a similar religious or spiritual reverence for daily things and for nature. She often lets images from the natural world stand as metaphors in her writing, just as Stanley does. Students should include any examples they may find from Dillard's writing as points of comparison with Stanley's.

2. Students may agree or disagree with the idea that they are "fat emperors ruling a kingdom of inanimate serfs" (para. 11), and they should provide evidence as to why they do or do not see themselves in this light. Some may feel Stanley overdoes his argument about the effect humans have while some may feel swayed by the way he has presented his case.

3. Students can choose from a variety of problems Stanley presents here. They should be able to describe themselves as "consumers" much as he does in the essay and explore their effect on the world from one particular angle. They may be able to include information on how to slow or stall the negative impact by choosing to behave in a certain way or engage in any sort of beneficial activity.

Jacob Swede (student essay)

Remembering Johnny Appleseed

[*The Minnesota Daily*, University of
Minnesota Twin Cities, March 10, 2010]

Vocabulary/Using a Dictionary

1. A *legacy* is something that gets handed down from an ancestor or predecessor. In this essay, Johnny Appleseed's legacy, the story of his planting of apple orchards, is honored on Johnny Appleseed Day.

2. An *ecosystem* refers to an environment in which organisms interact, an ecological community that functions as a unit. Words that begin with *eco-* usually deal with the environment or nature. A *system* is a combination of things functioning as a whole.

3. If something is *rampant*, it is unchecked or widespread. In this essay, Swede refers to the use of cheap labor as rampant in poorer countries.

Responding to Words in Context

1. A *critique* is a criticism or comment on something. In this case, the critique is of modern life—Johnny Appleseed's legacy points out the ways in which people today have grown disconnected from the land and what they eat.

2. Swede means that what we don't know about our food can hurt us—physically. Our bodies suffer from our lack of knowledge—we can

quickly become obese and suffer myriad health problems that come as a result of obesity.

3. *Land degradation* is the spoiling of the environment as a direct result of human activity. *Degradation* is the reduction or breaking down of something. As a geographical term, it often refers to erosion.

Discussing Main Point and Meaning

1. Swede points out that the American public views food only as it is presented to them on the grocery shelf or a plate and that we have little or no idea of where it comes from, what it is treated with (in terms of chemicals), the effects of farming on our world, or even of the nutritional values of different foods (fast food vs. fresh). This ignorance is dangerous to our environment, to our physical well-being, and to our sense of ourselves in the world (our relationship to the land and to food—the very things that sustain our life).

2. Land degradation due to current food production practices is the main environmental concern voiced in the essay. Land degredation destroys ecosystems, which in turn creates an economic concern for those who work in those ecosystems. Poor working conditions and poor pay are other economic concerns, since cheap labor often supports the production and distribution of imported foods.

3. The example of "the apple at breakfast, the half-price turkey on Russian rye you had for lunch" illustrates that most people know no more about their food than the fact that it somehow gets put in front of them. People know where they buy their food, but they have lost their connection to where the food *really* comes from. At one time people grew their own food or at least knew where it was grown and by whom.

Examining Sentences, Paragraphs, and Organization

1. Johnny Appleseed was someone who traveled the countryside planting orchards. As Swede points out, Johnny Appleseed Day is a largely forgotten holiday in the United States. The point is made in the essay that just as people have forgotten a man who was so connected to the land he lived on and who could help sustain people by growing food, so too have they forgotten their own relationship to the food they eat. Not many of us could grow food ourselves—we have become entirely dependent on unseen forces to create food and feed us. Swede would like us to remember a time when food was much more important and fathomable to us.

2. The Appleseed reference is made in the introductory paragraph and at the end of the essay. The body paragraphs deal largely with our ignorance of the food we eat and the undesirable effects of that ignorance. Students may feel the Appleseed reference is necessary to the essay and a good way to present the information that follows; others may feel it is extraneous to the point being made about our lack of relationship to the food we eat. If more information had been brought out about Appleseed

and tied into the body paragraphs, students might feel the reference is more important to the essay.

3. "Americans have forgotten what Johnny Appleseed achieved and that forgetting has led to a lack of connection to farming in general" is one attempt at a rewrite using simpler language. Answers will vary.

Thinking Critically

1. Consumers no longer know what they put in their bodies—they don't know which foods are healthy. Producers no longer care about producing healthy foods, and the way they produce destroys the land instead of maintaining it for production.

2. Some may agree with Swede's claim that our relationship to the food we eat has become so disjointed, but some may feel that bad food choices also have to do with lifestyle choices and apathy instead of ignorance.

3. Students may think Johnny Appleseed Day has to do with awareness, or with self-sufficiency, or with conservation and a more intimate pretechnological relationship to the earth.

In-Class Writing Activities

1. Students can research the life and legacy of Johnny Appleseed and discuss their familiarity with the man and the holiday. Their writing about why it is a neglected holiday should both echo and enhance the information found in Swede's essay.

2. Depending on what they eat and where they buy, students may or may not know what countries their foods came from or what companies packaged them or what each food's nutritional values are. They may or may not know what farming practices were used and what type of labor was employed.

3. Students should pick one of the topics and stick to it through this brief essay. Focusing on one topic will challenge students to go deeper than Swede in terms of their responses, since he tackled a variety of issues in one essay.

Discussing the Unit

Suggested Topic for Discussion

There is a growing trend to pay more attention to what we consume, but you may want students to explore whether or not this has had any effect on their eating habits. Did any of these articles make them rethink what they eat on a daily basis? In addition to the advice given by the authors of these articles, what do the students think would make a difference in our relationship with food?

Preparing for Class Discussion

1. Good food is harder to come by because of the changes in the farming industry (the move to agribusiness, as Sabin mentions), which has left the poor of this country, particularly, with the difficult choice of paying much more for simple, healthy food. Swede looks at similar problems that stretch across economic lines. Stanley discusses how we have become divorced from the understanding of our own needs—because we are in a consumer society, we eat without thinking, "constantly eating, and for contradictory reasons." Domini has hope for the fast food industry, but she thinks the fast food tradition is too entrenched for us to get around it.

2. Most of these essays show us to be consumers in a consumer-driven society. Based on our choices about how we eat and how we grow our food, we seem to have little interest in or respect for the world we live in and the people we live with. Domini has hope for how we can change the fast food industry, but the damage is already being done, socially and environmentally (Swede points out similar actions and damage in his essay). Stanley speaks of our conscience and calls for a deeper awareness of what we eat and what we do.

From Discussion to Writing

1. Answers will vary depending on what essays students choose to compare.

2. The history provided by most of these authors highlights the contrast between how we used to view food and how we view it now. They show the gulf in our knowledge of food production and what foods are good for us that would not have been the case for someone in another time. The rise of agribusiness and fast food is made manifest, as are the differences between the situation and needs of our ancestors and our own.

Topics for Cross-Cultural Discussion

1. Students should consider what sorts of choices about food Hispanics bring from their original countries, or people of Asian or African descent. Then examine the cultures of particular regions of this country. Students should take into account not only regional and cultural differences, but also the role of economics when answering this question.

2. The role of the United States in the world post–World War II (when products like fast food came into being) should be discussed. The role of technology and advertising as influences on our choices and the choices of the rest of the world should also be discussed. Students may want to think about how globalization affects food and consider how our choices about food are influenced as well.

4

Photography: Can We Believe What We See?

In "This Photo Is Lying to You," Rob Haggart writes, "The old trope 'The camera never lies' is, in fact, backwards—the camera *always* lies." Each of the essays in this unit explores the relationship between photography and truth. Haggart focuses on the common practice of manipulating and enhancing photographs. He begins with a discussion of photographer Ed Freeman, who uses Photoshop to create striking—and unrealistic—pictures. Haggart concedes that photographers have always tampered with their work, going back to nineteenth-century "pictorialists." But he argues that the prevalence and acceptance of such practices now is "screwing up our concept of reality." He ends on an optimistic note: All this artifice has created a "growing hunger for truth"—and a growing number of photographers in pursuit of it.

Jed Perl writes in the context of a photographic and political controversy: the Obama administration's decision not to release more photographs of prisoner abuse at Abu Ghraib. Perl agrees with the administration's position in his essay "Picture Imperfect." His argument touches upon the idea of photographic "truth" as a "particular kind of truth," as well as the ways in which pictures can "skew the truth" or "collapse a complex story into an image that, however horrific, is only one piece of evidence in a story that is even more terrible." Perl's case is subtle and counterintuitive; he argues that truth might be better served by suppressing photographs than by releasing them. As he writes, "information does not always advance knowledge . . . ."

For Elizabeth Svokos, digital photography has removed spontaneity, excitement, and imperfections from picture-taking. In "Head to Head—Print Photographs," she laments the loss of all her photographs after her computer crashes. The occasion leads her to consider the differences between digital and print photography—and argue in favor of the latter. Not only does she like the red eyes, blemishes, and spontaneous "bad" photographs captured by film cameras, she also prefers the experience of handling weathered pictures: "life captured in those imperfect and beautiful photographs with their smudge marks and rips on the edges from passing them around so much."

Rob Haggart

This Photo Is Lying to You

[*Outside*, September 2009]

Vocabulary/Using a Dictionary

1. The prefix *Franken-* derives from Mary Shelley's novel *Frankenstein*, which features a fictional monster pieced together from human body parts. The word connotes both artificiality and monstrosity. Haggart uses it to describe Freeman's photographic creation as an unnatural hybrid.

2. A *trope* can be any literary or rhetorical device, such as a metaphor, simile, or irony; it may also refer generally to a turn of phrase. The word comes from the Greek *tropos* (turn, direction, figure of speech). It shares this origin with terms such as *trophy* and *tropical*.

3. The term comes from the Latin *verus* (true). *Veracity* means conformity to truth or fact.

Responding to Words in Context

1. The phrase often appears as a euphemism for unintended damages, injuries, or deaths caused by a military operation, especially civilian casualties. Haggart uses it to refer to the unintended and negative consequences that artificial or composite photographs have on both photography and our "sense of reality" (para. 5).

2. *Hallowed* usually refers to places, objects, or people who are regarded as holy or sacred. In the context of Haggart's essay, however, the word suggests certain curators and photographic images are venerated and revered.

3. The quotation marks highlight the word's double meaning for Haggart. In one sense, photographers and photo editors "tweak" images—darken skies, adjust coloring, sharpen the contrasts—to make their pictures more appealing and compelling. But for Haggart, such tampering degrades the practice of honest photojournalism, as well as the viewers' trust.

Discussing Main Point and Meaning

1. *Migrations* appeared four years after the introduction of Adobe Photoshop. Wolfe was an "early adopter of digital tools" and used them to "enhanc[e] images" as a painter would (para. 10). These deliberately altered pictures "started a stampede of accusations" that such work would break the trust "between nature photographers and viewers" (para. 11). According to Wolfe, however, these practices have become so common that "nobody would bat an eye" if the book were released now (para. 12).

2. In Haggart's view, people are "finally fed up with all the tampering" (para. 23). He also sees the professional photographic community "policing" photographs (para. 23). Haggart cites a *New York Times Magazine* portfolio of altered images, which was spotted by viewers and ultimately pulled by the magazine's editors. He sees this as evidence of a "growing hunger for truth" (para. 24).

Examining Sentences, Paragraphs, and Organization

1. The detail signals Freeman's distance from his subject and suggests the inauthenticity of his photographs. At the same time, Freeman's justifications—that he was capturing "how surfing feels to me," as opposed to "how it is"; that he's an "artist" who "couldn't care less" if the images were "'real' or not"—set up Haggart's main points about the value of truth in photography.

2. In this section, Haggart demonstrates that "truth in photography has always been fuzzy" (para. 6). He provides a brief but evocative account of photographic deceptions, from fake images of Abraham Lincoln to altered photographs of the Kent State massacre. These paragraphs provide historical context. They also demonstrate that dishonest photography is not a recent development.

3. Haggart begins the essay with specific examples of photographic dishonesty; he then moves to the long history of photographers manipulating or altering images. But after examining the present "crisis" and placing it in historical context, he closes the essay by arguing that tampering has led to healthy skepticism and a "growing hunger for truth" (para. 24). You might note how this is a corollary to the "collateral damage" Haggart refers to earlier in the essay. In this case, though, the unintended consequences—a "more savvy public," photographers looking to "pursue truth"—are a benefit, not a problem.

Thinking Critically

1. Freeman raises provocative questions about the relationship between photography and reality, as well the one between art and reality. He concedes that his goal is to represent how "surfing feels to me," rather than produce "sports photography" (para. 1). Students may agree that he can alter his photos, but only on the condition that he disclose that they have been altered. That way, "our concept of reality" (para. 5) is not affected.

2. Haggart could have chosen to make a more general argument, supported with specific examples of altered photography. He might have merely summarized the counterarguments of photographers like McLean. Instead, Haggart quotes their own language, which gives his own argument a grainy specificity. The choice demonstrates his good faith in letting people explain themselves: Haggart takes their point of view seriously and addresses it honestly, even though he largely disagrees with them. The choice also suggests Haggart's trust in his readers to draw their own conclusions.

3. Haggart hopes and suspects that we are fed up with simulation and tampering: "Too many published photographs are unhinged from reality, morphed by a few mouse clicks into slick advertisements for perfect moments in time." There may be a case to be made for artifice over "reality." Students might also broaden the context to question assumptions about "truth" or "authenticity" that Haggart may take for granted.

In-Class Writing Assignments

1. Answers will vary depending on students' choice of image.

2. Students might consider how images from the media, advertising, movies, or popular culture affect our sense of "reality." Models in magazine ads are probably the most obvious example, but even more straightforward photojournalism may create iconic images of people and places that are "unhinged from reality" (para. 24).

3. While Wolfe is writing about the world of photography, the notion of being a "purist" is applicable to innumerable contexts — music, food, movies, hobbies, traveling, sports, fashion, religion, politics, etc. Purists can be seen as uncompromising, honest, and devoted; they may also appear stubborn, close-minded, and dogmatic. Haggart's essay concerns matters of "taste" (as he makes explicit in the final paragraph), and students can use this prompt to examine their own tastes.

Jed Perl

Picture Imperfect

[*The New Republic*, June 17, 2009]

Vocabulary/Using a Dictionary

1. *Propaganda* is information, images, ideas, or rumors spread deliberately to help or harm a person, group, movement, cause, institution, or country. The word originates from the Latin *propago* (that which produces offspring) and *propagare* (to breed plants); the origin suggests dissemination. The term *propaganda* was originally used by the Catholic Church in the seventeenth century for its missionary organization, the Congregatio de Propaganda Fide or "congregation for propagating the faith."

2. In this context, the word *grotesque* suggests that the photographs are unnatural, fantastically ugly, absurd, distorted, and bizarre. It comes from the Italian *grotta* (cave) and *grottesco* (of a cave); it was first used to describe paintings found in the basements of Roman ruins during the sixteenth century, with a connotation of the fantastic or fanciful.

3. The word *sadism* derives from the Marquis de Sade (1740–1815), a French writer infamous for the cruel sexual practices he described in his novels and short stories. It denotes the tendency to derive pleasure or sexual gratification from inflicting pain or emotional abuse on others.

Responding to Words in Context

1. Perl elaborates in the next part of his sentence on the "ability to comprehend horrors we have not ourselves experienced or for which there is little or no documentation." The term "moral imagination" is related to both empathy and sympathy: our capacity to imagine ourselves in the circumstances of others. In the context of philosophical ethics, the "moral imagination" may also refer to our ability to imagine various possible actions and evaluate the possible consequences—harmful or helpful—of those actions.

2. These words—both French—are often confused. A *cache* is a hiding place or a stash of hidden goods; it is pronounced like the word "cash." In contrast, *cachet* refers to a mark of prestige, distinction, or superior status; it is pronounced with a long *A* sound in the second syllable.

3. *Pathological* refers to disease: Perl sees the perpetrators' behavior as sick and disturbed. He worries that placing such actions in the context of sociology (as well as art history and psychology) will explain away the ugliness of the behavior, frame it as a sociological symptom, or even "make it all seem somehow interesting, the material for a novel or a movie" (para. 7).

Discussing Main Point and Meaning

1. Perl argues that photographs can only "represent an aspect of the truth," even when they are accurate, unaltered, and unedited (para. 3). If the images are made public, a photograph that "represents a single act of brutalization" will be distorted by repetition in the media—repetition that is a "form of editorializing" (para. 3). Ultimately, "Islamic militants" will exploit these "true" images to "create lies about the United States" (para. 3).

2. Some social and cultural observers have tied the Abu Ghraib photographs to the prevalence of online pornography; others have compared them to the work of Robert Mapplethorpe; still others have connected the images to works by Picasso, Goya, and the ancient Greeks. Perl resists these comparisons. He argues that they dress up an "ugly truth" and bestow "catchet" (para. 7). For Perl, the images are "evidence of particular, terrible things done by particular men and women at a particular moment" (para. 8). Associating them with art only diminishes their meaning and horror.

3. In addition to its distortion-by-repetition (para. 7), TV news is "always looking for the next flashpoint": the medium demands sensational stories. But as a result, TV news "can collapse a complex story into an image that, however horrific, is only one piece of evidence in a story that is even more terrible, if understood in its entirety" (para. 7). This problem is related to Perl's idea of "photographic truth" (para. 3).

Examining Sentences, Paragraphs, and Organization

1. Students may point to specific examples of this strategy. For example, Perl begins by asking: "What is there to say about photographs we have not seen?" (para. 1). The deceptively simple question introduces the broader themes and issues in his essay—especially because he argues that these images should remain unseen by the public. In paragraph 2, he asks: "So is the Obama administration standing in the way of truth? If we do not see these photographs, are we being denied some information that we need to have now?" These questions allow Perl to frame his argument in his own terms: For example, he can answer the first one (as he does in the next paragraph) by explaining that photographic truth is a "particular kind of truth" (para. 3).

2. The writer's long, carefully developed paragraphs match the complexity and graininess of his arguments. In paragraph 8, for example, Perl discusses his resistance to those who make connections between the Abu Ghraib photographs and "various works of art." The length of the paragraph gives him room to include examples of these connections; but it also gives him time and space to reflect on them—as in his ambivalent response to Stephen F. Eisenman's book *The Abu Ghraib Effect*. Obviously, paragraph length is relative. You might point out to students, however, that all the sentences in this paragraph support and extend the topic sentence. Magazines like *The New Republic* provide an opportunity to examine complex issues in ways that briefer news stories or television reporting cannot. Notice that the writer presumes his reader is familiar with the Abu Ghraib prisoner abuse stories and images, as well as with artists like Francisco Goya and Robert Mapplethorpe.

3. Perl acknowledges opposing viewpoints: "The arguments of the American Civil Liberties Union and other organizations that support release cannot be taken lightly" (para. 2). In paragraph 4, he writes: "The argument has been made that the wide distribution of torture photographs helps to concentrate the public's imagination, rendering ideas of brutality and suffering concrete." Yet, you might point out the lack of specificity about the ACLU's claims, as well as the passive voice in the previous sentence ("The argument has been made . . ."). Perl summarizes opposing views in his own words, as opposed to citing specific language. He seems to do so fairly, even to the point of conceding the merits of some of his opponents. However, his framing of these counterarguments allows him to respond to them in ways that further his own case.

Thinking Critically

1. Perl wants to focus on the particularity of the photographs—images of "terrible things done by particular men and women at a particular moment" (para. 8). He makes a measured, almost bland statement about the possibility of "violent power relationships" being "appealing to certain individuals" (para. 7). But he equates attempts to provide any larger meaning or context with "amelioration" (para. 8). This seems

like a problematic stance. Even his own claim against psychological analysis is undermined when he refers to the "pathological behavior" at Abu Ghraib, which implies a psychological disorder. Students may connect the images to history, culture, sociology, and psychology to attempt to understand the reasons for such behavior.

2. Students' answers will vary depending on whether or not they agree with Perl. Those who do agree with him may use examples such as Obama's defense of the photos depicting torture (para. 3) and explain that these photos cannot possibly tell the whole story of the war, nor can they be sufficiently contextualized. Those that disagree may state that as long as a photo is unedited, it captures a moment of truth, and therefore cannot be disputed. Students on both sides may want to discuss media manipulation of an image, although those who agree with Perl's statements may say that the ability to manipulate images is a good reason to keep them secret; those who disagree may say that the image cannot be blamed for the subsequent manipulation and should not be withheld regardless.

3. Students' answers will vary depending on their stance, but both sides may see similar connections to knowledge, information, and democracy. It would seem that a well-informed society has a better chance of being a successful democracy, but Perl's idea that "information does not always advance knowledge" complicates that theory (para. 9). Perl seems to argue that knowledge is more important than information in creating a successful democracy, and therefore withholding information does not always negatively affect the voting public.

In-Class Writing Activities

1. While most students will define propaganda in the most historical political sense, or even equate it with "lying," students might also choose other examples: advertising, college brochures, cover letters and resumes, anti-drug campaigns, movies or TV shows with a "message," political punditry, etc. Students will most likely say that their chosen example of propaganda is ineffective, perhaps because it is too easily identified as pushing an agenda and not conceding merit to any opposing views. Propaganda is often so radical it may be hard for students to imagine it being effective.

2. Students should use this prompt to examine their own assumptions and ideas about information, knowledge, photographic truth, and the need for an informed public in a democracy. Students might respond to a specific aspect of Perl's argument—e.g., his points about "photographic truth"—if the scope of the assignment seems too broad.

3. For this assignment, students may want to consider the way they control the dissemination of their own images—on Facebook, for example. They might even look at photographs of family or friends that conceal something, or create a false impression.

Elizabeth Svokos (student essay)

Head to Head—Print Photographs

[*The Bi-College News*, Bryn Mawr
College/Haverford College, November 18, 2009]

Vocabulary/Using a Dictionary

1. In the context of computers and cameras, the word *digital* refers to devices that can generate, record, receive, transmit, or display information that is represented and processed in numerical form. *Digital* derives from the Latin *digitus* (finger or toe); it took on a numerical connotation because numbers were counted on fingers.

2. The word derives from the Latin *monstrum* (monster, misshapen creature, omen, portent) and the root *monere* (warn). *Monstrosity* carries the connotation of something unnatural, abnormal, and hideous. The word seems better chosen than "deformity" or "horror," for example, which do not evoke the comic overstatement of "monstrosity." But the synonym *atrocity* might be suitable to Svokos's tone and purpose.

3. In its broadest meaning, *technology* refers to all the ways that social groups create the material objects of their civilization by drawing on subjects like engineering, the industrial arts, and applied science. It originally comes from the Greek *tekhne* (art, skill, craft) + *logos* (word, speech, discourse, theory, thought).

Responding to Words in Context

1. The word *weathered* is usually associated with objects like stone or wood, which are worn, disintegrated, discolored, or otherwise affected by exposure to weather. Svokos adapts it here to imply that old photographs are worn and seasoned.

2. In the context of her overall purpose, she wants the reader to understand the word ironically: Svokos does not think that photographs—and our experience of photographic images generally—are improved by alteration, retouching, editing, or the instant gratification that digital picture-taking allows. The quotation marks signal her detached and ironic attitude. Students might discuss whether this kind of irony can be overused.

3. The phrase *second nature* describes a habit or way of behaving so long practiced that it seems natural or innate. It can have a positive connotation when referring to a skill (driving in bad weather, for example). However, Svokos's use implies that our newer habits of mind toward photography reduce the pleasure of anticipation.

Discussing Main Point and Meaning

1. Svokos begins the essay with a literal loss: Her computer crashes and she loses all her photographs. But she moves to other kinds of losses: the

loss of entertainingly "bad" pictures in the pursuit of perfection; the loss of "weathered" physical objects—old photographs—which get passed through hands or saved in tins; a loss of spontaneity and excitement around picture taking, the "one-shot chance you get with a film camera" (para. 5). She argues that digital photography diminishes our sense of delayed gratification and anticipation.

2. According to Svokos, the bad photos—even a "monstrosity"—can become the most beloved and revealing in hindsight: "But isn't the best picture in your family album the one of your uncle looking constipated?"(para. 3). Such images result from the spontaneity and playful risk involved with printed pictures: "you just go for it, giggling, and hope no one's finger is blocking the lens" (para. 5).

3. The writer associates digital photography with false ideas about "enhancement," sterile perfectionism, instant gratification, and misplaced trust in technology. She associates print photography with authentic familial and social ties, spontaneity, the pleasures of anticipation, the bonds between generations, and the beauty of imperfection.

Examining Sentences, Paragraphs, and Organization

1. In this sentence, Svokos correctly uses the semicolon to join two independent clauses without a coordinating conjunction or a conjunctive adverb. She could have ended the first clause with a period and started a new sentence with the second clause, but the punctuation—and the breathless single sentence—help capture the spontaneity of her subject.

2. It does not matter if we know who Reyes is, specifically. Svokos presumes we can infer the subtext: Reyes is a friend of the writer's; readers can identify her as a type because we may all recall embarrassing photographs of friends. Similarly, when Svokos says she would use a bad picture of Juliana "as blackmail someday," we know that the writer was not planning a criminal act. Rather, she means the word "blackmail" in a friendly, playful way that matches the overall tone of the article.

3. Svokos begins with personal experience—her computer crashing, her memory of passing old photographs around, her decision to buy a film camera. She also ends her essay on a personal note, with the image of her mother's old photographs. But she uses this personal material to reflect on larger issues: how our relationship to photography has changed; our "world of instant gratification" (para. 4); the ways in which advances in technology do not always mean improvement. You might point out the value of connecting autobiographical information to larger themes and issues, rather than merely narrating anecdotes without reflecting on them and their larger significance.

Thinking Critically

1. Svokos writes in a style that is conversational, informal, even confessional. Most obviously, she drops into the second person: "Didn't you grow up looking at old pictures of your family and friends?" (para. 2).

She presumes complicity and intimacy with her reader: "But isn't the best picture in your family album the one of your uncle looking constipated?" (para. 3). She deliberately leaves some things unexplained, counting on her audience to understand: "Oh, that night! Where did we find a kiddie pool?" (para. 4).

2. Svokos means that we have grown accustomed to having exactly what we want immediately, without the pleasure of anticipation or the satisfaction of delayed gratification. She sees digital photography as an example of this. Students might discuss examples other than photography to support their agreement (or disagreement) with Svokos's statement.

3. The writer seems skeptical about technology, at least in her attitude toward digital photography. She implies that it severs our connection to other people—and even to cherished objects: "But now that we can't physically hold photographs, they are entirely in the hands of technology. They can be altered, enhanced, touched up, and even lost forever" (para. 7). Students may react in different ways to her skepticism about technological progress, generally, and digital photographs, specifically. Some might point out that people have been suspicious of photography itself since its invention (e.g., painters worried that photography would make them obsolete).

In-Class Writing Activities

1. For this prompt, students may argue from personal experience (as Svokos does). They could also take a more detached point of view and focus on the advantages of digital photography (or disadvantages of print photography). Svokos is nostalgic and even sentimental about the past. Students could begin with their own skepticism about her nostalgia—and about her suspicion of new technology.

2. This exercise should get students to consider not only the content or specific image, but the context around—or story behind—a favorite photograph.

3. This prompt should get students to consider technological advances more thoughtfully and skeptically, especially because our culture tends to place so much value on new technology. The examples are innumerable: cellphones, the Internet, iPods, text-messaging, etc. Students might focus on paradoxes like ways in which new devices both connect us and separate or isolate us.

Discussing the Unit

Suggested Topic for Discussion

Students may take this time to confess that they do not objectively analyze every image that they see. Perhaps they can cite an instance when photos of friends were posted on Facebook and taken out of context. Students may not have even thought about this question before because, as these sayings and "conventional wisdoms" point out, photos have long been thought to be the great truth-purveyors. And some students might still think they are. For example, in the Elián González photo, students might argue that it doesn't matter who the gun was pointed at, but simply that it was there—and the photograph is definite proof of that.

Preparing for Class Discussion

1. Of course, most people would claim to have a "hunger for truth": We do not generally see ourselves as eager consumers of dishonesty or artificiality. However, students might consider how that hunger is—or is not—reflected in their own lives, habits, and tastes. These considerations could go beyond photography—to film, television, video games, the Internet, etc. Perl suggests that we may understand the truth of the Iraqi prisoner abuse scandal better if we do not see more pictures—especially given the warping effects of the media. Svokos seems hungry (or nostalgic) for a particular kind of photographic truth, one that is best captured by imperfect print photography.

2. You might raise the question of "photographic truth" in the context of the González photograph. The image distorts and overpowers the facts behind the story, but does it capture and convey anything truthful? Or does it support Perl's claim that "information does not always advance knowledge, and photographic information in its raw form can mean many different things"? Despite the cliché about a picture being worth a thousand words, written language—used in good faith—can often provide a less visceral, more nuanced and accurate explanation of events.

From Discussion to Writing

1. There are many examples from history: the famous flag-raising photograph on Iwo Jima during World War II, Dorothea Lange's "Migrant Mother," Arthur Sasse's photograph of Albert Einstein sticking out his tongue, Eddie Adams's picture of a Saigon police officer shooting a Vietcong prisoner, the "Tank Man" image from the 1989 Tiananmen Square uprising, etc. Students may also consider why a particular image became so enduring and iconic.

2. Many students are immersed in contemporary technology. This prompt should get them to reflect on high-tech devices in the same way that Svokos does in her essay. The goal should not be to turn students into neo-Luddites, of course. But Svokos notes the way that our habits around technology can become unexamined "second nature," and this exercise should get students to think about those assumptions. You might even encourage them to consider these questions in the context of "retro" appeal—the renewed interest in vinyl records, for example.

Questions for Cross-Cultural Discussion

1. The prisoner abuse photos not only provided material for explicit propagandists and terrorists, they also sparked outrage more generally in the Arab and Muslim world. Similarly, after the September 11, 2001, attacks in New York, there was outrage when American television news networks showed Palestinians celebrating in East Jerusalem. Might a Cuban person look at the photograph of Elián González differently from an American? In all these cases, images shaped public perceptions. If the media will often "collapse a complex story into an image," the resulting distortions become even more complicated when they cross cultural borders. Ask students how they make sense of images of current events in other countries. Are they more skeptical? Do they notice a lack of context? Have they ever experienced a misunderstanding or misrepresentation of their own cultural or national background?

2. While such customs may be second nature, most of us are aware of unstated rules about photography. For example, we do not generally take pictures at funerals. If you wish to take a picture of someone, it is customary to ask that person first. This etiquette can become even more complicated when people travel. Have any students ever gotten in trouble for taking a picture? What were the circumstances? Did the rules seem sensible? Why would there be etiquette and customs around the practice of photography?

5

What Do We Fear?

International terrorism, massive economic downturns, flu outbreaks, an increasing national debt, global warming: We must face these problems and many more. But how can we react to them without giving into panic and hysteria? The essays in this unit address the problem of overreaction and fear in our culture. While their diagnoses and prescriptions overlap, the authors approach the problems from different vantage points.

In "What Should You Worry About?" Steven D. Levitt and Stephen J. Dubner begin by establishing that human beings are "quite bad at assessing risk." The writers present several "topics about which our fears run far out of proportion to reality," such as the "Summer of the Shark" in 2001, when the media overhyped the risk of shark attacks. Levitt and Dubner place real crises —like global warming—in historical context: Every generation has seemingly insolvable problems, from horse manure on the streets of nineteenth-century New York City to polio to global warming. The authors balance their dim view of our abilities to assess risk with their optimism about human ingenuity in the face of true threats: "A band of clever, motivated people—scientists usually— find an answer."

Irwin Savodnik takes a darker view than Levitt and Dubner. In "All Crisis, All the Time," he argues that Americans are addicted to overreaction. But rather than seeing overreaction as a common human impulse, he interprets it as a symptom of deeper cultural and social problems. Americans are in "retreat from reality"; they are succumbing to overemotional "mythical thinking," a practice usually "found in children, tribal cultures, and dreams." Savodnik also sees our addiction to crises as a moral problem: Increasingly, we are "acting in bad faith."

College student Erica Zucco writes as a self-diagnosed hypochondriac who's fed up with America's "Culture of Fear." Her immediate topic is the swine flu and her college's reaction to possible outbreaks. But she makes a broader argument about our tendency to "fear things we shouldn't" and not "fear the things we should." She advocates exercising good judgment, finding good sources of information, and ignoring the media's inclination to exaggerate crises.

The essays in this unit could be paired usefully with selections from Chapters 2, 8, 11, and 12. You might consider general overreaction in the context of specific issues: How does our ability to assess potential risks compare with our ability to predict our own future happiness? Do our strategies for preventing terrorists attacks seem sensible and effective, or do they suggest our addiction to crises?

Steven D. Levitt and Stephen J. Dubner

What Should You Worry About?

[*Parade*, October 18, 2009]

Vocabulary/Using a Dictionary

1.   *Flu* is a short form of *influenza* (an acute epidemic, a viral disease), which comes from the Latin *influere* ("to flow into"). It is related to the word *fluent* (flowing, easy) as well as to *influence*, a French astrological term that originally referred to the presumed power that stars had over the character and destiny of human beings.

2.   The word *hysteria* denotes an uncontrollable outburst of emotion or fear, characterized by crying, irrationality, laughter, or other unmanageable behavior. It derives from the Greek *hystera* (womb, uterus), which reflected the Greek belief that such disturbances were characteristic of women and originated in the uterus.

3.   *Paralysis* comes from the Greek *paralusis* (loosening or disabling) from *para* ("beside" or "on one side") + *luein* (untie, release).

Responding to Words in Context

1.   Levitt and Dubner do not mean that global warming is a problem in the Bible or a supernatural occurrence. Rather, the word suggests a disaster or catastrophe on a biblical scale or of an enormous size—such as the Old Testament flood.

2.   The writers put seemingly intractable problems in the context of other "impossible" historical challenges, such as polio or even horse manure in nineteenth-century New York City. The quotation marks suggest that we take the word ironically: These "unsolvable" problems were ultimately "solvable."

3.   Their point is that despite media hysteria (i.e., the "Summer of the Shark"), a more dispassionate analysis reveals that the number of shark attacks did not increase by much in 2001. These statistics, especially in comparison with the number of shark attacks in other years, provide the context necessary for people to accurately assess—and respond to—risks. The writers' bland headline illustrates the disparity between sensational media coverage and more empirical assessments of reality.

Discussing Main Point and Meaning

1.   According to Levitt and Dubner, "economics" offers "powerful ideas and tools, along with huge piles of data, to understand topics that aren't typically associated with economics" (para. 2). The writers argue that their professional discipline provides a way to analyze data and determine real risks in more objective and realistic ways than, say, typical news coverage of issues. They also see such analysis as a corrective to our emotional responses— "fear, blame, paralysis"—in the face of crises or potential threats.

2. The authors imply that our responses to uncertainty may be hard-wired: "Uncertainty also has a nasty way of making us conjure the very worst possibilities" (para. 15). But the authors also highlight how the media shapes our responses—and not just with the sensational coverage described in their opening paragraphs. In addition to the media, our own fear can "distort our thinking" (para. 13) to the point that we can no longer distinguish between a relatively harmless "threat" and an imminent one.

3. Nearly "every unsolvable problem we've faced in the past has turned out to be quite solvable" (para. 22). According to this historical "script" (or storyline), a "band of clever, motivated people—scientists usually—find an answer" (para. 22). The writers offer an optimistic view of science and progress: The "best minds in the world" can "focus their attention" and come up with solutions to problems like global warming.

Examining Sentences, Paragraphs, and Organization

1. The writers use fragments and one-word sentences for emphasis and for transitions. For example, they ask: "So how can we find out what's truly dangerous? Economics" (para. 2). The single word heightens the sense that this answer is both surprising and certain in its claim of truth. Paragraph 2 ends with a fragment that allows Levitt and Dubner to shift from the merits of economics to the topic of shark attacks. Later in the essay, they discuss the amount of manure produced by horses: "In New York, that added up to nearly 5 million pounds. A day" (para. 19). The two-word sentence adds to the sense that this is an enormous amount of horse manure. You might note here that these writers are choosing to use these fragments deliberately. Such choices depend on the writing occasion and the audience. For example, economists can write more informally for a publication like *Parade* than they can for scholarly journals in their field.

2. In paragraph 5, which quotes the lead paragraph from a news article on shark attacks, Levitt and Dubner demonstrate how such stories heighten anxiety and encourage fears "far out of proportion to reality" (para. 10). It supports the writer's argument by showing how the media influences our fears.

3. The writers see global warming as the seemingly "unstoppable" threat to this generation, in the same way that plague or polio appeared intractable to earlier generations. Before they examine approaches to global warming, however, Levitt and Dubner first establish that human beings are bad at assessing risk and tend to worry about the wrong things, generally. The authors ultimately concede that climate change is "an incredibly large and challenging problem" (para. 23), but the overall effect of their argument suggests that people may be panicking or responding in a way that is disproportionate to the threat. You might ask students how the essay would be different if the writers began with a more direct approach to global warming.

Thinking Critically

1. Strictly speaking, the writers are unconcerned with the production, distribution, and consumption of goods and services, which is the primary focus of economics as a social science. Instead, they want to encourage certain practices and habits of mind associated with their discipline: a preference for numbers and "huge piles of data," as opposed to subjective responses or human intuition. Students will most likely see this approach as a departure from their more traditional view of economics.

2. Students' answers will vary. Many may have difficulty believing that the horse manure problem is a fair comparison to global warming, simply because the negative effects of each are disproportionate. Some students, however, may see validity in an argument like this, especially if they are predisposed to thinking that global warming is somewhat overstated in the media. The authors attempt to downplay global warming by calling it the "problem" that our generation is faced with—just like the plague, polio, or manure (para. 14). The severity of these other "problems" however, may seem small compared to global warming and its potential effects.

3. While Levitt and Dubner think people are prone to irrationality and emotional reactions, the writers take an extremely optimistic view of human beings and human progress: "human ingenuity" will trump "large and challenging" problems (para. 23). The writers especially value groups of "clever, motivated people" and scientists (para. 22). Students' answers on whether they agree with this vision of people will vary.

In-Class Writing Assignments

1. This assignment should give students an opportunity to consider not only their own concerns, but those of others: Levitt and Dubner write in the context of generational problems. Students may find other issues more pressing: economic, political, educational, etc. They might also write about misplaced fears or priorities, which would build on one of the main points of "What Should You Worry About?"

2. Students may also use this prompt to consider the "media" more generally than just news stories. Levitt and Dubner note that our perceptions can come from other forms, like movies (para. 9). The assignment should encourage them to be self-conscious about how media shapes our perceptions. Point out that the authors cite specific language ("Summer of the Shark," a paragraph from a news story) to demonstrate how writing can be part of this distorting process. Students may mention specific examples such as global warming, terrorism, plane crashes, and natural disasters, among others.

3. You might note that Levitt and Dubner are the authors of *Freakonomics: A Rogue Economist Explores the Hidden Side of Everything* (2005) and *Superfreakonomics: Global Cooling, Patriotic Prostitutes, and Why Suicide Bombers Should Buy Life Insurance* (2009). Their work brings economic approaches, principles, and research methods to a broad

range of social and cultural issues. Students may consider the study of economics opaque and difficult, even as they are aware that their own lives will be shaped by economic realities.

Irwin Savodnik

All Crisis, All the Time

[*The Weekly Standard*, November 2, 2009]

Vocabulary/Using a Dictionary

1. *Animated* means full of life, action, or spirit; its root is the Latin *anima* (life, breath). *Animated* is related to words such as *animal* and *animus*.

2. A *mutation* is the process of change, especially a sudden change, in the context of genetics and inheritable characteristics. It may also refer to the individual or new species that results from such a change or departure. Mutation derives from the Latin *mutare* (to change). Words such as *mutant* and *immutable* share the same root.

3. *Volatile* comes from the Latin *volare* (to fly). In its literal sense, *volatile* means evaporating quickly or passing off regularly in the form of vapor. In Savodnik's context, it suggests something flighty, explosive, and quickly passing.

Responding to Words in Context

1. The term, which comes from construction and architecture, is most often used in geology; it refers to shifts and forces that move the Earth's crust. Savodnik uses the word figuratively to refer to major, fundamental historic changes that had widespread effects.

2. Savodnik is drawing a sharp contrast between reasonable, civilized, and enlightened adults, who use logic and empiricism, and primitive people who childishly rely on myth, emotion, dreams, and superstition. Students might find his usage condescending in this context or they might think it represents an important and valid distinction.

3. The phrase *bad faith* has several related definitions and connotations. It means that a person acts or speaks with the premeditated intent to deceive. "Bad faith" may also suggest that one acts knowingly and recklessly in a way that is inconsistent with accepted facts. It connotes self-deception, too: In existential philosophy, "bad faith" refers to people who deceive themselves about their choices and authentic identities. In this context, to act "in bad faith" means to reject the premise that we can make conscious decisions and shape our own lives. Savodnik's use of the term draws on all of these meanings.

Discussing Main Point and Meaning

1. Savodnik's thesis is that Americans are overreacting to events and turning them into "crises," which draw upon our illogical and emotional

responses. He introduces his main claim in the first sentence, as well as the first two paragraphs. Savodnik spends the rest of the essay supporting, unpacking, and refining this basic argument. You might ask students about the advantages of positioning the thesis at the beginning of an essay: Would the essay be less effective if, for example, Savodnik began with his discussion of the worldwide swine flu epidemic?

2. For Savodnik, *overreaction* is defined by "its reliance on emotion, its episodic time frame and, ultimately, its retreat from reality" (para. 4). He acknowledges that issues like widespread Attention Deficit Disorder or climate change do have "substance" and should not be ignored. But he aims to distinguish between reasonable responses to real problems, and overemotional reactions to "strings of events vying for crisis status" (para. 2).

3. The writer refers to a number of contemporary events and issues, including the "Great Depression" of 2009, the increasing prevalence of ADD, and global warming (para. 1). But his primary examples are an overreaction to a measles vaccine in 1998 and the responses to the recent worldwide swine flu pandemic. The example of the measles vaccine allows him to look at several aspects of overreaction (e.g., the role of the media), as well as the ways such responses can make problems worse rather than resolve them.

Examining Sentences, Paragraphs, and Organization

1. The gerund phrase "denying the value of either" as the object of the preposition "about," the repetition of "is," the strange word order—all make this an awkward short sentence. You might use it as a chance to talk about style and syntax. Would it be better as: "Those who overreact deny the value of both"? Or: "When we overreact, we deny the value of both"? "Overreaction denies the value of both"? Which choice is best, and why?

2. In paragraph 3, Savodnik examines the word *crisis*, which literally means "separation, and involves a break with the past by supplanting the existing order with a new one." He then gives examples of historical changes that meet this definition, such as the French and Russian Revolutions. In contrast, the credit card "crises" or education "crises," while "substantive concerns," do not merit the label in the "strict sense of the term." In the context of his overall argument, the paragraph demonstrates that we are overreacting to circumstances that are not "real" crises.

3. Savodnik builds his argument around a series of dichotomies. For example, he contrasts real examples of "crises" (on one hand) with events or "substantive concerns" (on the other) (para. 3). He makes a distinction between "overreaction" and a "forceful response" to the swine flu pandemic. But the writer uses these oppositions to discuss more fundamental contrasts: reason vs. emotion; science vs. mythical thinking; mature responses vs. childish ones; enlightened and civilized approaches vs.

primitive or "tribal" thinking; subjectivity vs. objectivity; reality vs. dreams. In each case, Savodnik's value judgment is clear: Science is superior to myth.

Thinking Critically

1. The writer discusses the controversy around a 1998 *Lancet* article about vaccinations and autistic enterocolitis. While the article itself caused little notice, a remark by one of the authors "ignited a furious reaction that caught the imagination of the media" (para. 7). Savodnik implies that the media is prone to such overreaction; it privileges "imagination," emotion, and "crises" over the less sensational aims of scientists, who value logic, fact, and "premises that are true" (para. 7). You might ask students if they can recall their own examples of "overreaction."

2. He considers "mythical thinking" a way of "embodying our emotions and impulses in tales of our fears, vulnerabilities, and guilt in strange, often colorful, stories" (para. 9). This "regressive" view helps us deal with our dread of being powerless and allows us to "concoct magical cures for our weakness" (para. 9). For Savodnik, mythical thinking is overemotional, childish, and primitive. It is also a "flight from reality" (para. 9). But you might ask how this applies, specifically, to contemporary problems. For example, Savodnik claims that Americans have overreacted to the economic crisis of the last two years. What is "mythical thinking" in this context?

3. For Savodnik, our tendency to overreact is not an unavoidable human reflex or an unfortunate-but-excusable result of contemporary culture. Rather, it is a matter of right and wrong: "We are not mere mythmakers. We know that fairy tales don't solve the problems that plague us" (para. 10). Our knowledge that there is a clear "right" choice and a clear "wrong" choice gives the problem of overreaction a "moral dimension." To knowingly revert to childish or mythical thinking in the face of serious problems is morally wrong. Students' answers about whether a moral dimension exists in this context will vary.

In-Class Writing Assignments

1. To get started, students may want to choose a problem (current or historical) that draws a range of responses. They may also want to challenge Savodnik's stark distinction between the two approaches.

2. Students' answers will vary, but almost all students should be able to easily describe a situation in which they overreacted. Students may want to test their specific examples against Savodnik's claims about "mythical thinking." They can also use this prompt to consider a time when they underreacted, or remained unaware of the seriousness of a particular problem or crisis.

3. Savodnik makes enormous generalizations here, even as he describes his conclusions as "self-evident" (para. 11). Students might argue that the

Internet and other new media forms can connect people and make them less "alienated." They should measure his account against their own experiences and observations.

Erica Zucco (student essay)

Quit Living in Swine Fear

[*The Maneater*, University of Missouri Columbia, September 4, 2009]

Vocabulary/Using a Dictionary

1. The word originally derives from the Latin *sanus* (healthy, sane). It shares this root with the English words *sanity* and *insane*.

2. The word comes from the Latin *quattuor* (four) and *quadraginta* (forty). It derives its modern meaning—the practice of isolating people to prevent the spread of disease—from the fifteenth-century Venetian custom of keeping ships from plague-stricken countries waiting in the port for forty days.

3. *Stress* is a shortening of the Middle French *destresse* (distress). It originates in the Latin *stringere* (draw tight). Words like *strain, stringent,* and *strict* share the same root.

Responding to Words in Context

1. A *hypochondriac* is a person who is excessively preoccupied or worried about his or her health. Zucco's self-diagnosis—even if she means it lightheartedly—is important because her fear of becoming ill is heightened even further by a "culture of fear."

2. Traditionally, *hysterics* referred to fits of weeping or laughing ("hysteria"). Now, the word includes more general outbursts of unrestrained emotion or fear. *Hysterical* now has the connotation of something funny or comical, but Zucco does not mean hysterics in that sense. She could have used the words *panic, madness,* or *frenzy*, among others.

3. Zucco chooses a slangy term, which fits with the informal, conversational style of her writing. Alternatives include "panicking" and "being frightened by," although the second choice does not carry the same connotation of a loss of control. Students might suggest that her wording here makes her essay seem less serious. They might also discuss the benefits and drawbacks of slang.

Discussing Main Point and Meaning

1. Zucco blames the "Culture of Fear" (para. 3). In the writer's view, the "interaction of the media, public policymakers and corporations, sometimes by accident and at other times on purpose, constantly issue widespread reports of danger" (para. 4). People tend to ignore more likely threats while they worry about sensational—but more improbable—dangers. Panic over the swine flu is only the latest example.

2. According to the writer, the media will overemphasize a "hot-issue story even if it wasn't really that newsworthy or a huge danger" (para. 4). The government may confirm these threats, and then companies find ways to exploit public fear.

3. She advises readers to "think about all of the realistic things we could be doing instead of preparing for the worst" (para. 6). She suggests avoiding the media when they create an "overblown threat" (para. 6). People should also use their own judgment and rely on trustworthy people to "discern between the actual and the exaggerated" (para. 6). She proposes that we try to avoid overreacting to overblown or irrational threats and focus on things we have control over.

Examining Sentences, Paragraphs, and Organization

1. The writer chooses a deliberately informal, conversational tone: She seems to be talking directly to the reader. Zucco's style implies her honesty and common sense amid a "Culture of Fear." Her diction is appropriate in the context of a college newspaper column. Ask students how the style might be different if Zucco was writing this essay for a media studies, sociology, or anthropology class.

2. In paragraph 5, she cites Marc Siegel's *False Alarm: The Truth about the Epidemic of Fear.* Zucco uses his thesis to support her own argument, but she does not include any specific language from the book. Her point would be strengthened if she integrated quotations from Siegel's work.

3. Zucco includes her professional background because it lends credibility to her statements about media sensationalism. Note that she uses the verb *reported* to indicate that she has experience gathering and presenting news.

Thinking Critically

1. The writer is referring to the panic and dire predictions that accompanied the turn of the century in 2000. In hindsight, the danger was overhyped. Her point might be strengthened, however, if she provided more specific evidence or examples of the overreaction to "Y2K," particularly as the media, the government, and businesses stoked public anxiety.

2. Ask students if their view is as skeptical as Zucco's. The media, in particular, has an interest in viewers and readers who are anxious or fearful: These people are likely to continue consuming media that plays upon these anxieties. Corporations can sell products (in Zucco's example, bottled water) by exploiting fear. What might the government's motive be? To increase control? To create consent or public support for certain policies? To get particular officials elected to office?

3. This question should provoke a range of responses. Students might discuss which crises, threats, and dangers fall under the purview of government responsibility: H1N1, terrorism, food safety, environmental issues,

national disasters, economic problems, etc. Is the government effective in its role? Ineffective?

In-Class Writing Activities

1. Zucco focuses on the swine flu as evidence of a "Culture of Fear." For this prompt, students will come up with their own examples that resemble Zucco's.

2. Zucco acknowledges that we "ignore the threat of more probable dangers" (para. 5). Students must discuss large threats—economic, environmental, political, medical, military, etc.—that people should be concerned about but are not. They could focus on what qualities make a threat newsworthy, or why some real dangers fail to capture the public's interest.

3. For this essay, students can choose from innumerable cultural and societal tendencies: consumerism, apathy, selfishness, patriotism, optimism, instant gratification, heroism, irresponsibility, etc. Encourage them to go beyond the obvious. They should support their generalization with specific examples. If students focus on negative qualities or problems, they should also provide possible solutions, as Zucco does in "Quit Living in Swine Fear."

Discussing the Unit

Suggested Topic for Discussion

These essays show that there are great costs for overreaction—Zucco shows the more personal side of these potential costs with her confessions about the swine flu, and Savodnik implies that we are becoming less able to reflect logically on events around us, which is actually affecting our ability to deal with threats. Students may offer ways such as critical analysis or logical reasoning to combat the sensationalized crises the media latches onto.

Preparing for Class Discussion

1. Zucco's suggestion may be appealing to some, but others may find it unrealistic. We are surrounded by media, in any case. This prompt should get students sharing their ideas and standards about what constitutes a trustworthy source of information. You might also ask if there are significant distinctions between "traditional media" (radio, newspapers, television) and newer media, like the Internet, in this context. For example, rumors and misinformation can spread much more quickly on the Web.

2. Savodnik and Levitt and Dubner take different approaches to the same general argument: that Americans are overreacting to relatively non-threatening events and situations. Levitt and Dubner provide an example-based, economic approach to the situation, trying to logically illustrate—with figures and data—that the most feared events, like shark attacks and plane crashes, are generally not worth worrying

about. Savodnik takes a more philosophical approach, showing the absurdity and overuse of the word "crisis" in American media, and highlighting the necessity for logical thinking and reasoning, something that overreaction tends to quell. The major difference in the articles comes at their conclusion: While Levitt and Dubner have faith in human ingenuity, Savodnik seems to think that we may not be capable of coming back from this state of overreaction.

From Discussion to Writing

1. Students' answers will vary depending on their position.

2. Students' answers will vary. If they agree with Savodnik, it may be because they have experienced this increased alienation due to popular forms of entertainment. Some students may disagree with Savodnik and argue that modern entertainment actually offers quite a bit of socializing: With massively multiplayer online role-playing games and social networking sites, personal entertainment has actually become a social activity.

Questions for Cross-Cultural Discussion

1. In the case of H1N1, many countries, like Japan and Mexico, seemed to react to the "crisis" in an even more exaggerated way than America— people there wore masks and stayed away from other people—but they were also reported to have been more severely affected. It is difficult, however, to accurately analyze these events when you are seeing them all through the same American media lens. There are crises, superstitions and overreaction all over the world, but exactly what you are afraid of and how you react are most certainly shaped by your individual culture.

2. Students' answers will vary depending on their views of how "over-blown" the fears surrounding cultural differences are. Many may point out that the biggest problem with creating fear of an entire culture is that it leads to stereotyping and, in many cases, racial profiling. Savodnik's idea that we are overreacting to the situations we are faced with may also fit here: There may be an immigration problem, but does that mean that immigrants are bad? And Islamic fundamentalism is behind many terrorist acts, but does that mean that Muslim communities should be persecuted? Some students may think that these connections are, in fact, warranted, and that the fear does not need to be alleviated, but others may suggest that we apply the logical analysis that Savodnik mentions in order to avoid conflict based on cultural differences.

6

How Is Today's Media Altering Our Language?

We are in the midst of a literary revolution, according to Andrea Lunsford, a writing and rhetoric professor at Stanford University. She is one of the experts quoted in Clive Thompson's essay, "The New Literacy," which argues that our writing now taking place largely online isn't changing for the worse, just changing. The writers in this chapter go back and forth on that statement. For some, the Internet has created a climate that redefines our writing and our understanding in positive ways; for others, the Internet has come between us and our ability to write well—and our ability to absorb information in an informed, educated manner.

Clive Thompson makes the case that our writing today is all about audience, similar to the Greek tradition of argument. Knowing one's audience, in his mind, holds the writing to a standard that academic writing might lack. It creates an enthusiasm and a focus previous generations never had.

Thompson would say Erin McKean is taking full advantage of the revolution taking place in the new media. Her essay, "Redefining Definition," describes how definitions and dictionaries come to be, and argues that the expansiveness of the Web can be channeled to broaden our understanding of the words we use. Her online dictionary, Wordnik.com, is already in place to begin this process. What a dictionary is will change to "involve more curation and less abridgment, less false precision and more organic understanding," all thanks to the seeming limitlessness of technologies now in place.

Rounding out the chapter, "How to Write an Incendiary Blog Post" by Chris Clarke turns the reader's attention to another facet of Internet writing: blogging. Aprille Hanson's student essay, "Stop Relying on Bloggers for News," covers the same issue. Clarke, a blogger himself, takes a look at how blogs appear to the general reader. His satirical essay points to the structures and subjects covered in a weblog, a phenomenon that has sprung up all over the Internet. Hanson chastises readers for taking the blogger's word as truth, providing data that shows the public now relies on blogs as trusted news sources. Today's media has changed the public's perception so much it would rather hear a satirist's delivery of the news than a seasoned journalist's.

Clive Thompson

The New Literacy

[*Wired*, September 2009]

Vocabulary/Using a Dictionary

1. Something *asynchronous* is out of sync, or doesn't occur at the same time. Something *synchronous* is something simultaneous, occurring at the same time.

2. *Rhetoric* comes from Greek. A *rhetorician* in ancient Greece would have been an expert in the art of rhetoric. Today, a rhetorician usually is someone who teaches rhetoric.

3. *Collaboratively* means jointly, and it is an adverb. When people *collaborate*, they work with each other on something.

Responding to Words in Context

1. The meaning of *bald* in this context is plain, or unadorned.

2. A *narcissist* is someone who loves himself (particularly his own body). Narcissus, in Greek mythology, fell in love with his own reflection in a pool of water.

3. This phrase refers to the amount of writing now devoted to the discussion of various topics on the Internet. Thompson uses the examples of "sprawling TV-show recaps to 15,000-word videogame walkthroughs." Anyone can write about anything at any length now on the Internet, no matter how ordinary.

Discussing Main Point and Meaning

1. According to the essay, we now write much more than we used to, largely because of the ease of writing on the Internet.

2. Because of technology today, Thompson says, people are writing more than ever. The Internet has created a public forum for anyone who wants to write, in the form of blogs, e-mail, and social networking sites. The resulting writing is perhaps less considered and more brief (consider status updates and e-mails vs. the letter writing that happened before the advent of the Internet), but Thompson claims more people are writing, and writing more frequently, than in the past.

3. The focus of writing happening today (outside the world of academic prose) is on audience and intention. A suggestion is made that it is a good thing that more people are writing than ever before. In the essay, this occurrence is described as a "literacy revolution."

Examining Sentences, Paragraphs, and Organization

1. Many people feel technology is destroying "good" writing. But Lunsford is an expert in her field (professor of writing and rhetoric at Stanford

University), and she is taking an unusual stance for an academic—suggesting that the writing that is taking place on the Internet does not detract from the study and practice of good academic writing in any way. Making this information evident at the beginning puts some weight behind Thompson's thesis. Lunsford's research runs through the essay to support the position that there is a "new" literacy.

2. *Kairos* is defined in the essay as "assessing their [students'] audience and adapting their tone and technique to best get their point across." Thompson states that the writing that is happening via technology today is becoming honed in a different way than ever before, with a focus on audience and the intention behind the writing. The use of the Greek word *kairos* is also relevant because of Lunsford's claim that "we're in the midst of a literacy revolution the likes of which we haven't seen since Greek civilization," connecting the dramatic changes that happened to thought and writing then with those that are happening now.

3. Midway through the essay, in paragraph 6, Thompson notes that Lunsford found that the writing taking place on the Internet shows an understanding of its audience since it is often directed to particular individuals and conversational in nature. The next paragraphs look at the students' perception of whom they are writing for and how that writing doesn't seem to have suffered any ill effects from a shift in medium. Thompson outlines some of the benefits of this writing: concision, the opportunity to write at length, and the ability to write in a collaborative way.

Thinking Critically

1. Students may believe that these forms of writing count as literacy and in fact promote literacy since so many people can participate. Others may disagree and feel that texting or other online writing is careless, encouraging writers to lose sight of the elements of "good" writing.

2. Students can imagine an audience for academic papers, and the assumed audience can help shape the tone and direction of the paper. Thompson examines the idea that writing today is shaped by the audience, because it is so public and often so directed (on a site like Facebook, for example).

3. Concise writing briefly expresses what the writer intends. It is possible that writers who text and update statuses are concise, and they could become that way with practice. However, it is possible to argue that texting and status updating, while brief, do not always cover what the writer intends, or do not cover that intention well, in so few words.

In-Class Writing Activities

1. Students will gather a good deal of varied information from Facebook. They may get a sense of a theme from some of the writing. They may believe they get a sense of the person from the writing—and it would be useful to try to describe that person based on status updates and other writing. The next step would be to try to describe the audience the person is writing for, using examples from the site. Students may disagree

that Facebook writers have a sense of their audience, and they may use examples to defend that position as well.

2. The preparation and revision students write about may be internal or may take place on paper. The essay will give students a chance to consider their academic writing and to what standards that sort of writing is held.

3. Technology is changing at an incredible pace and is changing the way we write and read. Students should research the pace and change felt by the ancient Greeks, and compare what is happening in our world with the Internet, rise of cell phones (and texting), and other technological advances. They should consider the literacy of the ancient Greeks and how they view the literacy Thompson describes in our current society.

Erin McKean

Redefining Definition: How the Web Could Help Change What Dictionaries Do

[*New York Times Magazine*, December 20, 2009]

Vocabulary/Using a Dictionary

1. When something is *primed*, it is prepared in some way or supplied with information.

2. A *lexicographer* is someone who writes, edits, or compiles a dictionary. The word *lexicon* comes from the Greek and refers to a dictionary (usually of Greek, Latin, or Hebrew).

3. The word *dissimilitude* means unlikeness. It shares its root with *dissimilarity* (noun) or *dissimilar* (adj.), both of which have to do with difference.

Responding to Words in Context

1. A *reputation* refers to how one is viewed by others and the opinion or esteem others have of one. A dictionary's reputation is established by how the words are defined and how helpful it is.

2. A book that is *abridged* is shortened in a way that still retains necessary information. Dictionaries are sometimes abridged.

3. McKean is working on an online dictionary. A colleague is an associate or partner, so McKean's colleagues would be people working together as editors, writers, and researchers on the online dictionary.

Discussing Main Point and Meaning

1. The child misuses the word in a sentence because the definition is given without context. There is a misunderstanding because the child constructs the sentence based on his understanding of the strict definition.

2. Definitions, in this essay, are shown to be limited without appropriate context. Meanings change depending on when the word is used and

how. Science implies some sort of laws or facts that govern the definitions, while poetry implies a freer, more associative or contextual way of looking at them.

3. The need to "cling to definitions" will change because the Internet provides lexicographers with more space to give examples of word use in addition to the definitions that have filled the pages of print dictionaries.

Examining Sentences, Paragraphs, and Organization

1. The examples of words and definitions clearly show the reader the power and limitations of words out of context. Without these examples, the discussion of "definition" would be too abstract. At times, McKean offers the definition first and then shows how the mind doesn't immediately jump to the word being defined. She also shows how definitions can be misconstrued. The reader is provided with concrete examples and context for the argument.

2. McKean is trying to say that words and their definitions are not meant to be seen as authoritative statements. We have come to treat dictionary definitions as "scientific pronouncements" or exact statements that somehow capture the word's "essence" or basic nature, and she wants to show another way of thinking about what definitions are and can do.

3. The phrase "According to *Webster's*" sets *Webster's* up as the overriding authority—it invests *Webster's* with a great formal power. She goes on to say that the lexicographer resists this sort of pronouncement because she knows that definitions alone should not hold that power.

Thinking Critically

1. Students may feel McKean's optimism about the Web and its "limitlessness." Or they may prefer the containment of dictionary definitions and want to argue from that position. They may have more ideas than the essay provides about how the Web can be used to build understanding of words and their meanings, or they may feel that "limitlessness" can create more ambiguity and confusion.

2. The definitions of words come from their use in context, which is something many people might not consider when they open a dictionary and look up a definition.

3. An Internet dictionary, as McKean points out, can make use of "infinite space" because of the lexicographer's ability to link to other sites and provide other ways of experiencing words without the boundaries created by paper. It can provide a more thorough experience of words and their meanings by providing contexts not physically possible in a print dictionary.

In-Class Writing Activities

1. Students can look at the format of wordnik.com and explore it. They may feel that the site is much more comprehensive than a dictionary, and they can explain why. They may also come up with ideas to expand

the site for even better word comprehension. Points of comparison and contrast with print dictionaries should be included, and examples of words and definitions via wordnik.com will vary.

2. Some students may never have used a "print" dictionary, but they may have used online dictionaries (www.merriam-webster.com or www .dictionary.com). These online versions can be used for the discussion. Most likely, students have used dictionaries for schoolwork, but perhaps some have used them in other situations. Responses will vary if students prefer to use resources that are not dictionaries. Some may try to find the words in context somehow, instead of looking up dictionary definitions.

3. Students may offer some history of the dictionary, reaching back to ancient times, but it would be useful in regard to this essay for them to examine a more recently established dictionary such as *Webster's*. They can examine Noah Webster's life and goals, the many revisions that the dictionary has gone through, and what about it has been lasting and important—what rules it established and what it includes.

Aprille Hanson (student essay)

Stop Relying on Bloggers for News

[*The Echo*, The University of Central Arkansas, April 7, 2010]

Vocabulary/Using a Dictionary

1. A *priority* is something given special attention or is highest in importance.

2. *Liberal* and *conservative* are political terms. A liberal favors progress or reform, and a conservative prefers traditional approaches and limited change.

3. *Professionalism* refers to the approach taken by someone with skill or experience in a certain field. In Hanson's mind, journalists are *professionals*, and their methods and knowledge are what creates a certain *professionalism* when they work.

Responding to Words in Context

1. *Spin* is a slang term that refers to a certain bias. When someone "spins" the news, he/she is influencing the news report in a certain direction.

2. "Platform of mistrust" is a metaphor Hanson created. She states that journalists have been placed in one area (a platform) that government finds itself on (since no one has trusted government since the Watergate scandal). She has grouped them together on a "platform of mistrust," which simply means that no one believes in what they say, as a group, anymore.

3. When someone or something is *credible*, it is believable. Something *incredible* is hard to believe or unbelievable. The words are opposites.

Discussing Main Point and Meaning

1. Hanson points out that journalists are trained for their work. while anyone can be a blogger. Journalists are required to be informed and objective about what they are reporting, while a blogger may or may not be.

2. Jon Stewart is an entertainer and not a trained journalist. In the poll taken, he comes out ahead of seasoned journalists as the most trusted newscaster in America. It is not surprising in some ways, though, because Americans have become less trusting of journalists and more likely to find their news from other sources. Stewart is also known for turning his sarcastic eye on most stories, no matter what the subject; a viewer might feel he provides a more objective viewpoint since he approaches all his work in this way.

3. Hanson says anyone can be a blogger. Journalists learn AP (Associated Press) style, interviewing techniques, how to do research, how to be objective, and are held to a standard of truthful reporting. They are accountable to people within the news organization for their work. Bloggers answer to no one but their readers.

Examining Sentences, Paragraphs, and Organization

1. Hanson offers two rhetorical questions in the final paragraph, asking the reader directly about whom we would rather trust for our news. The choices are an untrustworthy blogger vs. an informed journalist. She then states, "the answer is obvious, but the choice is yours," giving the reader the freedom to make an informed decision based on her argument.

2. The percentages highlight the startling choice that's being made between journalists and entertainers for news—Jon Stewart comes out ahead by 44 percent. The number acts as a sharper detail to bring the picture Hanson is painting into focus.

3. Hanson does not offer many examples of blogs and their lack of good information, but she does stress the difference between the potential blogger and the trained journalist. If anyone can be a blogger, the leap of faith involved in trusting him or her as a news source gets wider and more complex, just as it would if a nonsurgeon were to perform surgery. She describes the person who may be blogging the news as a "middle-aged man," unemployed, offering his latest thoughts instead of being a knowledgeable researcher and reporter.

Thinking Critically

1. Students may be able to find and cite blogs as valuable news sources, but they must offer some evidence that the bloggers are knowledgeable and/or objective about their subject matter. Others may also argue that blogs are not credible, but they, too, must provide evidence that the bloggers may not be trustworthy sources of news (the lack of credentials or an obviously biased approach may be enough to make their case).

2. Comedians can find what's funny about any subject. While comedians may be biased and poke fun only at one side of a story, they can still identify a "truth" about an event by using humor. The humor is what reveals a particular "truth" about a situation.

3. Journalists, unlike bloggers, must pass their stories through editors and "higher-ups" for review before the stories go to print or on the air. The stories can be examined for objectivity (or lack thereof) and the journalist can be questioned about his or her work *before* the general public reads it as news. A publisher or newspaper owner can create a set of guidelines for his/her journalists to look to, or create a standard for them to follow.

In-Class Writing Activities

1. Students may believe that bloggers are of more interest as news sources since the Web has made a proliferation of viewpoints easier to access. People may trust bloggers more because recent current events handled by "trusted" journalists have been communicated in ways that have eroded public trust. Examples should be provided to support whatever reasoning the student wants to follow. The examination of a particular "reporter," whether it is a trained journalist or not, should offer a picture of that person's background and field of interest as well as a description of their handling of newsworthy material.

2. Cronkite was a trusted reporter, and commentary will differ from student to student depending on what area of his reporting is looked at. Some information on the time period Cronkite was working in and a sense of the American public will be needed in this essay.

3. Students should look at topics covered, writing style, a sense of objectivity in the writing, and general layout of the newspaper for this assignment. They should make a case for whether or not it is Pulitzer-worthy (and if it isn't, perhaps give a sense of what kind of reporting would be Pulitzer-worthy).

Chris Clarke

How to Write an Incendiary Blog Post

[*Boston.com*, February 14, 2010]

Vocabulary/Using a Dictionary

1. The word *blog* is short for *Weblog* and refers to an online diary or personal thoughts of any nature published on a Web page.

2. Clarke speaks of those who have seen the *folly*—that is, the foolishness or lack of understanding—of people who disagree with the thesis of the blog post.

3. An *iconoclast* is someone who attacks traditional or strongly held beliefs (often religious beliefs). An *iconoclastic approach* would be one that goes against what is expected.

Responding to Words in Context

1. A *non sequitur* is something that doesn't follow from a premise. (It is Latin and translates as "does not follow.")

2. "To curry favor" is an idiom and means to try to gain favor through flattery.

3. Ironic words convey a meaning the opposite of the word's literal meaning. Words that are sincere are earnest or true.

Discussing Main Point and Meaning

1. Students' reactions to the writing itself may be enough to make them feel Clarke has indeed written an incendiary blog post. The examples used in the essay may be familiar enough for students to feel they know what an incendiary blog post is and how one puts it together.

2. This essay reflects on how people express themselves on the Internet, how others react to the blog posts, and how the dialogue is continued. Internet acronyms are particular to Internet writing and conversation conducted through new technology.

3. The writing in this essay is meant to call attention to itself. It is taking a hard look at how Internet writing is expressed and generalizes about that writing in a way that might make some people uncomfortable. Sentences like "This sentence is a wildly overgeneralized condemnation of one or more entire classes of people phrased in as incendiary a fashion as possible which claims to be an obvious corollary to the thesis and non sequitur" (para. 7) are examples of ones that are generalizations used to create a reaction.

Examining Sentences, Paragraphs, and Organization

1. The author calls attention to the writing and to his thought process by organizing sentences in this way. The writing feels highly structured and stylized. It creates distance between the writer and writing and between the writer and audience.

2. Students may be very confused by the self-referential nature of the sentences in this essay. The fact that each sentence begins with "this sentence" may be confusing (students will be looking for something more concrete from the writer). The sentences progress in a somewhat linear fashion, but there are leaps from thought to thought, and they often change course sentence to sentence and paragraph to paragraph.

3. The writer creates a structure for the writing that is followed through the entire essay. Readers must fill in for themselves what "this sentence" refers to. It can mean "this sentence that you are reading," but it must also connect to the sentences before and after it.

Thinking Critically

1. The writing here is abstract, but the writer uses occasional concrete examples to illustrate his points.

2. In the midst of all of the intellectual or abstract discussion of what makes an incendiary blog post, the writer must give readers something accessible and not just self-referential in the discussion. The references are to things that one might in fact find on the Internet, as over the top as they may seem. And they are things to which readers might have a strong reaction, as either funny, absurd, or offensive, in the discussion.

3. Blogs are open to public response. An "incendiary blog post" is bound to provoke response, but the author is trying to illustrate the irony of writing a post specifically for the purpose of sparking an uncontrollable response, and then trying to control that response. It shows the hypocrisy inherent in many of the blog posts Clarke is attacking, and concludes the piece on a humorous note.

In-Class Writing Activities

1. A student may better understand the purpose of the essay knowing that it first appeared as part of a blog. It may be hard to understand the writer's intent in writing the piece otherwise. The student may feel that the writing of this essay is an attempt to get a response from the reader (to find out if an incendiary blog post has indeed been written), and those responses would have appeared on the blog after the piece was published.

2. Student responses about the uses of a blog will vary and, depending on each individual's experience, the information covered in a blog will vary, too. Students may discuss the use of a blog to provoke a reader response. In this way, it is similar to other kinds of writing, but different in that the Internet provides a public forum for those responses.

3. The audience for this essay is made up of people who read Internet writing and for critics of that kind of writing. There may be others that students pinpoint as part of Clarke's audience. Students should be able to point to various examples in the essay that would appeal to such an audience. They should include that evidence in their essay.

Discussing the Unit

Suggested Topic for Discussion

You may want to ask students where they go for their news—do they agree with Hanson's assertion that they are ignoring traditional journalism in favor of a partisan agenda? What do they think makes a news source credible? How many news sources do they read on a daily basis? You can use this idea to discuss the new literacy discussed in Thompson's piece. If they get their news online, do they comment on the text? Interact with the author or blogger? If there are bloggers or Web sites that they trust more than others, have them name specific criteria as to why they trust those sites over others.

Preparing for Class Discussion

1. The writers in these essays describe bloggers as ignorant and bored, as predictable, as invested in their audiences, as people interested in creating a different version of tools like dictionaries. Answers will depend on which essays students draw from.

2. Many will feel the Internet is crucial to how they conduct their lives and may point to Thompson's arguments about the proliferation of writing on the Internet or McKean's discussion of the Internet dictionary in their essays. Others may refer to Clarke to show how blogs are unremarkable or expected. They may use Hanson to show how most people gravitate to the Internet and to blogs for their information and "truths," whether this is a wise choice or not.

From Discussion to Writing

1. Thompson and McKean are good examples to bring into this kind of essay because they support how the Internet can be used for knowledge. Students might use examples from Hanson, whether they agree that blogs are valuable sources of news or not—she shows how much we have come to believe in them as news sources. Clarke shows what we might find in blogs and looks at how we respond to them.

2. Thompson holds that writing for an audience is an example of "good" writing—and that writing standards don't necessarily vanish just because we are writing more online. Clarke exposes the writing of a blog as something we can anticipate and poke fun at. Hanson makes the distinction between the writing of trained journalists and the writing of the middle-aged, unemployed blogger. McKean reveals that dictionary writers are not simply people who have all the answers—definitions come from a variety of uses and contexts, and the Web can help further our understanding of words. Essays will vary depending on how students define "good" and "bad" writing and incorporate the authors' theses into their arguments.

Topics for Cross-Cultural Discussion

1. Students today, according to Thompson, define good writing as a way to persuade and organize and debate, no matter what they are writing about. Those who go to the print dictionary rather than the Internet dictionary might feel a lack of trust over the often faceless people who put the definitions together similar to the way Hanson distrusts the faceless people who put blogs together as a news source. People who loved Cronkite valued the person who was offering the information based on his credentials and track record while those who go to blogs for information might hope for subjectivity or a particular style (like satire) or a certain personality that comes across. (Followers of Cronkite may have been influenced by personality, too, and students should discuss how that personality might have come across.)

2. The question is whether it is subject matter and a knowledge of one's audience or something else that creates a good piece of writing. A Hispanic audience may have interests that differ from the interests of an African American audience. A Jewish audience might have different interests from a Christian or Muslim audience. Because Americans come from a variety of ethnic and racial backgrounds, interests in what's being written for the public will differ. Differences will also be apparent for those of different political and economic backgrounds.

7

Gender Roles: Should Women Act More Like Men?

In "Swagger Like Us," Ann Friedman writes, "Ever since women began making serious workplace gains in the 1970s, there has been a debate about the best way for them to climb the professional ladder." But the significance of gender roles transcends women in the contemporary workforce—and debates about the relative places of men and women (as well as their relative strengths and weaknesses) go all the way back to classical antiquity. No doubt, women have made enormous strides both socially and economically in the last several decades. Barriers remain, however. As Friedman notes, women comprised only 6.3 percent of corporate top earners in 2009. Each essay in this unit focuses on gender roles, especially conventional views of women. How can women achieve equality? In what ways do the biological differences between men and women matter? How should men and women treat each other in romantic relationships? How should women behave in the professional world?

Clay Shirky argues that women need to act more like men. In "A Rant about Women," he identifies self-aggrandizement, self-promotion, and even con artistry as distinctively masculine qualities. Shirky sees his proposal as part of a long-standing practice of crossing gender lines, as when men are encouraged to be more sensitive or women take self-defense classes: "I sometimes wonder, what would happen . . . if my college spent as much effort teaching women self-advancement as self-defense." In her essay, Friedman takes issue with Shirky's proposal, noting that women have faced a false choice for decades: Suit up in shoulder pads and be aggressively masculine or "embrace the idea that women promise to be different, somehow, from powerful men." According to Friedman, women's progress has stalled because of a "broad, cultural problem," not because of some innate biological difference between men and women. Her remedy is to "push back" against the gender dynamics that limit female advancement rather than participating in them.

In "Romance Novel Titles Reveal Readers' Desires," Tom Jacobs summarizes and discusses a study from the *Journal of Social, Evolutionary, and Cultural Psychology*. Researchers analyzed the titles of Harlequin Romance novels, hypothesizing that the language might "reflect mating preferences that have evolved over the millennia." The results suggest that "long-term commitment and reproduction are important to readers." Jacobs's tone is lighthearted, but he provides a good example of the summary form. His article should provoke lively class discussion as well.

Kim Elsesser's essay should also be provocative. In "And the Gender-Neutral Oscar Goes To . . . ," she proposes that Academy Awards should eliminate separate categories for men and women. Elsesser compares the different awards for "actor" and "actress" with the practice of racial segregation. She also argues that the separate awards have wider implications as well, as they "perpetuate the stereotype that the differences between men and women are so great that the two sexes cannot be evaluated as equals in their professions."

Shannon Morgan, a student columnist for the Boise State University *Arbiter Online*, focuses on gender roles in a more domestic sphere. She argues that we should bring a gender-neutral chivalry into the twenty-first century, a code that would "apply to any sexual orientation" and "cross cultures" as well. For Morgan, such chivalric ideals could help men and women cultivate compassionate, courteous, and committed relationships on an equal basis.

Clay Shirky

A Rant about Women

[*Shirky.com*, January 2010]

Vocabulary/Using a Dictionary

1. A *pseudonym* is a made-up or false name. It comes from the Greek *pseudes* ("false") + *onuma* ("name"). The prefix *pseudo* usually denotes falseness.

2. A *narcissist* is a person with excessive self-love or vanity. The term comes from Greek mythology: Narcissus was a beautiful young man who fell in love with his own reflection in a pool of water (there are various versions of the story from Greek and Roman antiquity).

3. A *con artist* is a person skilled at lying, dishonest persuasion, and self-serving talk; it is also synonymous with the term "swindler" or "rip-off artist." The word *con* is short for "confidence": Con artists operate by gaining the confidence of their victims, then deceiving them.

Responding to Words in Context

1. Shirky uses *gatekeeper* to label his professor as someone who controls access to something important or desirable. In this case, Warfel could facilitate Shirky's access to the college's theater program—and, indirectly, opportunities in Shirky's chosen profession. Warfel's status is essential to understanding the writer's lie. Shirky does not lie indiscriminately or aimlessly; rather, he knew that his professional future required him to get through his professor's "gate": "I can't say my ability to earn a living in a fickle profession was because of my behavior in Bill's office, but I can say it was because I was willing to do that kind of thing" (para. 12).

2. A *one-sided market* is one in which you have the autonomy to weigh options and then, as you balance "your preferences and your budget," make a choice: what to eat, where to live, etc. In a *two-sided market*, you weigh your options, but "those options are also weighing you" (para. 17). For example, your choice of where to go to college or what company to work for depends both on your own preferences and the preferences of the university or company. The distinction is important because in two-sided markets, self-promotion is a virtue—and perhaps even a necessity.

3. Shirky is using the word *lousy* to describe women's inability to act like "arrogant self-aggrandizing jerks" (para. 5). It is meant to be a bit playful—who wouldn't want to be bad at being a jerk? Shirky doesn't seem to think that it's necessarily a negative thing to not be able to act this way, but it does have a negative effect on women's abilities to succeed in the workforce.

Discussing Main Point and Meaning

1. Shirky worries that women are not as good at promoting themselves as men are. But he makes an important distinction: "This worry isn't about psychology; I'm not concerned that women don't engage in enough building of self-confidence or self-esteem. I'm worried about something much simpler: Not enough women have what it takes to behave like arrogant self-aggrandizing jerks" (para. 5). He may highlight this contrast because "self-confidence" and "self-esteem" are generally considered "good" qualities. He wants to shift the emphasis to personality traits that are necessary for success—but are not necessarily appealing or encouraged.

2. Hampton lies his way into restaurants, clubs, and affluent social circles—all the while realizing that he was taking an enormous risk. Shirky lies to get into Bill Warfel's theater design course. The writer sees the distinction as one of degree, not kind: "The difference between me and David Hampton isn't that he's a con artist and I'm not; the difference is that I only told lies I could live up to, and I knew when to stop" (para. 12). In Shirky's view, we all must occasionally take risks and behave like con artists to succeed in two-sided markets.

3. According to Shirky, it is now common to cross gender lines in this way. Colleges spend time and money teaching self-defense to women; men are asked to be better listeners or "more sensitive partners" (para. 14). You might ask if students agree with the writer that men are better than women at being "arrogant, self-aggrandizing jerks" and that women should strive to emulate their male counterparts. Does Shirky's analogy between learning self-defense and learning self-promoting behavior seem accurate or persuasive?

Examining Sentences, Paragraphs, and Organization

1. This section of the essay illustrates and exemplifies a concept that may be difficult for some readers to accept or understand: A certain kind of

lying is often necessary for personal and professional advancement. Shirky also qualifies his endorsement of temporary con artistry. He uses an example from his own life that illustrates the proper and necessary use of controlled dishonesty.

2. The writer begins his essay with a specific example of stereotypically male, self-promoting behavior. The third paragraph—and perhaps much of Shirky's essay—depends on readers recognizing that the former student is a male. If students did not guess the gender immediately, they may note that their trust in Shirky was undermined and therefore his argument was not as effective as it could have been.

3. The term *rant* implies that Shirky is writing in an exaggerated, extravagant, wild, or even violent way. But his style and tone are not "wild"; he presents arguments, makes a case, and proposes that women learn to be as good at self-promotion as men are, even if doing so requires them to become temporary con artists. He places the "rant" disclaimer at the end of the essay, reminding readers that he is only ranting; but the placement allows him to present all his ideas, and then distance himself from defending them. Ask students how the article might have been different had Shirky begun the essay by claiming he had "no idea how to fix the thing being ranted about."

Thinking Critically

1. Students may have different reactions. We generally think of lying as immoral or "wrong," but are there degrees of dishonesty or con artistry, as Shirky suggests? Does he frame his choice in moral terms? Is lying acceptable when you can "live up to" the lie (para. 12)? Some students may see Shirky's dishonesty as a necessary part of personal, educational, and professional advancement.

2. From Shirky's point of view, achieving, getting ahead, getting what you want, changing the world—all require narcissism, ego, self-promotion, and perhaps even dishonesty. Students might want to think of specific examples from history, politics, or entertainment that support Shirky's claim. Or they may find counterexamples. Students may discuss whether Shirky's statements apply to their own lives and ambitions. Is it impossible to be "forceful and self-confident without being arrogant or jerky," as he argues (para. 21)?

3. For this prompt, students may want to evaluate Shirky's stereotyping; that is, do they agree with him that women are less skilled at self-promotion, more risk averse, and overly concerned with what people think? We may think of sexism as something open and obvious. Yet, Shirky describes a subtler form, which is connected to gender tendencies: Women "wait for others to recommend them" rather than speaking for themselves; women are less assertive about raising their hands, etc.

In-Class Writing Activities

1. Encourage students to draw on their own experiences—job interviews, cover letters, college admissions interviews, applications to internships, etc. How does one play up strengths without sounding egotistical or even boorish? How does one downplay or cover over faults? They may also consider the line between honest self-promotion and lying, especially in the context of Shirky's essay.

2. In all likelihood, students have not encountered (or participated in) large-scale cons or scams. But they may have had the experience of being "taken" or lied to on a smaller scale, especially in their personal lives. They might consider how they felt or how, exactly, they were manipulated and "set up." Similarly, many students have probably engaged in minor forms of con artistry—exaggerating the symptoms of an illness to stay home from school, wheedling with their parents, trying to persuade a teacher to grant an extension, etc. What were their motives? What techniques did they use? Do they consider such behavior "wrong"?

3. Students' answers will vary depending on whether they felt Shirky successfully made his case or not. It will also probably depend on whether the student in question is a man or a woman. It is possible that students will take offense to Shirky's argument—he puts men and women into two distinct categories that students may not agree with—and if that is the case, he will have no effect on their behavior.

Ann Friedman

Swagger Like Us

[*The American Prospect,* March 2010]

Vocabulary/Using a Dictionary

1. A *mediator* is someone who settles disputes, brings about agreement and compromise, and removes misunderstandings between people or groups. The word derives from the Latin word *medius* ("middle"). *Mediator* shares its origins with words such as *media* and *intermediate.*

2. *Virtue*, which refers to excellence in conduct and morality, derives from the Latin *virtutem* ("moral strength, manliness, worth, valor"). The stem *vir* is Latin for "man" (see "virile"). These origins reveal how ostensibly gender-neutral language can carry a historical bias.

3. The word *uppity* denotes a self-important or presumptuous person who acts above his or her position in society. The first recorded use of the word is in Joel Chandler Harris's *Uncle Remus* stories, a collection of African American folktales published in 1881. *Uppity* still carries racial connotations from the post–Civil War, Reconstruction era.

Responding to Words in Context

1. Most students will be unfamiliar with *The Mary Tyler Moore Show*, a TV comedy from the 1970s. The program focused on a single, independent career woman in her thirties—a groundbreaking primary character for the time. The sentence is a line from the show's theme song. The lyric highlights the "serious workplace gains in the 1970s," even as it suggests the naivete of optimism about professional women today. You might use this example to discuss allusion more generally.

2. Friedman refers to "shoulder pads" literally; the suit of a stereotypical professional woman includes padded shoulders. The visual effect minimizes femininity. At the same time, the writer evokes the image of a football player in shoulder pads, trying to gain yardage or cross into the end zone against determined opposition. Both meanings reflect the idea that women have tried dressing and behaving like men in the workplace.

3. You might ask students how else she could have worded this. Would the sentence be as effective if she had written: "The idea that your sexual organs determine your management style is nothing new"? Friedman's wording is surprising, informal, and direct; it seems neither clinical nor precious. It also highlights the absurdity of this common assumption.

4. The phrase is from Christina Hoff Sommers, whose book Friedman quotes. Although Friedman characterizes Hoff Sommers as an "antifeminist crusader," the phrase "responsible femininity" (para. 4) sounds promising: an approving way to characterize the talents and skills of women in the workplace—and in the world. Later in the essay, however, Friedman writes, "When was the last time you saw 'responsible femininity' among desired qualities in a job listing?" (para. 6). Here, in the context of a real job search and the "real" business world, the phrase sounds naive and overly idealistic.

Discussing Main Point and Meaning

1. According to Friedman, women are supposedly "natural mediators"; they are "levelheaded" and know "how to multitask" (para. 3). They are better communicators and "kinder, gentler" leaders (para. 4). Do students agree with these generalizations about women?

2. Women can act like men in a male-dominated business world by being aggressive, demanding, and self-promoting: "if you can't beat the boys' club, join it" (para. 1). Alternately, women can "embrace the idea that powerful women promise to be different, somehow, from powerful men" (para. 3). As Friedman considers the "stalled progress" of women in the working world, she concludes that "neither of these two options is working" (para. 5).

3. Friedman thinks it is a "broad, cultural problem," rather than a matter of any one person's choices: "This is much bigger than women's individual behavior" (para. 7). While she addresses the issue as a writer, Friedman moves beyond abstraction and reporting: "I not only write publicly about

the 'byline gap' between men and women in political journalism—I actively seek out women writers and encourage them to pitch their ideas" (para. 8). Her ultimate goal is to change an "unjust system," rather than compete within it (para. 9).

Examining Sentences, Paragraphs, and Organization

1. The writer lists common presumptions about women's skills and aptitudes. Women are "natural mediators"; they "know how to multitask"; they are "more levelheaded." The repetitions build to the final sentence: "If women ruled the world, it would be more stable, less violent, and color-coordinated." She takes an ironic attitude toward these clichés—a sense heightened by the inclusion of "color-coordinated." For Friedman, the presumption that women are better business leaders than men is just another example of the fallacy that "what's between your legs determines your management style" (para. 4).

2. In paragraph 4, Friedman cites specific authors who believe that women's superior business skills have a biological basis. She lets them speak for themselves; the prominence of their books shows that their views are influential. Friedman wants to move beyond these essentialist arguments, however: These writers only reinforce the notion that "what's between your legs determines your management style" (para. 4). She engages the specific claims and specific language of those she disagrees with. Doing so allows her to show the naivete of a phrase like "responsible femininity" in paragraph 6.

3. Shirky represents the view that women should act more like men—a position Friedman finds unsatisfactory. But more important, his blog post provides a timely occasion for Friedman to make her case. She is not conjuring a controversy out of nowhere or debating straw targets; rather, she is participating in a lively, contentious, and relevant conversation. You might point out to students that writing often comes from responses to other writing—especially when we are active and thoughtful readers.

Thinking Critically

1. Friedman offers her evidence in a single parenthetical phrase about corporate top earners. She implies that the practice of acting more like men or embracing distinctly female aptitudes is ineffective or has even "stalled" women's progress, but she does not demonstrate it conclusively. The writer could provide more substantive proof—statistical trends, etc.—showing that women's progress is at a standstill; then, she would have to demonstrate causal connections between the two approaches (acting like men, embracing femininity) and "stalled" progress.

2. Friedman rejects biological explanations. Instead, she believes that "we are shaped by the society in which we live," and that "there are cultural, structural reasons why men are typically more assertive, more self-promotional, and more successful everywhere from the boardroom

to the op-ed pages to the halls of Congress" (para. 7). Students might reflect on the relationship between internal, biological differences and external, social factors in shaping the fortunes of men and women—professionally and otherwise.

3. Students might have fun with this premise or they might question it altogether (e.g., are there spheres in which women already "rule"?). Friedman focuses on positive stereotypes (e.g., that women are "natural mediators"), but what about more pejorative conceptions of women? There is a serious side to this question as well: Demographic trends indicate that within a few years, the United States will have more living female college graduates than male college graduates. Increasingly, women are primary "breadwinners" for families. Do these trends complicate Friedman's argument?

In-Class Writing Activities

1. The image of the "professional ladder" is a clichéd metaphor that students will most likely agree is still in place. Most professions require that people start from the bottom and work their way up, although there are exceptions to this, especially in more creative professions. Students may note that this idea of a "ladder" is what encourages them to work harder in school; some may say it motivates them to avoid the corporate world altogether because they don't feel comfortable with the concept. Students may also mention clichés here like "glass ceiling," "pulling yourself up by your bootstrap," and the like.

2. Friedman does not cite a specific study, and her word choice ("wary," "high-achieving") is vague. But students can use this prompt to consider their own attitudes about "high-achieving women": Why would they be "wary"? Are such women stereotyped? Do students see this dynamic at work in academic contexts?

3. Students will bring a wide range of aspirations to this prompt. The assignment should give them a chance to consider how "cultural" and "structural" factors (to use Friedman's words) will affect their careers. In some cases—students with athletic ambitions, for example—biology will play a direct role. Other professions might still carry strong gender connotations (nursing, preschool teaching, human resources, carpentry and other trades).

Kim Elsesser

And the Gender-Neutral Oscar Goes To...

[*The New York Times*, March 4, 2010]

Vocabulary/Using a Dictionary

1. *Ceremony* comes from the Latin *ceremonia* or *cærimonia* ("awe, deeply respectful ritual").

2. *Laud* means "to praise." It derives from the Latin *laudere*. It's related to words like *laudatory* and *laudable* and persists in the academic honor *cum laude* ("with praise").

3. Strictly speaking, the English does not have gender in its structure the way languages like German or French do. But since the fourteenth century or so, English has appropriated some feminine French nouns (which use the *-ess* ending) as well as added the French feminine ending to native English words. The suffix has its roots in both Latin and Greek, which use *-issa* for feminine nouns.

Responding to Words in Context

1. "Separate is not equal" carries associations of the civil rights era, particularly the 1954 Supreme Court case, *Brown v. Board of Education of Topeka*. In that decision, the Court ruled that state laws establishing separate public schools for black and white students was unconstitutional. The so-called separate but equal doctrine had been put in place by the Court's 1896 case *Plessy v. Ferguson*. Elsesser draws upon these connotations in making her argument about separate Oscars for men and women.

2. There is no strict definition of a "strong female character," but students should have some ideas about what the phrase means. Such characters might be independent, strong (emotionally, psychologically, physically), active (as opposed to passive), complex, and multidimensional. Usually, they are not helpless victims; they do not need to be "saved" by male characters. Students might provide examples. Following Elsesser's argument, however, you might ask whether we still need a separate category for "strong female characters," rather than just "strong characters."

3. In this context, *genre* would mean that movies are divided by theme, subject, and form—musicals, comedies, dramas. Other categories might include documentaries, action movies, and science fiction films. Ask students if they think this is a better way to divide the awards process.

Discussing Main Point and Meaning

1. The writer compares the awarding of separate Oscars to men and women with the practices of racial segregation—especially the doctrine of "separate but equal." Her use of the words *segregate* and *segregated* also emphasizes this analogy. In Elsesser's view, there is no significant difference between dividing these awards based on gender and giving them based on race.

2. Elsesser points out several upsides. First, she suggests that the gender divisions are inherently wrong, in the same way that racial segregation is wrong. Second, making the Oscars gender-neutral would help eliminate the stereotype that men and women "cannot be evaluated as equals in their professions" (para. 5). Third, this gender neutrality would better reflect the increasing parity between men and women in the Hollywood film industry. Last, it would reduce the length of the Oscar broadcast, "a move that many viewers would laud" (para. 8).

3. Elsesser's attitude seems to be that gender-segregated Oscars are inherently and self-evidently wrong. She also points to general progress toward equality between the genders. But she does not give an extended analysis of why the segregation endures, other than acknowledging that it stems from the early days of the awards, when women "had only recently won the right to vote and were still decades away from equal rights outside the voting booth" (para. 3). She does not take a hostile or angry tone toward the academy: The sexism appears institutional, rather than personal. Her final sentence implies that in the future perhaps having an award for best actress will seem as silly as having an award for best "directress." Would the essay be more persuasive or effective if Elsesser's tone was more indignant? Why or why not?

Examining Sentences, Paragraphs, and Organization

1. Elsesser begins with a hypothetical situation: "Suppose . . . that the Academy of Motion Picture Arts and Sciences presented separate honors for best white actor and best non-white actor . . ." (para. 1). She then moves from this hypothetical to a rhetorical question: "Why, then, is it considered acceptable to segregate nominations by sex . . . ?" (para. 2). In beginning this way, she evokes a response from her reader (repulsion at racially segregated Oscars), then ties that response to the issue of gender segregation. This analogy structures her entire argument.

2. Elsesser addresses a counterargument in paragraph 4: "Perhaps the academy would argue that the separate awards guarantee equity, since men and women have received exactly the same number of best acting Oscars." She also acknowledges that the academy might want to "preserve the number of acting awards" (para. 8). However, Elsesser does not quote any specific counterarguments, nor does she cite anyone with an opposing point of view. This fits the general idea that gender-segregated Oscars are largely a matter of tradition and custom, rather than the deliberate work of people who oppose equality between men and women. Still, she might have contacted the academy to include their view on the issue.

3. Elsesser makes her fullest thesis statement in the last paragraph of the essay: "For next year's Oscars, the academy should modify its ballots so that men and women are finally treated as full equals." When restating or summarizing the thesis, students may want to include the analogy between racial segregation and gender segregation. You might discuss the advantages of placing the thesis statement in the last paragraph. How would the essay be different if this essay began with this concluding paragraph? Would that placement work as well? Better?

Thinking Critically

1. Elsesser implies that women have achieved equality, which may be true in legal contexts. Socially and culturally, however, men and women are still treated differently. Those differences can range from disparities in salaries and glass ceilings for female executives to the persistence of

chivalry and customs of polite behavior toward women. They might also include different expectations about men and women—their roles, potential, aptitudes, behavior. Is it possible to acknowledge gender differences without creating systems of inequality? Does separation always lead to inequality?

2. The writer sees gendered awards at the Oscars as similar to racial segregation. In contrast, she accepts the separation of male and female athletes because of "biological differences" (para. 5). Notice that she does not use the word *segregation* when referring to sports. Do students agree with this standard? Biological differences do not apply to acting skills in the same way that they do in sports. However, what about cases where the distinctions are not so obvious? Several years ago, then Harvard President Lawrence Summers proposed that there might be "issues of intrinsic aptitude" that limited female achievement in math, science, and engineering. How do we distinguish gender differences determined by society and culture from those which are biological or intrinsic?

3. Elsesser emphasizes the analogy of racial segregation. Yet, she does not succeed in making the case that separate Oscars for separate genders is the moral equivalent of racial segregation (in their consequences, for example). You might note that her article appeared during the Oscar season. Is the issue important enough to be covered at some other time of year? Some students may agree that Elsesser evokes the absurdity of this separation—especially in the last line of her essay. Why is "directress" any sillier than "actress"? She also highlights unexamined biases in our popular culture and our language.

In-Class Writing Activities

1. Direct students to examples of gender-neutral language that may be second nature to them: *server* instead of "waiter" or "waitress"; *first-year students* instead of "freshmen"; *police officer* instead of "policeman." They should consider the significance of these changes. Students' responses will vary depending on their use of gender neutrality in their writing. They may bring up confusion with the fact that they are discouraged from using the phrase *his/her* even though gender neutrality seems to be an important issue. They may have examples of how they write around gender, and try to justify which pronouns they tend to use more often.

2. Students' answers will vary depending on the strong female characters that they choose to write about. Some of the attributes that students may discuss are intelligence, resilience, and determination, but they may also talk about more typically feminine attributes like compassion and generosity.

3. Elsesser reads the divided categories as an "insult," which implies that women cannot win otherwise. However, the division leads to a kind of rough equity: Male and female actors each receive the same number of awards. Her example of the "directress" may be questionable, as well.

Acting roles in movies are often determined by gender; women play female characters—mothers and daughters, for example. In contrast, there is no corresponding determination for directors. As students consider what would happen if the academy took Elsesser's advice, they should ask themselves if there are more—and weightier—roles for men in films, would that make it difficult for women to win Oscars?

Shannon Morgan (student essay)

Defending Camelot: Chivalry Is Not Dead

[*Arbiter Online*, Boise State University, February 24, 2010]

Vocabulary/Using a Dictionary

1. *Chivalry* comes from the French *chevalrie* ("horsemanship") and *chevaler* ("knight"); these French terms have their roots in the Latin *caballus* ("pack horse").

2. In this context, to be *patronized* means to be treated in a condescending way. The word ultimately derives from the Latin *pater* ("father"). It is related to words such as *patron, paternity*, and *pattern*.

3. *Antiquated* means old-fashioned, out-of-date, and no longer in use. Synonyms include *obsolete, unfashionable, antique, dated*.

Responding to Words in Context

1. In a literal sense, "weaker" might mean physically weaker. But the phrase connotes emotional and psychological fragility, as well. In this context, Morgan is using the phrase to show that women are not the *lesser* sex.

2. The word *discreet* denotes the practice of being careful and wise when speaking, as well as respecting privacy. Morgan argues that chivalrous people should be careful and thoughtful when offering criticism of their romantic partners; they should also keep such criticism and disagreement private. This fits in with the traditional idea that avoiding scandal is part of chivalry.

3. The writer is using the word *romantic* in the context of romantic relationships. You might note that romance is commonly characterized by a preoccupation with love, but *romantic* and *romance* also carry connotations of impracticality, fancy, idealism, and even a desire for adventure. Romance is associated with passion, too, yet Morgan sees chivalry—which is certainly part of a Romantic literary and historical tradition—as a "check on our urges" and passions (para. 4). Is this paradoxical?

Discussing Main Point and Meaning

1. Morgan wants to redefine chivalry so that it is "gender-neutral" rather than sexist (para. 2). She notes that the idea originates in a medieval

code for knightly men. For contemporary people, however, Morgan argues that chivalry should help both men and women cultivate "rewarding and supportive relationships" (para. 4).

2. Her writing is not specific, as she refers to chivalry as a "compass to ensure we are behaving in ways that cultivate rewarding and supportive relationships" (para. 4). But Morgan seems to mean that chivalric attitudes and behaviors will help us think long-term about our connections with others (support, commitment, affection), rather than following our instincts for more immediate gratification. In the context of romantic relationships, this appears to refer to sexual desire, but she is not specific. Morgan does note, however, that chivalry is not "spontaneous" (para. 4). Spontaneity usually has a good connotation. What problems can it cause? Why would a chivalric code prevent them?

3. Morgan sees chivalry in the attitudes and behaviors that support long-term and committed relationships—fairness, faithfulness, compassion, dependability, strength, kindness, and discretion. She also refers to the small, daily acts, like "brewing coffee in the morning, picking your wet towels up off the floor, or taking time to write a love letter or plan a romantic evening" (para. 4).

Examining Sentences, Paragraphs, and Organization

1. Morgan refers to "some women" and "antiquated gestures of chivalry," which are relatively general. The sentence could be more specific if Morgan had quoted a specific woman or even given brief examples from her own experience to support her statement; doing so would make the purpose and timeliness of her essay clearer to the reader.

2. Morgan lists some "polite gestures," which men and women both make "in situations that extend beyond the pursuit of romance" (para. 2). She then moves to a dictionary definition of *chivalry*. Ask your students what they think the distinction is between "chivalry" and "good manners." Is the difference that chivalry exists only in the context of romantic relationships, while good manners do not? Is the distinction between the superficiality of manners and the depth of chivalry?

3. Morgan's tone is serious and earnest, for the most part (rather than, say, ironic or flippant). She takes chivalry, manners, and romantic relationships seriously; she believes in decorum and discretion. Appropriately, her diction tends to be relatively decorous as opposed to slangy.
   "Chivalry should be a check on our urges, a compass to ensure we are behaving in ways that cultivate rewarding and supportive relationships" (para. 4). You might have students rewrite this sentence in a different register: "Without chivalry, we'd do nothing but hook-up all the time." Morgan wrote her article for Valentine's Day, but she is not preoccupied with the saccharine or passionate aspects of love; rather, she writes about chivalry as "respect for yourself and your lover—and the commitment to serve and honor each other" (para. 4).

Thinking Critically

1. As the writer acknowledges, chivalry has traditionally been linked to a code of male behavior toward women. She also refers to good manners, generally, as something that both sexes can practice. Still, some polite gestures have a gender connotation: giving up a seat on public transportation to a woman, avoiding certain kinds of language around women, standing when women enter a room, etc.

2. This prompt should get students to consider their own views and expectations about gender roles within relationships. For example, do the men see themselves as "protectors" of women, on some level? Do women see themselves as "nurturers"? Morgan refers to "balance": Does balance in a relationship imply equality as well?

3. Students may bring a range of definitions, practices, and expectations to these questions. You might also note the perennial complaint that people are not mannerly anymore or that politeness is a thing of the past. Do they agree? Some might argue that manners can be anachronistic, superficial, false, or inhibiting. But do manners reflect deeper truths or essential rules—about mutual respect, tradition, civilization itself?

In-Class Writing Assignments

1. Of course, people bring a range of attitudes and behaviors to their romantic relationships. But there seem to be enduring customs, codes, and rules. These questions should get students thinking about their own views—and perhaps even the views of their peers. Implicitly, Morgan writes from the standpoint of a person seeking to maintain a long-term and committed relationship. Does this seem like a particularly "feminine" point of view? Are there different "codes" for men and women?

2. While chivalry is most associated with male courtesy toward women, it traditionally includes such qualities as selflessness, religious devotion, obligations toward fellow citizens, care for the poor, and protection of the innocent. Certainly, if society moves toward less formality and more equality (particularly between men and women), that trend would undermine ideals of courtesy and decorum. But chivalry—as evident in much medieval literature, for example—helps bind society and social classes together through rules and customs. Do we have such codes now that encourage us to be selfless or protect the innocent? Where do we find them?

3. This prompt provides an opportunity for students to make their own arguments for—or against—chivalric ideals. Generally, we value qualities such as compassion and kindness, but does it make sense to see them as part of a chivalric code, as Morgan proposes? Does it seem like a practical model for romantic relationships?

Discussing the Unit

Suggested Topic for Discussion

You may want to begin this discussion with Shirky's "rant." Perhaps women are getting ahead because they are adapting "masculine" behaviors and becoming more aggressive at self-promotion. At the same time, the increasing number of women in professional positions and academic institutions might be changing the "system" in fundamental ways, as Friedman prescribes. Biological differences probably make less of a difference in white-collar careers than they do in fields like construction and manufacturing—a distinction that made blue-collar work implicitly masculine. So is it possible that women—with their corresponding stereotypes as good communicators and social connectors—might be better suited to dominate the business and professional world? Conversely, what qualities—whether determined by biology or culture—might be causing men to lag behind?

Preparing for Class Discussion

1. For this prompt, try to get students to move beyond the obvious topical descriptions (e.g., "gender," "men and women") to more subtle inferences and thematic patterns that allow for debate and discussion. For example, the essays address gender differences, but they also investigate the origins of these differences, attempt to highlight the consequences of these differences, and (most important) recommend ways of managing these differences equitably—e.g., Shirky argues that women should act more like men, while Elsesser argues for gender-neutral Oscars as a way eliminating gender disparities. You might also encourage students to look for two essays that might play well off each other. Friedman and Shirky are an obvious choice, but Jacobs's report on romance novels would also pair well with Morgan's analysis of chivalry.

2. In some of the essays, the stereotypes are obvious. Shirky refers to male tendencies toward self-promotion and con artistry; Jacobs tries to analyze the desires of women through the lens of romance novels. Even Morgan's column about chivalry elevates values like long-term commitment, supportive relationships, and nurturing—characteristics that are often associated with women. At the same time, students might quibble with Shirky's assertions: Are there stereotypes of conning, deceitful, or self-aggrandizing women as well?

From Discussion to Writing

1. Students' responses will vary depending on their opinion. Shirky and Friedman both present arguments about what women would have to do in order to achieve workplace equality, and students may base their answers to this question on which author they thought made a more compelling argument. Students who agreed with Shirky may think that equality is attainable as long as women start acting more like men, while those who were more persuaded by Friedman might think that

equality may not be attainable in the near future because her idea—changing the system itself—is more daunting than changing individuals' behavior.

2. Students' answers will vary based on their opinions and their gender. There will most likely be students who do not feel that their gender has limited them in their career choice or path thus far, but that does not mean they will not be affected in the future. Students may want to talk about the gender make-up of their classes, why they chose their major, or even their particular school.

Topics for Cross-Cultural Discussion

1. Gender is already a sensitive topic for students. Religious and ethnic differences can heighten that sensitivity, so approach these questions with respect and care. Remember, suspending judgment and remaining civil does not mean that you cannot hold an opinion—even a strong opinion. But tolerance and open-mindedness require us to test our ideas against contrary ideas and arguments. The point of this prompt is not to arrive at a bland, everyone-is-right consensus or (alternately) elevate a single view of men and women as "correct." Rather, the questions should give students a chance to understand how their opinions and ideas have been formed—and how they may continue to change.

2. The essays provide a range of views on this dichotomy. Friedman, for example, views gender as something "shaped by society" rather than purely biological; Elsesser wants to eliminate the distinction related to awards between male and female actors—and, implicitly, that distinction as it applies to other professions. Jacobs's essay suggests that these differences may be hardwired and "natural." Do writers like Friedman and Elsesser seem to want a "genderless" society? Are there definite "male" and "female" qualities that need to be maintained? Why or why not?

8

Does Our Need for Security Threaten Our Right to Privacy?

The years since the terrorist attacks of September 11, 2001, have brought an increased awareness of safety and security issues. Umar Farouk Abdulmutallab's 2009 unsuccessful attempt to blow up a Northwest Airlines flight from Amsterdam to Detroit, as well as Faisal Shazad's 2010 failed car-bomb attack in Times Square remind us that real threats persist—as do questions about the best way to prevent such attacks. How do we maintain security without infringing on people's privacy or civil liberties? To what degree is the federal government capable of protecting us? What role should ethnic and racial profiling play in our security efforts? How do we distinguish between effective safeguards and mere "security theater"?

That last question animates Jeffrey Rosen's essay "Nude Awakening." He argues that highly touted, new body-scanning machines at airports not only raise major privacy concerns, but also provide a false sense of security: "The next plot rarely looks like the last one. But, if we need to waste money on feel-good technologies that don't make us safer, let's at least make sure they don't unnecessarily reveal us naked." In "New Airport Policy: Grin and Bare It," Connie Schultz takes the opposite view—and a more lighthearted approach. Privacy concerns about these new scanners are overblown, according to Schultz. She sees those who distrust the government's travel-safety measures as a laughable "cast of angry Americans"; for her, their skepticism is unfounded, given that they trust the state to provide safety in so many other areas of their lives.

Student writer Mohammed Khan focuses on the pervasiveness—and ineffectiveness—of racial and ethnic profiling. He notes that such profiling would have likely missed the 2001 "shoe bomber" Richard Reid, as well as Umar Farouk Abdulmutallab. Khan also writes from personal experience, having been detained at Chicago's O'Hare Airport apparently because of his name. He argues that while the "need for safety is paramount," security protocols must adapt to meet a terrorist threat that is always changing and evolving.

Jay Griffiths's "The Tips of Your Fingers" discusses border crossing, biometric identification, and the meaning of privacy. Her essay has a much broader scope than the others in this unit. While Rosen, Schultz, and Khan focus on airport security, Griffiths meditates on individualism, modernity, art, and spirituality. She is less interested in government competence or the nature of terrorist threats than she is in more fundamental questions about identity and the reach of the state.

Jeffrey Rosen

Nude Awakening

[*The New Republic,* February 4, 2010]

Vocabulary/Using a Dictionary

1. *Enthusiastic*, which means passionate, devoted, or excited regarding an interest or pursuit, comes from the Greek entheos (*en-* "in") + (*theos-* "god"): inspired or possesed by a god. In the seventeenth and eighteenth centuries, the word had a negative connotation related to excessive emotion or religious zeal.

2. *Contraband* means illegal goods, especially in the context of trade importation or exportation. It derives from the Latin *contra-* ("against") + the Italian *bando* ("law").

3. *Hypothetical* comes from the Greek *hypo-* ("under") + *thesis* ("proposition"), meaning the basis of an argument, especially something taken as true for the purposes of argument or investigation. It is related to the words *thesis* and *hypothetical.*

4. *Ephemeral* means short-lived and fleeting. It originates from the Greek word *ephemeros*: lasting only one day.

Responding to Words in Context

1. To "mince words" means to sugarcoat, euphemize, or otherwise blunt language so that it remains inoffensive or hides more straightforward facts or truths. Here, Rosen implies that those who support the use of body scanners might downplay or avoid the reality that the scanners are a "virtual strip search," while he (in contrast) is more honest in his assessment.

2. The word *rogue* suggests a person—in this case, a government official—operating outside the bounds of laws or rules. It connotes unpredictability and even destructiveness.

3. The adjective *feel-good* is often used to describe movies that leave viewers with a pleasant feeling. In this context, "feel-good technologies" suggests sophisticated devices that make people feel safe and secure, while not actually providing substantive safety or security.

Discussing Main Point and Meaning

1. Rosen argues that the machines are an example of "security theater," which gives people the "illusion of safety without actually making us

safer" (para. 3). They cannot detect lower-density explosives, nor can they detect explosives hidden in body cavities. In addition to being ineffective, they require people to sacrifice privacy—and pose a "serious threat to the dignity" of many people traveling in the United States (para. 7).

2. According to Rosen, the scanners constitute a "virtual strip search" (para. 7). He cites the customs of certain Muslim sects, which "forbid men from gazing at Muslim women unless they are veiled" (para. 7). His greatest privacy concern, however, is that images may later be leaked (para. 8) or used by "rogue officials" (para. 8). Because the Transportation Security Administration is "free of independent oversight, it's impossible to tell precisely how [the scanners are] being used" (para. 5).

3. There are scanners "with an alternative design that is more sensitive to privacy" (para. 4). They allow images to remain anonymous and ephemeral. Rosen suggests that President Barack Obama—with a "few simple technological and legal fixes"—authorize the use of "blob machines" instead of "naked machines" (para. 9).

Examining Sentences, Paragraphs, and Organization

1. The quotation points to a balance between two competing values: the need for aggressive security measures and the need to respect privacy. In citing the president's specific words, Rosen suggests that Obama needs to institute policies in line with his own stated goals and values. In the context of Rosen's essay, that means requiring the use of "blob machines" instead of "naked machines" (para. 9).

2. Rosen deliberately argues against popular wisdom. He implies that many people are reacting emotionally, especially "in the wake of the failed Christmas bombing of Northwest Flight 253" (para. 2). But according to Rosen, a closer, more rational analysis of the full-body scanning machines and their implications reveals that they are merely "security theater" (para. 3). The main point of his essay is to get readers to think more carefully and thoughtfully about their security and their privacy, rather than reflexively embracing "feel-good technologies" (para. 9).

3. The opening paragraph recounts an airline passenger following the instructions of an airport security officer, even as the passenger remains unaware that "TSA officials in a separate room were staring at a graphic, anatomically correct image of his naked body" (para. 1). The anecdote evokes the themes of unawareness of—and "surrender" to—technological authority continued throughout the essay. But Rosen uses the indignant words of the TSA official at the gate to contrast with the general acceptance of these machines in the wider public: "Someone ought to do something about those machines—it's like we don't have any privacy in this country anymore!" (para. 1). The outburst allows the writer to move from personal observation to the broader issues in the essay.

Thinking Critically

1. Rosen relies on a limited number of sources: polling from *USA Today*, information from the TSA Web site, personal observation, an unnamed member of the British Parliament, and the words of officials and ex-officials such as Barack Obama and former Department of Homeland Security director Michael Chertoff. The writer also seems to be influenced by the thinking of Bruce Schneider, who is quoted but identified only as a "security expert" (para. 3). The article might have benefited from a more thoroughly sourced explanation of how the scanners are a "waste of money" (para. 9), as well as more direct and explicit engagement with those who support the use of the machines.

2. Most people would agree that people's privacy should be protected and that these images should not be "leaked." But Rosen builds his argument on the notion that a celebrity image will inevitably be sold "to the tabloids" (para. 8). He also refers to the possibility of "rogue officials" misusing the scanners' databases, citing the example of Erroll Southers, who searched confidential criminal records to impugn his estranged wife's boyfriend. Despite Rosen's implications to the contrary, however, Southers's example is not directly related to the scanners and may not support his point. Rosen's argument might be more effective if he addressed specific people who are willing to accept the risk to their privacy.

3. Rosen's article presents a skeptical view of the TSA, from the opening paragraph in which a TSA official refuses to describe the image on the scanner, but then blurts out his privacy concerns. He implies that the agency is complicit in the practice of "security theater," which does not actually keep people safe. He also notes that they operate "free of independent oversight," so "it's impossible to tell" exactly how the scanners are being used (para. 5).

In-Class Writing Activities

1. Students' answers will vary depending on their experience and views on privacy, but many may use personal experience to back up their claims. Most students will have experience with airport security, some even with the body-scanners that Rosen describes. It could be interesting to hear their perspective since many students may not have known airports before this heightened level of security.

2. Rosen clearly takes a suspicious and even cynical view of the TSA. This assignment should encourage students to reflect on their own attitude toward government authority in the context of national security: Do they trust officials to make the right choices, act wisely and efficiently, with respect for both the privacy rights of citizens and also our need to remain secure? They may also broaden their scope beyond issues of terrorism and airport security: Do government agencies usually take care of the public interest?

3. Rosen provides no explicit examples in his own essay, but students may be able to propose some of their own—for example, in the contrast between the phrases "necessary security procedures" and "virtual strip searches." They might also consider how people soften or blunt their language when discussing (or arguing about) other potentially controversial subjects: abortion, torture, gay marriage, race, etc.

Connie Schultz

New Airport Policy: Grin and Bare It

[*Cleveland Plain Dealer*, January 10, 2010]

Vocabulary/Using a Dictionary

1. The word *privacy* comes from the Latin *privatus* ("set apart, belonging to the individual rather than the state") and *privare* ("to separate or deprive"). The word is related to terms such as *deprived* and *privilege*.

2. In its contemporary meaning, *visa* refers to an official endorsement on a passport that authorizes the bearer of the passport to enter or travel legally in a country. The term originally comes from the Latin *videre* ("to see") and the French *charta visa* (paper that has been seen).

3. The word *violation* means an infringement or the breaking of a law, but it also connotes desecration, disrespectful treatment, and even sexual violence. It originates in the Latin word *violare* ("to treat with violence") and shares its origins with words such as *violent* and *inviolate*.

Responding to Words in Context

1. We tend to think of a "travel accessory" as some harmless object—a piece of luggage or a child safety seat. Schultz uses understatement and irony to describe hidden explosives as a "travel accessory." She makes light of a serious subject, but then moves in the same sentence to the more substantive claim that such an accessory "probably would not make it through a full-body scanner" (para. 5).

2. The writer argues that the news media sensationalizes the full-body scanners by referring to "graphic images" when the images are (in Schultz's opinion) not graphic at all. Similarly, the "brave" and "courageous" volunteers demonstrating the machines are not actually acting bravely or courageously; rather, they are participating in a manufactured controversy. The quotation marks indicate that the writer is being ironic.

3. In paragraph 2, the word refers to the supposedly controversial and "graphic" images displayed on the full-body scanners in airports. She states (humorously) that the bodies of her readers have "more bumps and bulges than the Appalachian foothills" (para. 3). At the end of the essay, the image remains comic. Rather than referring to the out-of-

shape physiques of airport travelers, however, the humorous image now becomes that of people who trust the government to regulate innumerable other aspects of their lives, but not airport security.

Discussing Main Point and Meaning

1. Schultz believes that the scanners are an improvement over standard metal detectors, which failed to stop Umar Farouk Abdulmutallab. But she also makes a broader argument that we should generally trust the government to provide safety and security. Additionally, most of her essay focuses on the spuriousness—and even absurdity—of arguments against using the new machines.

2. Schultz does not believe the images are truly an invasion of privacy in the first place. But in paragraph 10, she notes that the screener who waves passengers through the scanner is not the same person who sees their computer images; she also points out that the images are immediately deleted and cannot be stored or shared in any way. TSA officials are not allowed to bring cell phones or cameras into the room where the scanning takes place. You might ask students whether these precautions seem thorough enough.

3. Schultz makes several generalizations about those concerned by the new scanners. In paragraph 4, she suggests that those who worry about the images being pornographic have "issues." She refers to the American Civil Liberties Union, which (according to Schultz) argued against the use of the machines by "champion[ing] the rights of celebrities" who "regularly expose themselves for money and attention" and consequently "don't make the best victims" (para. 12). The writer also points to the "usual cast of angry Americans who insist you can't trust the government" (para. 13). According to Schultz, these people trust the government in many other aspects of their lives, so their opposition to the scanners is "curious" and (implicitly) illogical.

Examining Sentences, Paragraphs, and Organization

1. Students should recognize elements in the essay that are informal and comic. For example, Schultz uses a sentence fragment (para. 6) and slangy diction like "c'mon" (para. 15). In addition to her sustained irony, the writer relies on hyperbole: "Now we're talking about how Grandma should be able to keep her waist-highs to herself" (para. 12). She pokes fun at celebrities (who "probably don't make the best victims"), as well as the "usual cast of angry Americans" (para. 13). Schultz even places a would-be terrorist in a comic light: "Not exactly Secret Agent Man" (para. 6). You might ask students if they think the topic deserves a more serious tone.

2. In particular, her choice to use the second person allows her to address the reader directly and conversationally—even in the first sentence of the article. But her transitions are effective as well. After she discusses the "usual cast of angry Americans" who do not trust the government

(para. 13), she shifts to the second-person plural ("We" in paragraph 14), and then asks her readers a question in the second person: "So, c'mon, you're going to stand there and tell me you don't trust the government?" (para. 15). The grammar here carries a sense of immediacy, as well as the implication that it would be absurd to disagree with the writer's logic.

3. The writer addresses implicit claims and counterarguments that the images of "virtually nude, lumpy" (para. 2) airline passengers are prurient or sexually suggestive. She characterizes such views as absurd, suitable only to those whose "sexual fantasies steer toward cartoon characters and robots" (para. 4). This dismissal supports her point that the machines are not a real threat to privacy—and her goal of "making light" of the controversy (para. 4). The sentence also implies that those outraged by—or concerned about—the scanners for such reasons are ridiculous.

Thinking Critically

1. The writer relies upon personal observation. For example, she dismisses the notion that the images are graphic by claiming, "I saw these computer-generated images close-up and personal last summer . . ." (para. 4). Schultz also makes a qualified statement about the effectiveness of the machines, stating that a person carrying explosives (such as Abdulmutallab) "probably would not make it through a full-body scanner" (para. 5). Students might note that more substantive evidence that the machines work better than metal detectors or other devices would improve her argument.

2. Schultz cites no specific counterarguments, choosing instead to generalize—perhaps to the point of engaging in an "Appeal to Ridicule" fallacy. Schultz might have included a particular example of an argument she finds specious or unpersuasive, rather than using such a broad approach. Her characterization of the ACLU's opposition to the scanners appears exaggerated and perhaps unfair as well (para. 12). Students might investigate the degree to which the writer caricatures the organization's position.

3. Schultz uses analogies to get her point across, but often her main purpose seems to be humor. For example, her arguments that "lurking under what's left of your clothing are more bumps and bulges than the Appalachian foothills have" (para. 3) and that the images created by the monitors "are not pornographic unless your sexual fantasies steer toward cartoon characters and robots" (para. 4) serve not only to show that the airport scanners are not dangerous, but that people are severely overreacting to them. She finds humor in a situation that many, like Rosen, find incredibly disturbing. Whether students think these analogies are successful will vary, but most will probably concede that they are entertaining, whether they agree with Schultz's point or not.

In-Class Writing Activities

1. After September 11, 2001, the threat of terrorism became far more vivid and prominent in our society. The possibility remains a serious and persistent concern; at the same time, the likelihood of any particular American dying in a terrorist attack remains statistically low, compared to other threats (car accidents, etc.). Students' answers will vary depending on their own experiences and beliefs.

2. Schultz generalizes broadly about attitudes toward government competence and its ability to keep us secure. Students should consider her logic carefully: We trust the government when it comes to paving roads or licensing drivers, therefore, we should probably trust it in the case of airport security. This assignment might also be an opportunity to investigate how much trust in the authority of the state is unexamined and taken for granted.

3. This question should encourage students to evaluate how they balance issues of safety, privacy, and trust in the government. Schultz notes that the TSA is ordering hundreds of the scanners over the next year; it appears that they will soon become standard. Do students think that the machines have been adequately evaluated for their effectiveness and their privacy safeguards? What choices would students have if they believed their privacy was being compromised?

Mohammed Khan (student essay)

The Need for Safety Is Paramount

[*The Daily Evergreen*, Washington State University, January 13, 2010]

Vocabulary/Using a Dictionary

1. *Feasible* means capable of being done or accomplished. Its roots are in the Latin *facere* ("to do, perform").

2. *Paramount* means "most important" in Khan's sentence. It comes from Old French, *par* ("by") + *amunt* ("up") and the Latin *per ad montem* ("to the hill"). *Paramount* is sometimes confused with *tantamount*, which means "equivalent."

3. In this context, *protocol* denotes a code of correct conduct or procedures. The word originally comes from the Greek *protokollon* ("first sheet glued onto a manuscript, table of contents"). You might note the prefix *proto* refers to "first" or "primary" in other words, as well: *prototype, protoplasm*.

Responding to Words in Context

1. Even before the attacks of September 11, 2001, these terms were contested. The language we assign to people has consequences: foreign and domestic terrorists or "enemy combatants" may have different legal

status than, say, soldiers from a foreign military. Students will have different ideas of how to define a *terrorist* or *terrorism*, but most will agree that terrorism cannot be directly linked to a recognized state or government.

2. *Racial profiling* refers to the use of a person's race or ethnicity by law enforcement or security officials as a factor in deciding whether to investigate that person or engage in enforcement (search someone at an airport security checkpoint, make a traffic stop or arrest). The term can carry racist connotations, e.g., the presumption that some races are more likely to commit crimes and therefore more likely to be stopped by police.

3. In its precise meaning, *strategy* refers to large-scale, long-range, "big-picture" planning, especially military planning during both peace time and war time. In contrast, *tactics* denotes the deployment of specific troops, devices, or procedures in carrying out such plans. Khan uses the term correctly: Airport screenings are ostensibly a tactic in a broader, strategic campaign to reduce the threat of terrorism.

Discussing Main Point and Meaning

1. Khan argues that racial profiling is ineffective and impractical, and that we must instead emphasize "intelligence-based" tactics such as full-body scanners. Despite concerns about these techniques, the need for security is paramount and must ultimately override concerns about privacy. You might point out that Khan frames his argument in a way that implies a false choice: "An enormous amount of evidence indicates racial profiling is not sufficient to protect us from terrorists" (para. 2). Ask your students: Is anyone arguing that racial profiling—alone—is "sufficient to protect us from terrorists"? Might profiling be just one part of an overall strategy?

2. For Khan, Reid and Abdulmutallab demonstrate that (presumably) conventional ethnic profiling methods are ineffective. Reid is half English, half Jamaican; Abdulmutallab is Nigerian and comes from an affluent English family. Neither fits the ethnic profile of an Arab, Iranian, or Pakistani. Ask students if we can draw broad conclusions about profiling from these two examples.

3. Khan writes that discomfort with "invasive" security procedures is "understandable" (para. 6). After conceding that new protocols must "address people's qualms," he proposes that those who are uncomfortable with body-scanning machines come to the airport early so they can undergo a "thorough search" from security officials. You might note that such searches could raise other privacy concerns. But for Khan, safety, not privacy, is "paramount."

Examining Sentences, Paragraphs, and Organization

1. Khan believes that profiling is part of a "facade": a superficial, illusory, or false appearance of safety and security. Instead, he proposes

"intelligence-based" measures, like full-body scanners. Some students may note that the use of "intelligence" here is ambiguous—Khan could either be referring to being smart and informed, or he could be referring to "intelligence" in its security and military context. This reading could affect how a student answers the question. In terms of a contrast, Khan is trying to illustrate that intelligence, not racial profiling, would have been effective in stopping the Christmas day bombing attempt by Umar Farouk Abdulmautallab—he was not Arab, he was Nigerian, and therefore not targeted for racial profiling.

2. Rather than just referring to "many people" (a generality), Khan could have cited a specific example or quoted a person with a particular privacy concern. A quotation (from a news source, for example) would allow his argument to move from the general to the specific. It could also provide his column with a more explicit connection to the timely and ongoing public conversation about terrorism and security issues.

3. When Khan writes about the ineffectiveness of profiling, he does so from experience. He was held at the airport for two hours—in large part, because of his name. The example supports his overall point. Note that the anecdote is subtle, given its placement: Many arguments against profiling are based on the idea that stereotyping is wrong and dangerous. But Khan focuses on the ineffectiveness of profiling, rather than making a moral argument about racism or civil liberties.

Thinking Critically

1. Khan writes that determining individual religious beliefs is difficult. Additionally, Muslims comprise "more than one-fifth of the world's population" (para. 3). Notice that he emphasizes that profiling all Muslims would be ineffective or impossible, rather than making a moral argument about the "rightness" or "wrongness" of profiling.

2. Khan does not delve deeply into the specifics of privacy concerns or "qualms" about privacy. However, he acknowledges that "privacy infringements" raise "important questions" (para. 6). What might those questions be? What concerns do students have?

3. While he refers to an "enormous amount of evidence," Khan does not cite much of it in his essay. He relies primarily on the examples of Reid, Abdulmutallab, and himself. He could strengthen the argument by citing expert sources, airport security workers, or scholarly research on the subject.

In-Class Writing Activities

1. Students should use this prompt to reflect on their own images and presumptions about terrorists and terrorism. As the backgrounds, goals, nationalities, ethnicities, and religions of terrorists can vary, students may want to explore current research on the topic and measure their assumptions and impressions against more empirical data.

2. Khan's essay provides an excellent basis for a response, either pro or con. If students agree with his claim that racial profiling is not sufficient to protect us, they may want to elaborate on the moral and legal aspects of racial and ethnic profiling. If students disagree, they might highlight the dichotomy implicit in Khan's column: Racial profiling, on its own, is "not sufficient to protect us from terrorists," but perhaps the practice—if used in a limited and careful way—could have some place or value.

3. This prompt will give students the chance to consider their own fears—or lack thereof—in (to use Khan's words) "this age of global terrorism" (para. 1). How did they react, for example, to Faisal Shahzad's failed attempt to attack Times Square with a car bomb? Do they trust the U.S. government to keep citizens safe? Do they agree with Khan's emphasis on safety over privacy?

Jay Griffiths
The Tips of Your Fingers

[*Orion*, January/February 2010]

Vocabulary/Using a Dictionary

1. An *idiosyncrasy* is a characteristic, habit, or mannerism that is peculiar to an individual. Deriving from the Greek *idios* ("one's own"), the word is related to terms such as *idiom* or *idiot*, as Griffiths notes in her seventh paragraph.

2. The writer's usage suggests not only the psychology or mind of a person (which is the common contemporary usage), but also the human spirit or soul. The word comes from Greek and Roman mythology: Psyche was a beautiful girl loved by Cupid. As a Latin and Greek noun, the term means "soul, mind, life, or animating spirit of the body."

3. *Panopticon* derives from the Greek *pan* ("all, everything") + *optikon* ("sight"). It denotes an object that is all-seeing.

Responding to Words in Context

1. Here, *diviners* suggests that fingertips have the power of prophecy, insight, and intuition. The word connotes a god-like power to reveal the self—and achieve a transcendent connection with others.

2. The term *cache* refers to a secret space for hidden valuables. Griffiths is especially tuned to the sound of her words. *Cache* evokes a small, soft, inner "tenderness" or space: the "sh" sound connects it with the word *shelter* in the same sentence, which is an example of consonance.

3. *Individuation* is the act or process whereby social individuals become different from one another. *Individuality* refers to the specific character or qualities that distinguish one person or one thing from others.

Discussing Main Point and Meaning

1. Griffiths sees biometrics and national ID cards as a threat to individuals on different levels. For example, in the context of border protection, she states that practices like identification and tagging are "used to intimidate those at the margins, the borders of society": refugees, political dissidents, protesters, and people who threaten dominant cultures of "intolerant homogeneity" (paras. 4–5). They become a tool for modern surveillance, which encourages conformity and political docility. Such identification and surveillance practices also allow the "state" to cross into the inalienable, idiosyncratic, and personal spaces of our private selves—an "ugly act" (para. 10).

2. The writer sees the "state's assault" as part of larger and interconnected trends toward homogeneity. Such forces support "monoism, destroying variety from biodiversity to linguistic diversity" (para. 5). They range from our food and our politics to our entertainment: "Like the mono-culture of Hollywood and the monocrops of agribusiness, the monopolitics of world powers erase the particular . . ." (para. 5). The contrast is between individuality and diversity on one side, and "monoism" on the other.

3. For Griffiths, state intrusions into the "private self" are "ugly," especially when they are enforcing boundaries at the expense of the marginalized and the idiosyncratic. She contrasts such intrusions with a different kind of border crossing: the "self reaching outward," which is an "act of beauty and transcendence" (para. 10). Such acts seek to escape the "confines of the single self" and connect with others (para. 10). Humans find "benevolence" in these border crossings. In Griffiths's view, art, spirituality, environmentalism, and movements for social justice all partake of this benevolent transcendence.

Examining Sentences, Paragraphs, and Organization

1. Students should be able to point to several examples of her stylish, figurative, and sonorous prose. For example, Griffiths uses rhyme to refer to those who stand out for their beliefs, "who poke and provoke with the demeanor of a pitchfork in the cutlery drawer" (para. 4). She is fond of alliteration: "These laws of life agree with the law of love . . ." (para. 14). Such rhetoric can be powerful, persuasive, and even dazzling to readers. At the same time, her claims and arguments can be more poetic and associative than strictly logical; sometimes, they are not clear: Who, exactly, are the "insane with their flashes of specific mind-lightning" (para. 4) and how, exactly, do they pertain to her main point? In a larger sense, a practical reader might also wonder how the "perennial philosophy of a universal oneness" (para. 11) might be reconciled to the more prosaic, real-world concerns of patrolling national borders.

2. Griffiths traces the etymology of the words *private* and *idiot* in paragraphs 6 and 7, respectively. She uses the original meaning of the terms to reinforce the idea that most people today are "deprived of public

life" (para. 6) and must be "purely private persons," as if governments preferred "their subjects to remain idiots, disengaged from the state's process but suffering its intrusions" (para. 7). The etymologies do not "prove" her point on their own, but these linguistic recoveries do reveal and reinforce her notion that citizens are increasingly deprived of connection and political power.

3. Griffiths begins with a practical example of people searing their fingers to get through border checkpoints: Fingertips and fingerprints have obvious associations with identification procedures. But she moves in the next two paragraphs to the other associations of fingertips—with touching, feeling, connecting, idiosyncrasy. As the essay develops, their significance becomes more figurative than literal: "Burning away the signature of individuality, at the borders of those very countries that most profess individualism, is a metaphor of terrible reproach" (para. 5). Indeed, the removal of fingertips becomes a metaphor for the way our society is not "individualistic." She returns to fingertips again in the final paragraph of the essay—the way they delineate an "exquisite uniqueness" in their ability to both reveal ourselves and touch others, even through time.

Thinking Critically

1. Griffiths makes broad generalizations in this essay. In this instance, readers may even have a hard time determining what, exactly, the "dominant culture" and "society" refer to here. Whether or not students agree with her statements will vary. Students may interpret Griffiths's argument as unsupported—she makes many big claims in a short space. Other students might argue that this is exactly what she set out to do, and was successful in her argument.

2. In paragraph 6, Griffiths writes: "A vote every few years does not constitute a political voice." This suggests that citizens are largely voiceless—particularly people who hold idiosyncratic or dissenting points of view. Students may argue that there are many other ways for your political voice to be heard—in polls, rallies, protests, etc.—but that people do not take full advantage of these possibilities. Students may also disagree with Griffiths completely, and think that the current voting process is the best way to maintain a representative democracy. Students may want to discuss how anyone on the "fringe" can be heard, and whether or not they are fairly represented by the current voting process. Griffiths obviously does not think they are, but some students might disagree with her.

3. Students should be able to understand the possible dangers of too much surveillance: invasions of privacy, the implicit presumption of guilt, the reduction of freedom. They might also be familiar with novels like *1984* and other dystopian representations of police states. Yet, on a daily basis, is surveillance always sinister? For example, security cameras in convenience stores or large parking lots? Airport security? Customs procedures? Griffiths seems more concerned about surveillance practiced

by the state: Is there a difference between government surveillance and that practiced in the private sphere (e.g., security cameras in a mall)?

In-Class Writing Activities

1. The words that Griffiths lists—*solidarity, trade unions, co-operatives*, and *collectives*—may be difficult for students to analyze because they may not have much experience with them. Students may think that these words have positive connotations, therefore undermining Griffiths's argument, or students may also think that these concepts are outdated, which somewhat proves Griffiths's point, even though students might not realize it. Students may also take this time to explore their own views on the difference between *individualistic* and *hyper-privatized*—many may not have been aware that there even was a difference, and some might still believe that there isn't.

2. For the writer, true individualism reveals and values the "'this-ness,' the essential specificity of the beloved person" (para. 14). She also associates with the marginalized, the eccentric, and all of those people who urge us to "see it otherwise" (para. 4). Students should be well-versed in the clichés of individualism, so it may be difficult to get them to think beyond platitudes and conventional wisdom. You may want to prompt them with Griffiths's provocative statements. For example, she seems to suggest that all attempts to encourage "normality" within a dominant culture are hostile to individualism. Moreover, she tries to separate individualism from "hyper-privatization": the tendency of people to become atomized, separated, and isolated from one another. Whether or not students agree with her view of individualism will vary.

3. Griffiths chooses the example of solitary television viewing. Students may consider other kinds of entertainment, including new media forms like Internet social networking sites and video games. Do they prefer "hyper-privatized" entertainments to communal ones? Moreover, are online role-playing games or Internet communications "communal" or are they still isolating, even when they do bring people in contact with one another? Is there a significant difference between listening to music on an iPod and going to a concert? What kind of communities are being built around contemporary forms of entertainment (e.g., music file sharing)?

Discussing the Unit

Suggested Topic For Discussion

These essays suggest a range of responses about the role of the state, from Griffiths's deeply philosophical skepticism to Schultz's pragmatic trust. You might also note the government's role in issues less sensational than border security, terrorism, or outbreaks of disease: food safety, day-to-day police protection, traffic laws, etc.

Preparing for Class Discussion

1. Most of us are familiar with the use of fingerprints as a biometric for identity, especially in the context of police procedures. But you might get students to discuss the broader implications of biometrics and biometric identification. For example, one immigration reform proposal in circulation would require a national biometric ID card for employment eligibility and Social Security purposes. Would students agree with this? Do they worry about the "state" crossing the borders of their "private selves" (as Griffiths does), or would the benefits of such a requirement outweigh any possible drawbacks?

2. Encourage students to be specific in their responses and assessments. Do diction and style play any part in their judgment? Each of the essays addresses security issues, but the authors also reveal broader attitudes and assumptions. Griffiths, for example, provides a meditation on identity; Schultz discusses how Americans view the role of government in their lives. Student responses will vary depending on which essay they find most effective.

From Discussion to Writing

1. There are a number of ways into this exercise. Rosen writes from personal observation, and students may want to begin with a specific example from their own lives that helps define the right to privacy. Griffiths notes the old argument that "if you have nothing to hide, you have nothing to fear." Do students accept that point of view? If not, how would they go about refuting it in the interest of privacy? They might also rely on their sense of rights and liberties as enumerated in the U.S. Constitution, although that document does not explicitly name a right to "privacy."

2. Khan gives no definite sense of the official's tone. We do not know whether he or she was being completely serious, flippant, grimly honest, or even sympathetic. The essay does not include his response at the time, either. Students might write about how they would react if they were profiled because of their names or backgrounds.

Questions for Cross-Cultural Discussion

1. Immigration is a perennial controversy in the United States. Griffiths seems to value "universal oneness" and the inviolability of the individual over national and state identities. Immigration and national identity are contested issues in many countries and students views will most likely be varied, and possibly polarized. Students should consider the practical necessity of national borders and border security, in particular.

2. Khan refers to his own experience traveling as a person with an Islamic-sounding name. Rosen points out that new body-scanning machines pose a "serious threat to the dignity" of travelers such as Muslim men, who may be forbidden to view unveiled women. To what degree do people need to sacrifice such cultural, religious, or even individual notions

to participate in contemporary life? Griffiths writes that surveillance "creates conformity," and compares this process to the creation of a docile herd. But is the modern world—airline travel, for example— possible without surveillance, a certain level of conformity, and accepted conventions of behavior?

9

Barack Obama:
What Does His Election
Mean to America?

Americans' discussion of race has always been fraught and difficult, weighed down by the legacy of slavery and discrimination, and occasionally opting to avoid the painfully difficult question of poverty in the African American community. As the charismatic and wildly popular Barack Obama soared in the polls during the 2008 election cycle, many began to wonder what it would actually mean to have a black president. Would Obama bring a real change to a Washington establishment many Americans felt was out of touch? Or would he just represent a superficial manicure, putting a new face on old ideas and ways of governing? Would he help to defuse racial tensions and bring the country together? Or would his policies—or even vestigial prejudices—widen the race-based rift in American society?

The answers to these questions have become no clearer. Many have faulted the president for failing to live up to his initial promise, while others consider his administration a welcome departure from the past and argue that real change will take real time. In these essays, though, written around the time of Obama's election and inauguration, several writers from several different backgrounds consider the implications of the Obama election to American policy and the American social fabric.

Diane McKinney-Whetstone and John Edgar Wideman observed the election of Obama in November of 2008 from two very different angles: McKinney-Whetstone ("The First Family") watched the actual acceptance ceremony in Grant Park in Chicago, while Wideman ("Street Corner Dreamers") considered a group of African American youths outside an underserved school in New York City, going about their routine as if nothing had changed. Both writers hold out enormous hopes that President Obama will make real changes to the state of black America, symbolized in the smiling faces of his family and the crumbling facade of that school. But both also seem to harbor doubts and concerns.

Student essayist Pearl Wong is more direct: She embraces the more race-blind opinion that Barack Obama must be, as her title asserts, a "President for All," not just black Americans. Wong appreciates the enormous mantle Obama has taken on—he is not only subject to the hopes and fears of critics like McKinney-Whetstone and Wideman, but must actually govern a large and complex country with the interests of all its citizens in mind. Wong suggests the only way to do so is to act without race directly on the agenda and offers a related lesson for the way we can all improve race relations and race dialogue.

The most skeptical essay in the chapter is by critic Christopher Hedges, who derides the notion that Obama will represent a real change on either front, calling him a celebrity brand used to repackage the regressive ideas of the past. In "Celebrity Culture and the Obama Brand," Hedges focuses on the political and policy dimensions of the Obama presidency, but students should keep both of these themes—our policies and our larger discussion of our diverse heritage—in mind throughout the chapter.

Diane McKinney-Whetstone

The First Family

[*Essence*, January 2009]

Vocabulary/Using a Dictionary

1. To know something *intimately* is to know it very closely, as you would know a good friend. One possible opposite would be *sketchily*.

2. *Culminate* is a verb, meaning to finish in a particular state, usually a climax. Typically, a series of events *culminates* in an interesting peak.

3. *Ebullience* is a very bright and optimistic demeanor. It comes from a Latin word meaning "bubbling."

Responding to Words in Context

1. "Norman Rockwellesque" means in the style of Rockwell, an illustrator known for painting scenes of ordinary, wholesome suburban American life in the first half of the twentieth century. A Rockwellesque diner would be one that's clean and well-ordered, most likely in a small town. McKinney-Whetstone implies that the scene was one typical of a loving, intact family unit.

2. *Supplant* is a verb, meaning to replace. It typically means to serve in something's place, and here it means filling in for absent parents.

3. *Buoyant* means afloat, and has come to mean very excited and cheerful, giving off an air of optimism and happiness. We imagine the president-elect smiling widely, moving around, embracing his family, etc.

Discussing Main Point and Meaning

1. McKinney-Whetstone is describing a feeling of solidarity with the Obama family, who achieved great things despite humble beginnings and low expectations, combined with pride that a black family had achieved so much.

2. McKinney-Whetstone implies that many people only see the "fractured part" of the black experience in America — dire poverty and dysfunction in families. The Obamas, by being a loving, intact unit, challenged that notion.

3. The author is referring to African Americans, and particularly to African Americans from families that encouraged them to achieve despite their humble beginnings. She says this group understands the poverty and adversity Barack and Michelle faced—especially the single-parent home in which Barack was raised—but also empathizes with a spirit of perseverance they represent.

Examining Sentences, Paragraphs, and Organization

1. These details show us how much McKinney-Whetstone sees herself in the Obama daughters; we imagine from her description that she owned similar dresses and at least recognizes a hairstyle from Sunday school. (She later refers to being in church as a child.) It also illustrates how carefully she examined every detail of that night, further underscoring how the image of the Obamas on stage was so important to her—as important, perhaps, as the speech the president-elect gave or the policies he backed during the campaign.

2. The paragraph lists the many obstacles the Obamas had to overcome to succeed, obstacles McKinney-Whetstone says are familiar to all African Americans. The long sentences listing these adversities illuminate the depth of their adversity, while the terse final sentence ("And for the Obamas, the moment came.") underlines how triumphant the moment of the election felt.

3. The essay alternates frequently between the two scenes, beginning on stage in Chicago, switching into the homes, we presume, of the black audience, and then back and forth repeatedly. This confusion of the scenes highlights McKinney-Whetstone's main point, which is that the black audience on election night was able to see itself in the Obamas: They are one and the same.

Thinking Critically

1. A good response will address the tensions between American society as a whole and the black community, particularly in terms of America's image of African Americans. Obama has the potential, as McKinney-Whetstone argues, to counter harmful stereotypes of blacks, and particularly of the black family. Another tactic for answering the question is the more race-blind one: The election means very little, because most Americans already encounter a politician like Obama outside of the context of his race.

2. This question asks students to confront the problem of stereotyping, which the essay both attacks and partially relies on. Responses should note that there is a huge diversity—socioeconomically, politically, and otherwise—within black families. But students are likely to divide on

whether a "typical" black family is a useful construct: Some will describe families broken up by poverty and neglect, others strong, vibrant communities bound together by a larger sense of family, and still others will argue that the group is too large to typify, and that doing so borders on the offensive.

3. McKinney-Whetstone wants to avoid entering the political fray directly, especially when writing about a candidate and a president as controversial as Obama. Rather than discussing the issue of his race analytically, she relies on a visual narrative nobody can dispute, one whose images are familiar to all Americans. This makes her point stronger and more compelling than if she were to discuss Obama's significance to the black community from an immediately political or philosophical point of view.

In-Class Writing Activities

1. Responses should focus on the centrality of the family, rather than the politician, throughout the acceptance: the way Michelle and the couple's daughters really are front-and-center. Some students may notice the large bulletproof glass that separates the Obamas, physically and figuratively, from the crowd, and also responds to an atmosphere of danger for the president-elect. This very salient danger is one example of something absent from McKinney-Whetstone's essay.

2. This is likely to be a divisive question that raises some passions. As above, students may argue that the idea of a typical black family is too reductive to be useful and may even be offensive. But some may write that there is an archetype, however many aberrations there may be from it, of a black family in America, and that poverty and dysfunction are facets of it. Some students may blame these hallmarks on endemic American racism that still denies blacks opportunities, and others will argue the community itself is to blame for failing its members. The most important thing to look for in this essay is that students engage Obama's *impact* on relations between blacks and whites. Will an Obama administration, in which a black man both leads the country and absorbs its criticisms, help defuse tensions between blacks and whites who feel alienated from their fellow Americans of other races? Or could he make things worse, particularly for the way whites see the black family?

3. Responses will vary widely, but prompt students to replicate the visuality of McKinney-Whetstone's essay—the way a public figure's posture, clothing, manner of waving, etc.—said more than the words or ideas associated with the event. If students can't come up with such an event in their lifetimes, challenge them to look for one through their study of history: a photo of Lincoln at Gettysburg, for instance, or a video of Kennedy's famous speech at the Berlin Wall.

John Edgar Wideman

Street Corner Dreamers

[*Essence,* January 2009]

Vocabulary/Using a Dictionary

1. To *marginalize* something is to make it feel or appear unimportant—to put it on the margins. Wideman is arguing that America's urban youth has not been a priority for society over the last few decades, that they have essentially been treated as insignificant.

2. *Motley* means mixed in color or fabric, and is used to refer to the many-colored costumes worn by jesters. Wideman uses it to describe the outfits worn by the inner-city kids, which are not coordinated or styled, but patched together.

3. *Amalgamated* means mixed together, related to *amalgam*, a chemistry term meaning a mixture of mercury and another metal.

Responding to Words in Context

1. A *scowl* is an angry expression, typically on a human or even an animal face. Wideman is using the word metaphorically when referring to the facade of a building, indicating just how ugly and unpleasant the broken-down school is to look at.

2. Wideman is continuing the metaphor he started when he referred to the building's "scowl"—comparing its front to a human face. A *facelift* is a surgery that changes a person's face but does not change what's behind it; Wideman is implying that the change to the school may not have improved the education offered within it.

3. A *blight* is most literally a disease of a plant, caused by neglect and decay. Wideman is suggesting by this metaphorical use that society has neglected these youths and thus caused their potential to wither and decompose.

Discussing Main Point and Meaning

1. The students stand for poor, urban youths, who are mostly black. Wideman witnesses these particular students living near their school in New York, but they come to represent, for the author, the "missing ones" throughout the nation.

2. Wideman writes that urban poverty is a product of marginalization—a sense that America decided long ago not to deal with poor, mostly black urban youths, because "we could get along just fine without them, thank you." As a result, these kids are often in prison or dead, and the students who remain don't see themselves as part of America or think they have a real voice within it.

3. Wideman declares he will do no "crystal-ball gazing" to keep the essay in the present, and announces that he has no specific prediction for the

future. But the tone of the essay can be read as either optimistic— especially its last paragraph describing President Obama firmly in charge and willing to do what it takes to improve the lot of these students—or pessimistic—since it gives a large space to describing just how large and apparently insurmountable the problem of urban poverty is.

Examining Sentences, Paragraphs, and Organization

1. Wideman is illustrating the contrast between Washington politics and reality on the street—he doesn't mean to imply that these two things literally happened at the same time, but their *juxtaposition* serves to show us the disconnect politicians can have from the very reasons they do things like, for instance, raise taxes.

2. All three sentences are questions—specifically, rhetorical questions posing difficult problems in the war on poverty. The paragraph therefore advances Wideman's general feeling of exasperation at the problem, and his aspiration to provoke action from his readers, whom he directly engages with the series of questions.

3. The essay begins by describing the rotting front of the Seward Park High School building in Manhattan, giving us a vivid sense of how neglected the children who attend the school have become. The essay gradually shifts from a literal description of the crowd of students exiting the school to an argument about what needs to be done to secure their future. By beginning with something so concrete, Wideman makes his argument more vivid and makes us feel the urgency that underpins it.

Thinking Critically

1. Students should recognize that Wideman's term means not that the children are literally missing, but that they've been ignored—particularly by the media in its depiction of American life and by the government in its allocation of resources. Students are likely to divide on whether they really are ignored, with some placing the blame on black communities themselves for the problems Wideman is describing, and others concurring that the problem of black poverty is one many Americans, and especially the American media, do not want to confront, let alone solve.

2. There are two potential arguments for the positive impact President Obama could have on urban poverty. He could change policy in a way that alleviates it somehow, such as spending more money on urban renewal or education; he could also improve race relations in a way that ultimately benefits blacks. The argument against his influence would be grounded in the empirical evidence of his first few years in office— many critics claim he's had very little impact and has not been active enough in effecting the change his campaign promised.

3. Wideman's comment is not meant to endorse total race-blindness, but students may read it to endorse a society where our traditional racial

identities are less salient in everyday life. Some students may feel we make too much of race, while others are likely to think we as a society, or our government, need to do more to tackle race problems, particularly economic inequalities between the races. Look for all responses to acknowledge the differences between consciousness about race in everyday life—like, say, being conscious of what race someone is when deciding to hire him or her—and consciousness about the racial tensions facing America.

In-Class Writing Activities

1. The most startling facts involve unemployment, which is considerably higher for blacks than for whites. Students will divide on the causes of this disparity—whether racism or inertia is to blame, or whether the community itself has not done enough to bridge the gap. Encourage students to propose solutions that do more than just redistribute wealth: They should be aware of the roles that culture and discrimination play in poverty.

2. Look for responses that stress the visual impact of the school and its surroundings—not just the facade of the building, but how well manicured its lawn and hedges are, how welcoming it looks, what (if anything) is advertised outside. Better maintained schools, of course, suggest that more money is going into them.

3. Again, students will divide between cynicism and optimism about politicians, but look for them to pay particular attention to the special potential of an Obama administration, namely to help improve race relations and bring a major change to the tone and policy of Washington.

Pearl Wong (student essay)

Obama—President for All

[*The Santa Clara*, Santa Clara University, February 25, 2010]

Vocabulary/Using a Dictionary

1. *Dis-* is a general negative prefix. *Discontentment*, in turn, is a lack of satisfaction, which Wong is here ascribing to the African American community.

2. A literal *milestone* is a stone set up on a road to mark an important place or to indicate a distance. Figuratively, which is the way Wong means it, it means an important moment or turning point in time.

Responding to Words in Context

1. Something *conspicuous* is highly visible. Wong is referring to activities like ethnic pride parades and literature and art with an ethnic focus, which are very conscious of heritage and make it very open.

2. To *embody* means to be a visual representation of an abstract idea—literally to become the body of something. Wong is suggesting that the "milestone" in American history is an expanded acceptance of African Americans in public life and that Obama represents that milestone physically.

Discussing Main Point and Meaning

1. Wong is describing a fine line between an overly conspicuous embrace of ethnic identities, which she believes can be showy and divisive, and being ashamed of who we are.

2. Wong says individuals have to act locally in their communities to achieve real change, and that minorities cannot expect politicians, even Obama, to improve their lot.

Examining Sentences, Paragraphs, and Organization

1. "Red pill or blue" refers to *The Matrix* (see gloss), in which it represents an exceedingly difficult choice, where either option has serious downsides. Wong is describing the choice politicians like Obama face between protecting minority groups and representing all Americans. She is emphasizing what a challenge this is for the president and how significant the ramifications are.

2. Wong quotes Obama declaring that he is responsible for all Americans, very directly and literally reiterating her main idea. She also quotes Mother Teresa making a perhaps more profound point, which rounds off the essay by making us think about our responsibility to care for each other without judging each other.

Thinking Critically

1. Some students will argue, against Wong, that individuals can have a racial consciousness without defining themselves entirely by their heritage or ethnicity. Prompt students to think of membership in clubs as a concrete manifestation of this sort of identification: They, or their peers, may be in ethnically based clubs, but does that preclude membership in other clubs as well? Is it the most defining organization one can belong to? Why or why not?

2. Responses should consider thoughtfully and carefully the pros and cons of both local and national efforts. Government attempts to alleviate racial problems include more money for local urban-renewal programs, and large-scale political and social efforts akin to President Clinton's "national conversation on race." Some students will argue that these efforts have often failed in the past, while others will argue that local, individual efforts, while important in their own right, are too small to account for any real change.

In-Class Writing Activities

1. Examples are split into two major categories: 1) reallocation of funds and efforts to projects like urban renewal and education; and 2) defus-

ing racial tensions and working to depolarize Americans psychologically about race. Specific examples will vary widely, but look for students to come up with original ideas that go beyond throwing money at problems.

2. This works well as a group exercise: Have students break into small groups and write out specific proposals for improving race relations locally. Then have the groups critique each others' proposals. The important thing here is specificity: Look for concrete examples like programs to bolster after-school clubs where students of different ethnicities work together on community service projects, rather than "more money for education."

Christopher Hedges

Celebrity Culture and the Obama Brand

[*Tikkun*, January/February 2010]

Vocabulary/Using a Dictionary

1. *Imperial* comes from "empire," and describes actions by one country intended to dominate or rule other parts of the world.

2. *Tilting* means leaning very slightly, in order to change the meaning of these concepts without being conspicuous.

3. A *demagogue* is any politician or leader who appeals more to people's emotions than to their sense of logic or reason. It comes from Greek *demos*, meaning "people," and *agein*, meaning "to lead," and thus originally meant "a leader of people." It has a decidedly negative connotation.

Responding to Words in Context

1. To *grease* someone's *palms* is to bribe him or her, whether directly or, as in this case, simply by offering campaign money in order to secure favorable policy stances, as lobbyists often do to politicians.

2. *Trivia* means anything unimportant, and is familiar to most of us as a designation of quiz-type questions. Here, it refers to the objects of media attention (presumably celebrity gossip and the like) that Hedges considers insignificant.

3. *Deflation* means letting the air out of something, and in this context Hedges is illustrating an advertising strategy that has lost its "hot air," the rhetoric that has puffed it up. In other words, it no longer has an effect on people's opinions.

Discussing Main Point and Meaning

1. *Brand* is an advertising term, meaning a way of thinking about a product controlled by the producer, and not necessarily completely accurate. Hedges considers Obama a brand because his backers are selling the public a particular image of him at odds with reality.

2. Hedges, a liberal, is viciously opposed to the policies of the Bush administration, which he characterizes as lawless and imperial. He points especially to the administration's secrecy laws, suspension of habeas corpus, wars in the Middle East, and neglect of domestic problems. He implies that Obama promised a substantial departure from these policies, but writes that he has not lived up to those promises, extending Bush's policies and altering only the image of the presidency.

3. Hedges says explicitly that corporations "control our politics" (para. 3) and describes our system of government as "corporate" and "consumption-oriented." Hedges believes that the corporate interests that control America have rolled Obama out as a new brand to replace Bush, much as they would replace a failing product with a new one; he does not believe, however, that the new president actually represents a new set of ideas or policies.

Examining Sentences, Paragraphs, and Organization

1. Both of these terms are in scare quotes, representing Hedges's skepticism that they represent the kinds of changes they claim to and casting them as more empty corporate branding. Nuclear energy is not, Hedges says with those quotes, actually green; the bill in question did not reform anything.

2. With these short, choppy sentences, Hedges mimics the workings of a mind that has been numbed to any real nuanced thoughts. All we know is that we feel entertained and happy; and we are ignoring the larger problems that still face our country.

3. Hedges is writing for *Tikkun*, a left-leaning magazine, and seems to presume that his readers share most of his conclusions. To take one example, Hedges faults Obama for expanding the war in Afghanistan, not an effective argument for a reader who believes the war is justified or necessary.

Thinking Critically

1. Hedges's premise is essentially that commerce and politics should be kept separate, and there is certainly a strong philosophical argument to back that premise up. Some students might worry that an expanded commercialism in politics will invite a situation where the candidate who spends the most on branding wins—some may think we're already there. Others may argue, as Hedges does, that a corporatist state will never allow for any real change, since corporations are known to thrive on stasis and inertia. Others, however, may take the position that there's nothing wrong with branding a politician, or that it may be inevitable. We've been trained to think in terms of brands, for better or worse, and a unified sense of who a candidate or leader is and what he or she believes in may be the best avenue Americans have to connect to their government.

2. Answers will vary depending on the way students interpret the given definition of "junk politics," and whether or not they agree that America

is functioning under a junk politics system. The definition given may be a bit confusing, and it might also lead to some debate over what constitutes issues "at home" and "abroad." Politicians have been criticized for downplaying the wars in Iraq and Afghanistan, but those would appear to be the "threats from abroad" that Hedges implies are being magnified. Students may not be able to completely agree or disagree with this definition, simply because the current political and socioeconomic landscapes are so complex.

3. Hedges would likely answer that the dissent, whether its practitioners are aware of it or not, is all "part of the show," an entertaining, competitive contest meant to distract Americans from the way their country is actually being run by both parties. Ask students to consider this point of view, particularly in light of the partisan rancor that was especially vitriolic leading up to the 2010 midterm elections. Are there real differences between Democrats and Republicans?

In-Class Writing Activities

1. Hedges is referring to media coverage of celebrities and minor news events that, while perhaps temporarily interesting, do not do, in his opinion, the media's job of informing the country about what's really going on. Students should give examples of coverage of the latest celebrity breakups or scandals, and consider 1) whether this is really such a bad thing, and 2) whether Hedges's characterization of the media as made up entirely of this sort of triviality is accurate.

2. Prompt students to think of a specific, concrete issue. Health care, for instance, was legally reformed under Obama, but many people claim the reforms did not go nearly far enough or were simply window-dressing on the old policy. Alternatively, ask them to take John Edgar Wideman's approach from earlier in this chapter: Have them measure how much of an impact Obama has had on their communities by looking at the actual, physical landscape of the communities themselves. Has anything really changed on the ground in their towns and cities?

3. The typical meta-image of Obama is one associated with youth, vitality, and an urban spirit of liberalism and friendly cooperation. Do students believe this image matches the reality? Why or why not? Ask them what they think Hedges means by the "erotic appeal" of Obama. Is it just that some people find him good-looking? Or is there something deeper to this claim of eroticism? Do students agree with it?

Discussing the Unit

Suggested Topic for Discussion

You may want to pair this unit with Ira Berlin's essay "Migrations Forced and Free," at the end of Chapter 12. Berlin considers the extraordinary importance the African American narrative—particularly the legacy of slavery and discrimination—still has for black people in this country. To keep the conversation on this controversial topic civil, remind students how hard it is to imagine and access the consciousness of a person with a different heritage, a different ancestral history, and in many cases a completely different way of viewing the world as a result. Many students will disagree with this point itself, of course, preferring to see America as a country where everyone is equal in front of the law and, increasingly, in everyday social standing. Remember to keep the question focused not on what divides the races in this country, but on what binds them together.

Preparing for Class Discussion

1. This question, like many in this chapter, can engender some strong emotions and attitudes, so keep it analytical. Remind students who put more blame on the African American community itself that nobody wants to live in poverty, and also of how long the legacy of inequality was—Isn't it likely to last a lot longer? For students who consider discrimination the sole cause, discuss other groups (including poor whites) that live in similar penury: How do they account for them? The ultimate answer to this question must be that the problem McKinney-Whetstone and Wideman discuss is too complex to have a simple cause—otherwise, it would have a simple answer.

2. Note that Hedges does not dispute the psychological importance that Obama has had in the black community: He would likely acknowledge this importance and consider it a positive. But one of Hedges's main themes is that mass psychology is less important and far easier to manipulate than the real, radical political change he believes is necessary in America. While he might applaud the election of a black president that McKinney-Whetstone and Wideman take such pride in, he would be very skeptical of their hopes that Obama will make any substantial changes that could affect the "street-corner dreamers" Wideman observes in New York City.

From Discussion to Writing

1. Again, it's important to divide the promise both of these authors see in Obama between the political and the psychological. Both seem to believe that Obama can help repair race relations in America, but acknowledge that this will mean a combination of simple inspiration (which few can doubt Obama has on some level achieved) and actual policy change. Have students, if they're able, discuss the latter more substantively here. Based on their reading of the news (have them do

some research if they're behind), what do they think Obama has accomplished? Or do they agree with Hedges that he's the same soup, just reheated?

2. Look for responses that encapsulate the momentous importance of the 2008 election and inauguration itself—encourage the temporary historians to quote McKinney-Whetstone to illustrate the significance of the election for black Americans in particular—but use this question as an opportunity to consider the long-term historical importance the election has had on the population as a whole. Then prompt students to continue their account with either a contrast in tone or a continuation of it, depending on their prognostications for the coming years. Remind them of the ways history has judged previous presidents—Lincoln, Harding, Clinton, George W. Bush—as a template for their own judgments.

Topics for Cross-Cultural Discussion

1. A few examples of groups for fertile discussion are Native Americans, foreign-born citizens (and noncitizens), and even women. Is Obama, as Pearl Wong asserts, "president for all"? How will these groups fare in this administration? Why? Ask students to predict whether a broad selection of ethnic and other minority groups will vote for Obama's reelection or not, and why they make the predictions they do.

2. Ask students who have recently traveled internationally, or have relatives overseas, what the impressions of Obama were in the countries which they visited or to which they have connections. Or ask them to evaluate Obama pretending that they were not Americans but foreigners. Many believe George W. Bush's foreign policy damaged the image of America overseas, casting it as a selfish, bellicose nation callous to the concerns of the rest of the world. Do students agree? How, if at all, do they think Obama has altered the international perspective of America?

10

Social Networking— How Is It Transforming Behavior?

Start this chapter with a quick poll: How many students have used a social-networking site like Facebook or Twitter at some point in their lives? In an American classroom, the odds are extremely good that a large majority, even 100 percent, will raise hands. But see if the result even changes if you replace "at some point in their lives" with "today." Social networking is not an occasional diversion like team sports or movies. It's woven into the day-to-day fabric of life, especially for young Americans. The essays in this chapter raise the question: Is this a good or a bad thing?

Garry Trudeau's cartoon strip "Hi, Dad" opens the chapter neatly by presenting all the problems it will consider: whether social networking is "ruining" the lives of young people—as the daughter in the strip insists, with some irony, that it isn't, for instance—and how the generational gap can lead to a misunderstanding of the Facebook Age and its conventions.

Each of the subsequent essays examines one of those conventions, looking at the way some aspect of everyday life has changed, for better and for worse, since the dawn of the social-networking revolution. In "We Shall Overshare," Mary Katharine Ham discusses the basic ethics of communication (and over-communication) online. In student Brent Baughman's "Growing Older in the Digital Age: An Exercise in Egotism," the author considers the way Facebook has redefined something as basic as celebrating one's birthday. Finally, Professor Elizabeth Stone dissects her students' online responses to the tragic death of one of their peers in "Grief in the Age of Facebook."

This chapter obviously affords instructors ample opportunities to use their students' own lives as background and example: Again, even instructors who are not familiar with the details of social networking will find that almost all of their students are, and in depth. Continue to ask them, however, to see the issues the chapter raises objectively, and in terms larger than Facebook or Twitter.

Garry Trudeau

Hi, Dad

[*Doonesbury, Boston Globe* (syndicated), November 8, 2009]

Vocabulary/Using a Dictionary

1. *Secs* is short for "seconds." The daughter using this abbreviation, and even claiming what she had to do will take only seconds, is ironic considering how involved it turns out to be.

2. Here *blog* is a verb, though we often see it as a noun. It comes from the words "web log" and is just that—an online diary or record of events, usually associated with posting strong opinions or personal narratives online.

Responding to Words in Context

1. To *tag*, particularly on Facebook, is to identify someone in a photo with a link to his or her profile. To *strip* means to remove a tag.

2. Both of these terms are borrowed from corporate brand management and refer to the way a company controls the public's image of it or of its products.

Discussing Main Point and Meaning

1. Trudeau sympathizes with the father in the strip and casts doubt on the daughter's assertion that social networking is not ruining her life. The rigmarole she describes sounds truly painful and horrible, and we are led to agree with the father's befuddlement over why she goes through it.

2. The father is wearing his coat, suggesting he's ready to go outside into the world, a stark contrast with the hermetic, enclosed online life of his daughter. This is important in furthering the contrast between the two generations, and furthering our sympathy for the participant that actually wants to do something presumably more fun and meaningful than untagging photos.

Examining Sentences, Paragraphs, and Organization

1. The strip is set in a generic dorm room, which we can tell from the furniture—the short bookcase and the futon, for instance. This is important because it generalizes the discussion to one between all parents and their college-aged children, many of whom inhabit dorm rooms very similar to the one in the strip.

2. The strip is basically a monologue, with the daughter saying everything except her father's response of "Okay. Sorry." This underlines the strip's central idea that her activity is empty and meaningless compared to spending quality time with her father on parents' weekend—she says so much but none of it registers as personally as the father's short and sincerely perplexed apology.

Thinking Critically

1. Some students may raise issues with Trudeau's specific understanding of the mechanisms of social networking, or with his vocabulary—remind them that Trudeau is writing satire, and his details are unlikely to be perfect. Look for responses that argue for or against the general premise: that Facebook is ruining young people's lives. Do students think there's such a thing as responsible use of sites like Facebook, and do most of their peers (like the generic daughter here) use them responsibly?

2. The best arguments for a positive effect revolve around the binding effects Facebook and other sites have on communities that already exist and its ability to help forge new friendships and professional relationships. Students will likely have examples of occasions when Facebook or other sites have improved their social lives in some way. Others may argue, along the lines of Trudeau, that these sites absorb more time from socialization than they add to it, and that much of the human contact they provide is empty and artificial.

In-Class Writing Activities

1. Facebook estimates that its average user uses the site actively for an hour a day—a relatively enormous commitment of time. Ask students who both do and don't use social networking to break that hour down. How much of it is on a computer at home? How much is on a cell phone? What (if anything) is a waste of time, and what (if anything) is improving users' lives? Ask students to consider what that hour is supplanting: What did people do in that hour before Facebook came along?

2. Younger students will probably have stories of their parents or teachers misunderstanding their activity online: Ask them to elaborate on the causes. Do they just have a different vocabulary than their parents? Or do they approach and relate to technology in a substantially different way—perhaps trusting it as a part of their lives more than their forebears do?

Mary Katharine Ham

We Shall Overshare

[*The Weekly Standard,* June 8, 2009]

Vocabulary/Using a Dictionary

1. A *narcissist* is someone obsessed with him- or herself. It comes from the Greek mythical figure Narcissus, who was transfixed by his own reflection.

2. *Broadcast* is a word from television and radio, meaning to send out something (like a program) so that a wide audience can see it (i.e., send it "broadly"). Ham is making an analogy between her use of social media and a television or radio station sending out its programming over the airwaves.

3. To *cultivate* is to grow, or add culture; the term is originally agricultural. The word in this context means to develop an attitude by nurturing it.

Responding to Words in Context

1. *Erosion* is the process by which natural elements and weather gradually wear away land. Here, Ham is using the word metaphorically to mean the slow but steady diminution of oversharers' dignity.

2. An *antidote* is a medicine that counteracts the effects of a poison. Using it here, of course, implies that oversharing is somewhat poisonous.

3. Ham uses *pioneer* to suggest not only the first people to explore something (like the value of a technology) but bold and intrepid trailblazers like Lewis and Clark. Note that she also uses the word more ironically in paragraph 4.

Discussing Main Point and Meaning

1. Ham says she's more careful about what she posts online knowing it's all public: "It's amazing how reasonably you act when everyone you know (and many you don't) is watching you" (para 6). She's implying that someone with a more private profile on Facebook or Twitter, for instance, might be more casual about publishing something that could prove damning or embarrassing.

2. Ham mentions Facebook's role in raising money for cancer research, and its use by dissidents in Iran for spreading their message. These examples provide a stark contrast to the kind of casual sharing of trivial personal details Ham is criticizing.

3. Ham casts the revolutionaries as fighting a real battle against real tyranny, making the problems her Facebook and Twitter friends complain about seem extremely petty. Note how she sets this off especially against her friend whose status update makes her sound like she's in a gulag—the protesters in Iran actually have a right, Ham implies, to post such messages.

Examining Sentences, Paragraphs, and Organization

1. "We Shall Overcome" was the anthem of the civil rights movement, describing the eventual victory of justice over racial discrimination. Ham's title playfully contrasts the righteous goals and efforts of that era and movement with the inconsequential trifles shared online today.

2. Ham's example sets up the contrast with which the essay as a whole will deal—the contrast between the monumental struggles of the past (the struggles of Russian dissidents against the autocracy of the Soviet Union, for instance) and a culture in which, although we're constantly talking, we have very little of substance to talk about. The example also shows us, however, how well tapped in Ham is to her social network and gives us a preview of how aloof she simultaneously feels from it.

3. Ham juxtaposes throughout the essay to establish the conflict between the past and the present discussed above. Offer paragraph 9 as the

quintessential example of an effective juxtaposition: "When pondering another photo shoot for my profile picture the other day, I couldn't help recalling the Facebook users who raised $800,000 for St. Jude Children's Research Hospital only last week." The example of Alexander Graham Bell, an ossified figure from history, provides an especially stark and comic juxtaposition with the "serial masturbator" story.

Thinking Critically

1. Some students may feel that Ham jumps to a conclusion: Her friend could have been sharing something that, while not as physically harmful as imprisonment in a gulag, was nonetheless a psychological stress. Others may feel that nobody, at least nobody with access to Facebook, could possibly be in a situation that would warrant such a response. Ask whether the lack of context in the status update—notice that the friend explains a mood but does not articulate the circumstances that have brought it about—is in and of itself irresponsible? Is such a status update unusual?

2. Ham does not discuss the positive impact social networking can have on its users' social lives—introducing them to friends or tightening the bonds with friends they already have. Students may also mention academic uses on college campuses—Facebook has proven extremely useful for group studying in many instances—or further examples along Ham's lines, like political organizing or the establishment of volunteer networks.

3. Students should look up the "Twitter Revolution" in Iran in the summer of 2009: Not only were Iranian dissidents organizing their protest and spreading the word on Twitter and Facebook, but the site proved an extraordinary way of highlighting their struggles to the world, after journalists were restricted from the country. Some students may question the power of a resource to which not everyone has access and which the government can easily squash; others may feel that the political power of social networks is awesome and perhaps unrealized.

In-Class Writing Activities

1. *The Weekly Standard* is a conservative magazine; Ham's contention that her use of social networking follows a "quintessentially conservative formula" rests on the idea that she is taking personal responsibility for everything she posts, rather than putting the burden on the larger community. Ask students to imagine what a "liberal" way of using Facebook or Twitter would be.

2. Prompt students to ask what qualifies as "TMI" (too much information) on the Internet, and why. Think in terms beyond social networking—what is it we don't like about people talking about themselves too much? Some students may not mind any level of conversation on their social networks; ask them why. Have them break into groups and write ten sample tweets; then have the other groups vote on which ones count as an "overshare." Why does TMI turn us off in the way it does?

3. Ham makes the analogy on two levels—both she and Lewis and Clark are "pioneers," people at the beginning of a long journey whose destination is not entirely clear. She also notes that Lewis and Clark documented their journeys extensively, while she is doing the same, albeit in a much shorter format. Ham points out that some people on these sites are actual pioneers—like the users in Iran who were temporarily banned—but in terms of her own Twitter use, the analogy is mostly facetious.

Brent Baughman (student essay)

Growing Older in the Digital Age: An Exercise in Egotism

[*The Berkeley Beacon*, Emerson College, February 25, 2010]

Vocabulary/Using a Dictionary

1. *Egotism* comes from the Latin *ego*, meaning "I," and is the quality of self-absorption even to the point of self-worship.

2. An *interface* is the space where two systems meet, and is used especially for the computer users to connect and give commands. An operating system like Windows is the most familiar example of an interface.

3. *Mitigate* comes from the Latin *mitis*, "soft"; to *mitigate* something is to make it milder, easier, or less painful.

Responding to Words in Context

1. A *smirk* is a smile, usually with the connotation of smug satisfaction. The "collective smirk" Baughman mentions refers to a shared idea—here the possibility of revelry and sex on a twenty-first birthday—that is collectively understood but not expressed except by a subtle facial gesture.

2. The word *fester* usually refers to a wound or a sore, and means to suppurate or become septic. Metaphorically it means to rot or simply to become more intense from sitting still. Baughman means that at these bars sexual energy increases over time as young people gather.

3. A *fantasy* can mean a trip of the imagination unfettered by conventional rules, as it's used in music. It can also mean an idea with no basis in reality. Baughman employs both meanings in reference to modern birthdays.

Discussing Main Point and Meaning

1. Baughman writes that a twenty-first birthday is a major milestone, because it frees the celebrant to drink alcohol legally. The natural state of affairs, he argues, would be for subsequent birthdays (at least until another milestone) to be far more subdued. In fact, in the Facebook era, he suggests all birthdays become twenty-first birthdays.

2. Baughman points out superficial differences—on Twitter, for instance, one has to compact the birthday self-promotion into 140 characters and on Facebook he or she can monitor well wishes through e-mail alerts. But he maintains that all of the forms of social-network birthday celebration are essentially bound by self-absorption.

3. Baughman writes that the actual celebratory time with friends is the heart of the birthday and the reason it's celebrated. Today, he complains, a birthday is little more than an opportunity to count congratulatory e-mails and Facebook messages, which for many people has even become its *raison d'être.*

Examining Sentences, Paragraphs, and Organization

1. Throughout his essay, Baughman playfully criticizes his generation's practices online, but then indicates that he's just as guilty as any of his peers. Notice how he does so subtly and playfully, for instance, by calling generic passing birthday wishes "'Happy Birthday Brent!'s." Putting himself in the center of his own satire makes Baughman more relatable and makes his very valid social censure feel less like a direct assault.

2. He is referring to the robots Japanese men take to the movies, a phenomenon to which he alluded earlier in the essay. The comment both ties the essay together humorously and emphasizes the self-centered (even masturbatory) activity of young social networkers, which he equates with a romantic love for technology.

Thinking Critically

1. Baughman's essay is full of jokes—he jokes about the Japanese dating robots, for instance, and "Gmail bold." Ask students whether this style of writing would work if Baughman's subject were more serious than birthdays. Or does the humor perhaps take a subject that is quite serious (our increasing collective narcissism) and make it slightly more relatable? Have students dissect Baughman's joke about Social Security in the first paragraph—how does he connect to his (young) audience with it, and how does it help him set the tone for the rest of the piece?

2. Prompt students to think of examples beyond social networking or even the Internet. Are we addicted to our cell phones, to text messaging, to e-mail on our BlackBerrys? What do these addictions, if they exist, mean? What are they replacing—or could it be that they're just filling a void and improving our means of communicating with our peers? Remind students to think not just of what technology "addicts" are literally doing (staring at a computer screen, typing on a phone all day) but what they might be accomplishing by doing it. Compare it to the world before the technology existed. Is it an improvement?

In-Class Writing Activities

1. Many young people report that Facebook cements new friendships much more quickly than traditional, analog socializing. If your students make

this claim, ask them why: What is the Facebook environment like for meeting and chatting with new people, and how does it differ from the putative "real world"? What about with their existing friends? Is socializing online more or less sincere, more or less intimate, than socializing in a bar or student center? Don't assume the answer to this one is obvious.

2. Have students break into groups and guess which of the other group's messages correspond to which method of delivery. How does the medium direct the message, so to speak?

Elizabeth Stone

Grief in the Age of Facebook

[*The Chronicle Review*, March 5, 2010]

Vocabulary/Using a Dictionary

1. A *paradox* is an apparent contradiction drawn from apparently logical premises, or a statement that contradicts itself. *Paradoxically* is an adjective, meaning that something takes the form of a paradox—or more often, is simply complex and confounding.

2. *Virtually* can be an adverb from *virtual*, applied to something created by software but not in the real world; it can also mean "almost" or "nearly." Stone literally means the latter use here, but the former provides a poignant double entendre.

3. The verb *atomize* means to break down into very small parts, from *atom*, the smallest unit of a chemical element. Stone uses the word with its most popular contemporary meaning—a lifestyle in which there are many small, perhaps unconnected, components.

Responding to Words in Context

1. *Viral* means having the properties of a virus, an infective agent that enters a host and then multiplies. In the context of marketing, to call something *viral* has come to mean that it spreads fast by encouraging people marketed to to send the advertisement to their friends—advertisers achieve this by making the ad especially funny or making it appear that it isn't even really an ad.

2. Of a word, phrase, or speech, *colloquial* means informal and characterized by everyday conversational patterns. One possible antonym would be *formal*. "Hang out with" is a colloquial construction; "commune with" would be a more formal one.

3. *Uncharted* means unmapped, a term from cartography. (Note the shared root *carta*, Latin for "map.") Stone is using the word to mean a space in human relations that is unexplored, whose participants don't know what they're approaching.

Discussing Main Point and Meaning

1. The general tone of Stone's essay is anthropological, describing unfamiliar conventions in an objective, neutral way. But occasionally she sounds perfectly laudatory, or even in awe, of her students—especially those who reposted their profile photos with Casey—suggesting she thinks Facebook mourning may not only be an inevitable change in the social fabric but a healthy one. She also describes the classmates' grieving processes as preferable to the ones prescribed by Sigmund Freud.

2. Stone mentions the problem that initial displays of grief online can spread word of a death too casually and quickly, which is why she praises her students for using the phone to notify each other. She also delineates the issue of when to take down memorials: How soon should profile pictures with the deceased be changed back, for instance, or pages on which mourning has been registered return to their old exuberant uses?

3. Because of the effusion of mourners' expression, Stone learned things about her student that she wouldn't have otherwise known, like her acting talent and her love of horses. The Facebook memorial platform offers far more space, Stone suggests, than the traditional eulogy to bring out and illuminate the character of the deceased.

Examining Sentences, Paragraphs, and Organization

1. The essay is about the way the Millennial generation does things (namely mourns) differently from previous generations, and this idea—of being constantly connected and emitting a constant stream of information and update—is at the heart of that contrast. Because Stone was Casey's journalism professor, the characterization also helps illustrate the bond between teacher and student.

2. Stone wants to convey students' expressions of grief exactly, because it is precisely their colloquialism that distinguishes them from similar expressions in previous generations. Have students note how a Millennial who reads Facebook posts all day would read the wall post as Stone transmits it differently than an older person.

3. Although the essay is an exposition of an issue, it is told as narrative. This is important to bringing across the process of mourning, which even in the Facebook age unfolds gradually and in steps. It also helps us connect with Stone more personally as she undergoes the process.

Thinking Critically

1. Stone's precis of Freud is that we should "detach from the dead." Her experience of Facebook mourners is that they do exactly the opposite—continuing for a period much longer than traditional mourning to reminisce and even addressing the deceased directly. Have students list the potential advantages and disadvantages of each form of mourning, concentrating on the psychological benefits and drawbacks for the mourners themselves.

2. Some students will argue, in line with Stone's essay, that the social-networking revolution makes this kind of mourning inevitable, and that alternate policies—taking the profile down immediately—for instance, would be worse. Others will see this kind of continued intimacy as a psychologically healthier way to exhibit grief. Ask students to formulate other possible policies and compare them to Facebook's.

3. Stone brings us back to the bond she herself had with Casey, as her journalism professor. She reminds us of Casey's prowess as a writer and also furthers the intimacy of the connection she feels to Casey, who would be doing exactly what she (Stone) is doing had she lived.

In-Class Writing Activities

1. Have students with the experience who are comfortable sharing it compare their memories with Stone's essay, particularly focusing on how things would have been different in an age before online social media. Use the experience of another student who is comfortable discussing a pre-Facebook loss to compare the issues the essay raises: How did the bereaved express their grief? Was there anything inappropriate shared online? How long did the mourning last, and was that a good or bad thing?

2. If you're on Facebook, discuss your policy for friending your students and why having a policy is important. Have students consider the pitfalls of a close social connection with their teachers, and particularly those that express themselves in an era of oversharing. Press for specific examples of things Facebook allows us to know about our friends that teachers and their pupils are best off not sharing.

3. Ask students who present their stories to consider how the teacher looks back on the relationship. Are the salient details the same in the memory of both instructor and pupil?

Discussing the Unit

Suggested Topic for Discussion

Throughout this unit, keep in mind, and remind students, of what life was like before the conveniences (and inconveniences) of the modern Internet age. The central question the unit ponders is whether America before social networking was a comparatively impoverished place, yearning for a forum in which people could connect from their homes, or a much simpler, better, easier world to live in. Have Facebook and its peers made life better or worse for the average American?

Preparing for Class Discussion

1. If there are any students in your class who don't use social networking (a remote possibility), ask them to explain why they don't. Do they get along just fine without it, or do they feel its void in their lives? Do students have

friends who are not on Facebook or Twitter? How do they view these friends if so—as hopeless Luddites or as refuseniks who may even be too cool to log in? Ask them to deeply consider what life would be like without their social-networking sites. Perhaps the change would not be as monumental as some imagine.

2. Many critics fault Facebook especially for storing massive amounts of data on its users, data it could (if the site proves unscrupulous) sell to advertisers or otherwise use to betray its loyal users. Other critics also point out (as Ham does) that Facebook and Twitter users have often been caught in a serious jam when a boss, or some other person with whom a social networker is not on entirely open terms, sees something on a profile that person was not meant to see. Defenders counter that nobody is forcing anyone to sign up for social-networking sites, and a person puts everything he puts about himself online voluntarily. Ask students for examples of concerns they've had using Facebook and similar sites. Are they at all concerned about the wrong people seeing their profile? About being stalked? About other privacy concerns?

From Discussion to Writing

1. This question works well as a good, creative assignment and will especially appeal to students with a background in science fiction. Is a world without social networking a horrible dystopia or a pastoral regeneration of a simpler and better time? Prompt students to imagine what life is like in some of the spaces where social networking's impact has been most obvious: in dating, for instance, or, to borrow material from Brett Baughman and Elizabeth Stone, in celebrating a friend's birthday or grieving over a loved one.

2. Some possible areas of focus not covered directly in this chapter are dating and relationships, doing business and networking, learning and education, political and volunteer organization, etc. Notice how almost any aspect of life works for this essay—that in and of itself should provide students with a lesson about the impact social networking has had. Keep students focused on the broader anthropological aspects of the Facebook-age phenomenon they are dissecting.

Topics for Cross-Cultural Discussion

1. Students will likely be familiar with countries in which Facebook is used in much the same way as it is domestically. But have them tease out Ham's distinction: Facebook and other sites have become virtually ubiquitous, but in places where life is harder and more fraught with uncertainty than it is in the United States and Western Europe, the uses of social networking tend to reflect this fact. Students with experience making friends from other countries online, or students who have family members overseas that use social-networking sites, will be especially valuable in this discussion.

2. Some countries have banned or restricted social networks because they fear the large-scale organization these sites so enormously facilitate.

Others, including China, have expressed concerns about the leaks of state secrets on networks where anyone can make any contribution he or she wishes. Consider with students other reasons governments are afraid of Facebook and its peers. What does this censorship say more about—those governments or Facebook?

11

Saving the Planet:
Is It Too Late?

The global warming debate is one of the most peculiar in American life: In few other cases is the crux of a divide between Americans the question of whether a scientific conclusion is valid. At issue is simply whether the earth is rapidly warming, whether that poses a danger to human life, and whether human beings are to blame. Ask students to keep these questions in mind as they read the selections in this chapter, but also keep in mind the deeper issues that undergird them: Whether humans (and particularly human industry) can have an immediate impact on the natural environment, and what our responsibilities are as a society to alleviate this impact.

Bill McKibben begins the chapter by addressing one of the most familiar of our environmental responsibilities: recycling. But McKibben argues in "Waste Not Want Not" that it isn't only plastic bottles and rubber tires we're wasting. We live in a culture that epidemically wastes its resources, natural—economic, and even human.

In "Warming Gets Worse," *Rolling Stone* writer Jeff Goodell lays out the case for a state of climate-change emergency, while conservative Cal Thomas disputes both the premises and the conclusions of the argument in "Sinking 'Climate Change.'" Throughout these two essays, have your students consider why liberals and conservatives fall where they do in the divide: What is it about the conservative political disposition that rejects the premises of climate change?

Bill McKibben

Waste Not Want Not

[*Mother Jones,* May/June 2009]

Vocabulary/Using a Dictionary

1. *Hyper-* is a prefix meaning "too much" (as in *hyperactive*), and these terms refer to a social problem of too much consumption and consumer activity.

2. The word *particulates* is related to *particles*, and similarly describes small pieces of matter that float in the air. Particulates are finer than particles, however.

3. *Throughput* is a play on *input* and *output*, and refers to matter as it goes through the system.

Responding to Words in Context

1. Students are likely most familiar with the word describing a character— namely of a deeply unpleasant person. Generally, though, it refers to a sensory unpleasantness that is impossible to ignore, such as the large, visible forms of waste McKibben begins with.

2. *Margin* here is a term borrowed from the world of investing, where it refers to the capital available to an investor taking risks. It is related to the idea of a "margin of error," and thus to the more familiar concept of a border.

3. The word *thrifty* means hesitant to spend money, and *frugality* is the state of thriftiness.

Discussing Main Point and Meaning

1. McKibben argues that other societies (he mentions Tanzania) have enormous and expanding populations without using nearly the amount of energy Americans do. Costco, which sells excessively bulky quantities of consumer goods, is a symbol to McKibben of a kind of waste particular and endemic to Americans.

2. McKibben is referring, ironically, to a waste of human resources—the way a company that wants to lay off employees is likely to phrase its problem. McKibben doesn't believe a human being can be a "waste," and the reference is tongue-in-cheek.

3. The reference to "Harvard graduates" is meant more generally as an allusion to talented people, who McKibben believes are squandering their abilities working in the corporate world, for banks and other entities that add to the waste problem. McKibben would rather see talented youth go into jobs that are sustainable, help the environment, etc.

Examining Sentences, Paragraphs, and Organization

1. McKibben is referring to printed advertisements, particularly in catalogues and mailers. In addition to wasting paper, McKibben believes these ads contribute to our hyperconsumerist culture by fetishizing "stuff"—presenting the goods they're advertising in an almost pornographic way in order to increase Americans' lust for material possessions.

2. The list of forms of waste that literally exhausts McKibben here suggests that there are simply too many to list—he has to give up once he realizes how extensive a problem it is.

3. McKibben begins with the most obvious ("obnoxious," as he says) forms of waste: materials that are clogging the environment. As he moves on, his examples become more counterintuitive, until he is finally discussing social problems like employment and the use of our young people's talents that we would not conventionally place under the umbrella of waste.

Thinking Critically

1. Challenge students to think of the issue two ways: 1) Are the problems McKibben describes really all grouped under the heading of waste; and 2) Is it possible to have a truly less wasteful society? Ask students to imagine an America seriously committed to cutting down all of the forms of waste McKibben delineates. Is it really possible, or just a fantasy?

2. There are examples of humor throughout the essay. For instance, McKibben refers to a hypothetical Neanderthal tribe throwing out water bottles as having "no real effect except someday puzzling anthropologists," and summarizes the SUV craze by writing that "everyone in America thinks he requires the kind of vehicle that might make sense for a forest ranger." Students should note that McKibben isn't being flippant, however, but sardonic. His humor is expressing and encoding a sincere, if somewhat satirical, reproach for his society.

3. Many students will focus on the "waste of talent" argument as particularly ripe for disagreement. Ask them if they aspire to work in an industry McKibben considers wasteful after graduation. Why or why not? Could society function without those jobs and, if not, does that negate defining them as wasteful?

In-Class Writing Activities

1. Have students focus on the specifics here, particularly the ways government action needs to be coordinated with local, individual initiative. How can society encourage individuals—who are ultimately the key to changing large-scale behavior—to make more responsible, less wasteful decisions? How can individuals in turn change the patterns of wastefulness as they occur at higher, governmental levels?

2. McKibben is decidedly a liberal. He mentions wasting the talents of "gay folks," is incensed at environmental despoliation, and takes it for granted that corporations are often acting against the public good these days. Ask students who are more conservatively inclined what they think is wasteful about our society, and how we can fix it.

3. Have students consider whether these movements could make a real impact, especially when most Americans will likely find them incompatible with their lifestyles. Ask students to think up an advertising campaign for a postwaste movement they believe could make a real difference.

Jeff Goodell

Warming Gets Worse

[*Rolling Stone,* November 12, 2009]

Vocabulary/Using a Dictionary

1. *Permafrost* is land that is always frosted over, occurring near the North and South poles. The word has the prefix *perma-* from *permanent.*

2. *Microscopic* means "very small"—so small it requires a microscope to see. *Microscope* comes from Greek words meaning "small" and "see."

3. The noun *glacier* refers to a huge block of ice. The adjective *glacial* has come to mean "very slow," referring to the movement of glaciers in arctic waters.

Responding to Words in Context

1. *Greenhouse gases* are gases introduced into the atmosphere by various forms of pollution, and include carbon dioxide, methane, nitrous oxide, and ozone. They are worrisome because they contribute to the "greenhouse effect": They trap the sun's rays inside the atmosphere and thus raise the surface temperature on earth.

2. *Hosed,* to Jim White, means "completely finished"—or at least in deep trouble.

3. A *feedback loop* is another term for a *vicious* or *virtuous circle,* a process whose result accelerates or worsens the process itself. Familiar examples include the "poverty cycle," in which poor people, because of a lack of educational resources and other disadvantages, are likely to have children who will also be poor.

Discussing Main Point and Meaning

1. A furnace involves a central boiler that releases heat through ducts. Melting the Arctic will release more gases that would exacerbate the greenhouse problem.

2. A rise in sea level would sink low-lying coastal regions. Goodell is especially interested in poorer cities and countries, because they often lack preparedness and response mechanisms.

3. Goodell is likely to answer, besides providing his own numbers, that simple logical analysis of what is happening on the polar caps suggests that the problem will start getting bad soon, if it isn't already.

Examining Sentences, Paragraphs, and Organization

1. Goodell is illustrating just how cataclysmically major the effects of unchecked climate change will be. We shouldn't take this picture literally, but the incongruity of it should shake us—it's a far more effective image than simply citing figures of rising water levels would be.

2. The essay compares or quotes a comparison between the Arctic and a furnace, between the Arctic and a ticking time bomb, and between nature and a timekeeper. The subject of climate change can potentially be very dry, and using metaphor to enliven it is important in creating a reader's sense of urgency and personal investment in the problem.

3. The essay is quite pessimistic, but without fulminating or moralizing: It simply cites facts that read as incontrovertible. The effect of this tone is to make whatever a reader *can* do about the climate crisis seem worthwhile without a second thought.

Thinking Critically

1. The Copenhagen conference was widely regarded as a failure. The delegates did not agree on anything climate scientists regard as a long-term solution. Goodell's first sentence juxtaposes the delegates' meeting—we are tempted to imagine a large, slow bureaucratic process—with the problem they are seeking to address spiraling out of hand. The effect is to prime us to the idea that traditional solutions and approaches to the climate crisis are probably inadequate.

2. Goodell clearly thinks humans are to blame for the climate crisis, but does not feel compelled to argue to defend this point. He takes it for granted that the problem he's describing stems in part from our own policies: "thanks to our failure to reduce greenhouse-gas pollution," he says, "the fuse has already been lit."

3. Goodell clearly thinks reducing fossil fuel emissions is the only potential way to curb the warming of the earth caused by the greenhouse gas effect. But he implies throughout the essay that, because warming is accelerating in a feedback loop that's already in place, even large-scale action may be too late to be effective.

In-Class Writing Activities

1. Have students read this essay closely alongside the arguments of a climate-change skeptic like Cal Thomas (see below). Note how Thomas would regard the tone of Goodell's argument: as excessive, gratuitous fear-mongering. This question provides a good platform for a debate on the central thematic question of this chapter: Should we be afraid of a change in the climate, and why or why not?

2. Climate-change skeptics look to the warming of the earth, and the melting of the ice caps, as part of a cycle of temperature fluctuation that has been occurring on earth since its infancy and has little or nothing to do with human activity. They believe nature ultimately finds equilibrium, and any claims of total cataclysm as a result of the cycle are overblown.

3. Some skeptics have pointed to colder-than-average winters in many parts of the world—and to previous concerns about a "new ice age"—as rhetorical fodder against the existence of "global warming." As a result, environmentalists have adopted "climate change" as a more neutral term representing the irregular, but still catastrophic, changes in the earth's overall weather patterns they believe are caused by human behavior.

Cal Thomas

Sinking "Climate Change"

[*Townhall.com*, June 3, 2010]

Vocabulary/Using a Dictionary

1. A *consensus* is a general agreement within a community, particularly a community of experts on a particular topic. Thomas puts the word in scare quotes because he believes dissenting voices have not had their say.

2. *Domestic* means "at home," and here means within one's own country, as opposed to foreign. Domestic exploration of oil refers to drilling for oil locally, as opposed to importing it from elsewhere.

3. The adjective *dubious* means "doubtful or unlikely."

Responding to Words in Context

1. The word *myth* comes from the Greek word *mythos*, meaning "a story." It has come to mean a story that is widely believed but untrue, which is how Thomas uses it.

2. *Cuddly* means "cute and furry"; putting a cuddly face on the issue of climate change means making it more palatable by using the viscerally lovable image of a polar bear as opposed to colder, more objectively falsifiable statistics. Thomas obviously thinks using wildlife to promote the environmental agenda is a fallacious appeal to emotion.

3. A *cultist* is any member of a cult, a group that is swindled into subscribing on faith to precepts that are often false and promoted by charlatans.

Discussing Main Point and Meaning

1. Thomas believes that scientists and pundits who warn us about climate change are not well informed, but simply giving into a hysteria whose correspondence to reality they can not substantiate. The fact that thirty years ago *Newsweek* warned of global cooling and is now warning of global warming casts its concern as flimsy and malleable, and therefore ungrounded.

2. Most of our energy comes from fossil fuels, which are not renewable and which, when burned, introduce gases into the atmosphere that (people less skeptical than Thomas believe) create a greenhouse effect that is raising the earth's temperature.

3. Thomas believes we should be looking for more oil on our own coasts, which would not only have increased our supply of fossil fuels, but reduced the amount of money we send to oil-producing nations in the Middle East that have also been targets of the war on terror.

Examining Sentences, Paragraphs, and Organization

1. Thomas is playing on the concern that the polar ice caps are melting and the water levels on earth are rising, a belief he is ridiculing as false.

2. Thomas wants to establish immediately that he is a conservative and at the same time hopes to link the "liberal" doctrine of anthropogenic climate change to Obama and Pelosi. This helps him appeal to his audience, which has presumably been disappointed by Democrats in Washington, and will connect the fear of climate change to them.

3. The *Focus* article further confuses the causes and effects of climate change, and suggests an alternative explanation for rising temperatures—the meteorological phenomenon El Niño, and not pollution, it suggests, may be the cause of the recent spike in hot years.

Thinking Critically

1. Thomas is suggesting that environmentalists are less concerned with saving the planet from peril and more concerned with increasing the power of government, and particularly of the federal government, at the expense of individual liberties. Notice how this aligns with the rest of Thomas's conservative platform and agenda.

2. Thomas considers the media an arm of the liberal establishment in Washington, and suggests that they are not above fabricating or spinning the facts in order to sell a liberal package of responses to climate change.

3. Students should recognize that climatedepot.com is decidedly conservative and appeals directly to climate–change skeptics like Thomas. Use this question to consider the issue of confirmation bias in the climate debate—both sides favor sources that provide statistics in line with their preconceived views of the causes and seriousness of climate change.

In-Class Writing Activities

1. By now students should understand the breakdown of liberal and conservative positions on climate change and how they relate to the rest of the contemporary political philosophies with which they correspond. Liberals believe human beings should be responsible, on a large scale, for the environment; conservatives believe that environmentalism is an attempt to abridge basic freedoms and rights, particularly those of the businesses accused of polluting the environment. Many students are likely to feel passionate on the issue; those that believe climate change is real in particular may feel that our response should not be a politically divisive issue if the facts bear out that it is happening.

2. Challenge students to consider where they get their information on climate change. Is it possible that they are coming at the issue from a biased perspective? What ulterior motives could those who promote their opinions on the issue have besides the search for scientific truth?

3. There are dozens of examples of inertia in politics. Students may feel passionate about issues ranging from the war in Iraq to the refusal to legalize marijuana. Remind them of the importance of political will and political capital, and especially the amount of each that it requires to contravene a wide consensus and a widely held public feeling.

Yevgeniya Lomakina (student essay)

"Going Green" Misses the Point

[*The Daily Collegian*, University of Massachusetts, April 22, 2010]

Vocabulary/Using a Dictionary

1. An *initiative* is a proposal or an act designed to improve something; it comes from a Latin word meaning "to begin." One example of a green initiative would be a government plan to incentivize reducing auto emissions; another would be handing out more efficient light bulbs in a community.

2. *Novelty* is a noun meaning "newness," from the Latin word for "new." Here it means the relatively untested distribution methods of green products. Note that the relationship of the word to *novel* derives from a time when long-form fiction was a new literary form. Another use of the word *novelty* can refer to any amusing object with no real purpose, which is where the term "novelty shop" originates.

3. An *emission* is a noun, from the Latin for "to put out," referring to anything that is released by a system. *Carbon emissions* are simply the gases released by carbon-burning devices like automobiles.

Responding to Words in Context

1. Lomakina's catchphrase is "going green," and related phrases about the green economy and lifestyle. *Catchphrase* is a relatively pejorative term for a phrase repeated by people and spread by media without concern for its appropriateness to the situation. Another example might be "death panels," in reference to the The Patient Protection and Affordable Care Act. In this case, Lomakina wishes to cast the green movement as somewhat empty.

2. Produce is considered *organic* if it is grown without pesticides, which environmentalists believe have long-term deleterious effects on the environment.

3. *Consumerism* is the attitude of capitalistic covetousness for material goods. Our *consumerist desires*, in Lomakina's construction, are simply our desires for consumer goods.

Discussing Main Point and Meaning

1. Scientists say the emission of carbon dioxide, and other greenhouse gases, traps the sun's heat inside the atmosphere and raises the temperature of the earth, or at least leads to radical temperature fluctuations.

2. Lomakina is criticizing the materialism of the environmental movement, one she associates with the larger pattern of American consumerism. Americans, she writes, are so eager to buy things that their method of getting involved in environmentalism is to purchase more stuff, which, she argues, ultimately has destructive effects on the environment.

3. Lomakina endorses activities that are meaningful on a local level, rather than feeding into a general green fad. Examples could include unplugging cell phone chargers at night and driving less instead of driving more efficient cars. Underlying Lomakina's essay is the theme that traditional green behavior is actually quite easy and a way of placating consumers who need to make more sweeping changes in their overall behavior.

Examining Sentences, Paragraphs, and Organization

1. The implication of this phrase is that green initiatives are only words, not actions. Actions are much harder than slogans and catchphrases, but the environmental movement hasn't gone far enough beyond the surface.

2. Lomakina is setting up a contrast between behavior that will make a real difference in helping to save the environment and behavior that is merely a bandage that makes consumers feel better about themselves. The rhetorical questions, in particular, represent the way the modern consumerist culture addresses environmental issues.

3. Lomakina is suggesting that large environmental action groups like the Sierra Club are out of touch, and more concerned with preserving their own images than with preserving the natural environment. She implies that criticism from within is essential to keeping the environmental movement successful, and succinctly points out that this criticism comes only from individuals, not from nonprofit behemoths.

Thinking Critically

1. Have students compare other movements they're involved in to the environmental movement. They may even think of it outside of the context of activism: Does it make them like a band, or a TV show, any less to know that other fans appreciate it for different reasons? Why should the composition of the tent make any difference to the various committed members inside it?

2. Some students may point to the positive effects celebrities and other public figures can have even on the kind of private behavior Lomakina is describing. Campaigns for conservation and environmental consciousness on the level she advocates often thrive because of how publicly aware they are.

3. The United States emits a massively disproportionate amount of greenhouse gas and other pollutants, due to its inordinate industrialization. Some students will argue that that puts the burden on the U.S. government, or even on individual Americans, to take serious green action; others will likely feel that, as it's a dilemma that faces all human beings, human beings have to work together regardless of boundaries to fix it.

In-Class Writing Activities

1. Break the class into groups and have them assess each other's plans. In a matrix as complex as reversing environmental destruction, there are a number of factors to consider: Are the plans feasible? Will they be effective? Are they an easy way out where a tougher, less palatable course of action may be the only real solution?

2. Have students assess the green initiatives they have witnessed in the mass media. What kinds of large- and small-scale behavior are we taught will save the planet? Are these real solutions or just placebos? How, from our current vantage, can we tell the difference?

3. Look for press releases and strategies that take full advantage of the strengths of social media, namely organizing at the local level. How can students use tools like Facebook and other social networks to get their peers involved in solutions to the climate crisis, and other environmental crises, that require individual participation in large-scale efforts?

Discussing the Unit

Suggested Topic for Discussion

Some students may not fully believe in climate change, while others may be completely convinced of its existence and its severity. Students may want to discuss how public opinion can affect scientific findings—think of Copernicus and Galileo—and how politicians have used global warming as a tool for campaigning. Some may see the idea of politicians latching onto global warming as a good thing because it may inspire debate and more funding for research, while others may be skeptical of its place in politics, regardless of whether they believe it is real or not.

Preparing for Class Discussion

1. Conservatives tend to distrust environmentalism, perhaps in part because they see it as hostile to business and private development, issues near to their heart. Culturally, conservatives also tend (with many exceptions) to come from parts of the country closer to agriculture and where conservational sentiment is weaker. You may want to connect this to the debate over drilling for oil in Arctic reserves. Liberals believe in conserving these areas and developing other sources of energy, while conservatives ridicule what they see as a terribly misplaced concern for Alaskan caribou over Americans being squeezed at the gas pump. Remind students, however, that environmentalism is not an exclusively liberal domain: It was a Republican (Teddy Roosevelt) who created our national parks system, and another one (Richard Nixon) who presided over the creation of the Environmental Protection Agency. What is it about our modern political climate, though, that has made conservatives more automatically hostile to the idea that the planet is in trouble and that humans should do something about it?

2. Refer particularly to Jeff Goodell's essay, but turn this into a broader discussion about optimism and pessimism, environmental and otherwise, in America. Are there truly intractable problems, or is there always some solution—even when we're perhaps unwilling to brave it? Connect this question to other units in the book: race, immigration, etc.

From Discussion to Writing

1. McKibben and Goodell take for granted that a solution will come from some combination of government action and individual initiative. We all need to pitch in, but in the end the problem is so large that huge actors like the federal government need to be involved in solving it. Where do students stand on this question? Are their answers based more in their general convictions about the role of government in public and private life or more in their beliefs about what the solution (if one is needed) to climate change will actually be? Challenge the private-sector students to consider the possibility that the answer will involve some massive project, like shooting a cocktail of chemicals into the air. (This has been proposed.) Can the private sector really be trusted to undertake something like that? Conversely, ask students who have faith in the government whether Washington may be too slow and inefficient to deal with a problem essentially caused by inefficiency.

2. Scientists rarely write popular scientific articles, because the actual conclusions of science are far too complex and nuanced for a general audience with a typical attention span to understand and appreciate. Ask students if they think the preponderance of pundits in this chapter, and accordingly in the larger debate, suggests a larger problem in our public discourse. Should we aim to cultivate magazines and newspapers that treat issues of scientific import with more of a scientific approach?

Topics for Cross-Cultural Discussion

1. Many commentators have pointed out the cruel irony that the countries most likely to be affected by climate change are the ones that have contributed the least to its putative anthropogenic causes: poor countries like those in sub-Saharan Africa, South and Southeast Asia. Much of the hard work needed to overcome climate change will also have to come from developing countries like China and India, whose rapid growth comes at the cost of large-scale environmental damage.

2. Students should divide on the causes of American skepticism. Some will consider American optimism in the ability to fix the problems of the world quickly and easily the root of this divide, but others will argue that Americans are the least likely and the least willing to surrender the carbon-burning lifestyle that most scientists say is at least partially to blame for the problem.

12

Immigration:
Who Is an American?

In 2010, the state of Arizona raised passions throughout the country to a boiling point when it passed a law authorizing local authorities to ask for documentation from anyone they suspected of being in the state—and the country—illegally. The law, opponents said, not only gave the state a traditionally federal power of enforcing legal immigration, but would inevitably lead to racial profiling.

But the fracas reflected larger issues that remain at the forefront of America's debate over its borders: Who is an American? Who deserves to be in America? What protections, if any, do we owe people who are here illegally? And why, after all, do so many people want to come to the United States— particularly from Latin America?

The chapter begins with a debate on a question that often underlies our discourse on immigration: Are immigrants inherently harder working than native-born Americans, and is there an attendant economic value in having a large immigrant population? Tamar Jacoby answers that immigration does indeed "increase the virtues of hard work and fortitude in the United States," because the hardship of immigration reduces the immigrant population to only the most industrious. Mark Krikorian disputes both claims in his brief response.

"The Crossing," by an undocumented worked pseudonymously named Vicente Martinez, gives a first-person account of what the immigrant experience is really like, supporting Jacoby's view more than Krikorian's. Luis Rodríguez considers the experience of immigrants, legal and otherwise, already past the crossing stage; in "Slurring Spanish" he describes the plight of Spanish-speaking students in American schools and argues for more bilingualism there.

The final two essays in the chapter consider immigration from the angles of other groups affected by the debate. In "Uniting Families" student Elyse Toplin makes an argument for expanding citizenship to gay and lesbian couples with a foreign-born partner, and in "Migrations Forced and Free" Ira Berlin questions whether recent immigrants from Africa and the Caribbean belong to the history-rich African American community.

DEBATE: Does Immigration Increase the Virtues of Hard Work and Fortitude in the United States?

Tamar Jacoby (Yes)

[*In Character*, Spring 2009]

Vocabulary/Using a Dictionary

1. *Winnow* is an agricultural term meaning to separate wheat from chaff with a gust of air. Jacoby is using it with its metaphorical force, meaning to separate the weak from the strong over time.

2. *Norms* are social conventions; American norms include the idea of a two-parent family, a career, home ownership, etc.

Responding to Words in Context

1. Jacoby uses *scrappier* here to mean extremely determined, despite significant obstacles.

2. A *beacon* is a light used for guiding ships, but Jacoby is using it more figuratively to mean a shining example that guides the world and attracts newcomers—it is famous in this sense as a nickname for America, dating back to the Pilgrims.

Discussing Main Point and Meaning

1. Jacoby is trying to establish that immigrants do not come to America in order to leech off of American resources and the American way of life, as many detractors suggest. Nor do they come out of simple whimsical preference for America over their home countries. Rather, true economic exigency and emergency forces their migration. Jacoby uses the economic argument to suggest that we should sympathize with people whose motives are similar to our own.

2. Jacoby is referring to the types of jobs we often associate, usually accurately, with the majority of migrant workers: cleaning, busing tables, working on farms, etc., for very little money. Jacoby reminds us once again that the jobs immigrants take do not represent a threat to the American workforce—few of us would want such jobs. Krikorian, an opponent of immigration, does not focus on these jobs, turning his attention instead to the negative impact immigrants have on social entitlement programs like welfare.

Examining Sentences, Paragraphs, and Organization

1. The third and fourth paragraphs of Jacoby's essay are rich with statistics, but by the end she focuses on the more intangible aspects of immigration. This is an effective way of laying a theoretical groundwork, but bringing the essay overall back to the more specific and personal.

2. Jacoby is suggesting that hardworking immigrants who instill their values in their children should have even more hardworking descendants.

Some students might challenge this premise, preferring to assume that children born in the comfort of the United States, and immune to the vicious struggles of immigration and assimilation Jacoby describes, will be—for lack of a better word—lazier.

Thinking Critically

1. Jacoby is describing a process akin to biological natural selection, in which only the immigrants most suited to the harsh travails of their migration—and therefore the toughest and probably the hardest-working—will survive the ordeal without dying or returning home.

2. Jacoby suggests that immigrants (and particularly undocumented ones) get the advantage of relocating to a better life in America, while we get the advantage of their cheap labor in the short term. The first part is beyond much argument, though some students might wonder whether conditions in America are really worth the hardships required to get and stay here. Other students may argue with the second claim on the basis that it encourages an ugly sort of exploitation that dare not speak its name.

In-Class Writing Activities

1. Ask students to draw on their own experience in answering this question, and compare it to that of their classmates. How long have their families been in America, and where do they rank themselves against their forebears in terms of the "pluck and determination" Jacoby discusses?

2. In the context of the immigration debate, most of us assume "immigrants" are from Latin America. Some students will typify them as hard-working, winnowed as they are by the experience of coming here, and desperate as they are to make a better life for themselves. Other students may see immigrants less romantically, imagining them—more along Krikorian's lines—as somewhat greedy and no more productive than the average legal citizen. Encourage students to be imaginative with this activity, emphasizing the way we perceive immigrants (even visually) and how that perception lines up with reality.

DEBATE: Does Immigration Increase the Virtues of Hard Work and Fortitude in the United States?

Mark Krikorian (No)

[*In Character,* Spring 2009]

Vocabulary/Using a Dictionary

1. *Grit* is a term for small particles of stone or sand like dust. *Gritty* means covered with grit, suggesting hard work and courage. Krikorian puts the word in scare quotes because he disagrees that immigrants automatically deserve the modifier.

2. *Transnationalism* is defined as the philosophy of extending oneself, one's ideas, or one's efforts, across national borders. It comes from the prefix *trans-*, meaning "across."

Responding to Words in Context

1. *Decadence* can mean either moral or cultural downfall or decay, or luxurious self-indulgence. Krikorian uses it in both senses—he is referring to a putative American collapse caused by a collapse in our moral structure, particularly our sense of industry and hard work.

2. A *parasite* is an organism that lives off another; here Krikorian uses the word figuratively to cast immigrants, in the conception of the pundit he's imagining, as leeches living off the hard work of Americans.

Discussing Main Point and Meaning

1. Krikorian is saying that this labor, performed by unskilled workers, is not especially valuable because it's easy to find and commands less money than highly skilled labor.

2. A *miasma* is a deeply unpleasant situation—here Krikorian is referring to the fact that undocumented immigrants must openly break the law in order to survive in American society.

Examining Sentences, Paragraphs, and Organization

1. The essay thrives on a contrast between European immigrants from previous generations, who endured a degree of self-selection and whose labor was uniquely valuable at the time, and immigrants today, whose labor is less valuable and whose conditions of entry to the country obviate the "pluck" inculcated in their forebears.

2. This short paragraph delivers the major thematic punch of the essay: that immigrants do not provide the kind of general utility critics like Jacoby believe they do. Have students observe the rhetorical technique of building up evidence in longer paragraphs and then summarizing the conclusion in a one-sentence paragraph.

Thinking Critically

1. Jacoby's statistics suggest that immigrants take advantage of public welfare programs far less than do Krikorian's. Students may note that Jacoby only argues that illegal immigrants are not eligible for welfare, whereas Krikorian may be accounting for cases of welfare fraud.

2. Krikorian pictures the countries from which the immigrant population is drawn—namely those of Central America—as being without industrial mechanization and the attendant modern social advancement of the United States. Some students may argue this characterization represents a severe exaggeration, and that countries like Mexico are in fact quite advanced industrially and socially. All students should recognize that, because Krikorian's argument rests on the premise that immigrant

labor is not especially useful anymore, the characterization of these societies is central to his point.

In-Class Writing Activities

1. Remind students that Krikorian is writing in a magazine that is con-
    sumed almost entirely by middle-class or richer people. Some students
    might feel that his rhetoric would be different if he were writing with
    immigrants themselves in his audience; he might, for instance, be more
    sensitive to the difficulty and peril of the sorts of jobs they do. Have
    students discuss as a group whether it's possible to bring people into the
    dialogue —immigrants, the urban poor, etc.—who are central to it but
    often alienated from it.

2. Break students into teams for a lively debate on this interesting topic.
    Have them identify the cruces of the debate between Jacoby and Kriko-
    rian: whether the immigrant experience hardens and winnows people so
    that only the hardest working are left; whether immigrants in fact do
    work harder than native-born Americans; whether their work is valuable
    because Americans won't do it or relatively cheap because it's so easy to
    replace workers; and whether it's good and right for us to rely on this
    hard work to pick our crops and build our cities while immigrants them-
    selves often live in poverty. Encourage them to come up with other main
    points in their argument.

Vicente Martinez

The Crossing

[*Oregon Humanities,* Fall/Winter 2009]

Vocabulary/Using a Dictionary

1. The word *isolated* comes from the Latin *isola*, meaning "an island";
    isolated means not connected to other people or things, as an island is
    unconnected to a continent.

2. *Seep* is a verb from Old English *sipian*, meaning "to leak slowly through
    small openings." It is almost always used to describe liquids.

3. *Hypothermia* means simply a lack of warmth, from the prefix *hypo-*
    meaning "too little" and *thermia* meaning "heat." It is a medical
    condition, usually caused by exposure to the elements, in which a
    person's body temperature becomes dangerously low.

Responding to Words in Context

1. *Commerce* is the exchange of goods, and the adjective *commercial*
    means relating to that exchange. We're familiar with it from television
    commercial advertisements, but a commercial area is a part of a city or
    town that stands in contrast to a residential one.

2. *Terrain* refers to the topography, or the physical features, of a stretch of
    land.

3. The *shoulder* of a highway is the lane on either side of it usually reserved for broken-down cars.

Discussing Main Point and Meaning

1. Martinez is older than the typical migrant and slightly frailer; he also has HIV, which makes him weaker yet and also means he has to carry his medication with him.

2. The coyotes are vicious, motivated by profit more than altruism at every turn, and they treat the migrants terribly. One example of many is that they force their human cargo to take off their shoes when they go to the bathroom to discourage them from escaping.

3. The coyotes cover Martinez's head with a blanket to keep him from knowing, he suspects, exactly where they live. This detail reinforces the cruelty and inhumanity of the entire process, and particularly of the coyotes.

Examining Sentences, Paragraphs, and Organization

1. Martinez intends to put his reader directly into the scene visually and objectively. The descriptions of the terrain are a crucial aspect of this objectivity, both painting us a vivid portrait of the crossing—particularly its harsh landscape and brutal temperatures—and stirring sympathy for a man who had to undertake it, whatever our feelings about the legality of the situation.

2. The unbroken, objective narrative is a major facet of this essay's central style, and a reason the essay is so effective. Rather than considering the morality of immigration, the INS, or anything else, Martinez shows us the crossing exactly as he experienced it, and leaves it to us to decide what to make of it. This is a good strategy for an essay on a controversial topic.

Thinking Critically

1. "Undocumented worker" has far less negative connotations than does "illegal immigrant," which implies that the individual him- or herself is illegal. The first term also stresses the work the immigrants do, in contrast with the stereotype of these migrants as lazy drains on the system. Students are likely to divide on which term is more accurate and better roughly along the lines of their feelings on immigration and immigration reform.

2. The scene with the INS checkpoint strongly implies that the system is ineffective as well as unfair—some minor choreography gets Martinez past the checkpoint easily. But Martinez suggests that the checkpoint relies on racial profiling to catch illegal immigrants, checking cars not for papers but for Mexicans.

3. The community is close, tight-knit, and mutually supportive, paying coyotes, hosting big dinners, and generally doing what it can to assure

the survival and comfort, such as it is, of its members. Some students might be surprised to find this contrast to occasional stereotypes of migrant communities as especially competitive, dog-eat-dog populations.

In-Class Writing Activities

1. Martinez's writing style is extremely plain, rarely internalizing, and describing what he's seen and heard as objectively as possible. Most of the scenes in the narrative are especially effective because of this objectivity in making us experience what he went through. For instance, in the scene where the guide scans the horizon, Martinez gives us a few guesses of what he's looking for, but doesn't tell us for sure, because he doesn't know. We feel the uncertainty and confusion that accompanies Martinez's journey far more viscerally here than had he simply and explicitly asserted it.

2. Responses will vary widely, but look for them to draw on Martinez's style, focusing on what actually happened—especially the bitter hardships of the journey—rather than the broader implications or meaning of this journey. Remind students of how much this strategy puts us in the place of the actual immigrant, not just a participant in the debate over immigration.

3. This question offers the best opportunity in the unit for a conventional debate on immigration and immigration reform. Have students break into two groups and pick out points from their essays as cruces of contention for an oral debate. Then ask them to describe how reading Martinez's narrative changed, if at all, their thoughts on the issue.

Luis J. Rodríguez

Slurring Spanish

[*The Progressive,* March 2010]

Vocabulary/Using a Dictionary

1. A *curriculum* was originally a race course, but is now generally used to mean the course of education someone undertakes—that is, the requirements for completing a degree or the materials taught within a degree program.

2. *Bi-* means "two." Other examples include *bicolored, binocular, biennial, bisexual,* etc.

3. *Ramifications* is related to the verb *ramify,* which means "to spread or branch out." The word has come to mean the complex set of consequences some thing or action has.

Responding to Words in Context

1. *Multicultural* simply means embracing many (multi-) cultures. Rodríguez definitely uses the word as a general positive—an attitude we need to adopt more universally.

2. *Derailment* means going off a rail, and its literal meaning applies to trains. Rodríguez is using the word metaphorically.

3. Rodríguez means falling victim to drugs, gang violence, or other misfortunes measured by statistics. This construction suggests such a misfortune renders these young victims nothing more than fodder for analysts.

Discussing Main Point and Meaning

1. Rodríguez says that punishing students for speaking their native language, particularly Spanish, makes them feel marginalized and damages their self-esteem.

2. Rodríguez writes that Spanish-speaking students feel alienated from their education as a result of a single-language system.

3. In the penultimate paragraph of the essay, Rodríguez writes that other countries emphasize "the skill of speaking more than one language," and suggests that all students would benefit from the United States following suit.

Examining Sentences, Paragraphs, and Organization

1. The two narratives have a great deal in common, and Rodríguez is certainly inviting the comparison. In both cases, the students—Rodríguez and Zaragoza—were marginalized for being Spanish speakers. By juxtaposing them, Rodríguez is suggesting that things may have gotten a little better (Zaragoza is not "swatted"), but not nearly enough, since Spanish speakers are still treated as second-class students.

2. The paragraphs are 7, 10, 15, and 19. Rodríguez says he wants to "defer to the wisdom" of Zaragoza, but it's also important for his argument that his readers hear about the plight of Spanish-speaking students from one of them, particularly one who is eloquent and passionate; this lends the argument both a personal touch and some rhetorical gravitas.

3. Rodríguez uses *no problema* as a callback to the phrase that nearly got a student suspended. By repeating it in this upbeat context, he robs it of the negative connotations the near-suspension gave both the phrase and the general practice of speaking Spanish in school. By using a phrase we can all decipher and most of us know, he also illustrates how harmless, and even beneficial, bilingualism can be.

Thinking Critically

1. Students should have a sense of the larger implications of the argument —to what degree English should be treated as an "official" language, and what the implications of that question are for Spanish speakers. Many students are likely to sympathize with foreigners, often poor ones, who are having a hard enough time adapting to life in America without being forced to learn English immediately. Others will make the more pragmatic argument that government (and government services

like public schools) can not run efficiently in multiple languages, and including Spanish means by necessity including every other language as well.

2. Rodríguez mentions his many publications, an impressive feat even for a native English speaker. Ask students to consider how they would gauge their own success if they were forced to live in a country whose language they didn't speak at first. What could they expect to achieve as expatriates, and what do they think is a reasonable goal? With so many Spanish speakers in America, what sorts of standards should we have as a society for their success?

3. One example is Belgium, in which Dutch and French are spoken almost evenly. Canada, in which French is a minority language but appears on all official documents, may also be a familiar example. Both of these countries, of course, harbored speakers of each language before achieving nationhood, while America was principally English speaking through most of its early history. Challenge students to consider whether this really matters. What would it take to make America more like its multilingual peers in the world community?

In-Class Writing Activities

1. Three major arguments against bilingual education are: 1) it keeps Spanish-speaking students from learning English, an essential skill for their success in America; 2) it creates confusion and slows down education for students of all languages; and 3) it is impractical when students may come from countries where a language other than English or Spanish is spoken. Rodríguez would likely answer: 1) Spanish-speaking students will learn English from immersion in America; 2) exposing English speakers to Spanish will actually assure far more bilingual young people, which is good for everyone; 3) practical limits will of course have to be applied, but more exposure to foreign cultures and languages is never a bad thing.

2. When students are finished with this exercise, ask them to evaluate what could have made the difference in making their traits advantages. Were they burdened by them because of their own failures to exercise their potential? By other people's prejudices? Some combination of the two?

3. Students defending English-only laws will likely argue for them as a practical measure—to make things easier at the DMV or in school. The argument against them is typically more philosophical, focusing on giving people the right to live in a society that is not automatically hostile to their way of communicating. Conversely, challenge students to think of the philosophical reasons for having a single language in a country—and the pragmatic advantages of multilingualism.

Elyse Toplin (student essay)

Uniting Families

[*The Hullabaloo,* Tulane University, January 29, 2010]

Vocabulary/Using a Dictionary

1. *Deportation* comes from the prefix *de-* meaning "out of," and the Latin *portare*, meaning "to carry." It means the shipping of something, usually a person, out of a country forcefully.

2. *Homo-* and *hetero-* are Greek prefixes meaning "the same" and "different," respectively. Students should be familiar with the prefixes in the scientific words *homogeneous* (made up of the same material) and *heterogeneous* (made up of different materials).

Responding to Words in Context

1. In the context of law and government, to *introduce* a bill, or proposed law, means to suggest it formally.

2. Toplin is borrowing the phrase from the Declaration of Independence, tying the struggle of gay men and women to that of the struggles to found the country and overcome tyranny.

Discussing Main Point and Meaning

1. Toplin is referring to people who are not really in a relationship with someone pretending to be in one to get him or her citizenship. This is a very common form of fraud for which immigration authorities are constantly on the watch.

2. Toplin lists countries with similar legislation that are considered advanced, developed nations. The long list makes it appear that the United States is truly behind the times and maybe even backwards in its failure to recognize gay couples.

Examining Sentences, Paragraphs, and Organization

1. The first paragraph of the essay lays out a general legal problem theoretically, while the second transitions into a personal, anecdotal example with "Meet Gordon Stewart." Toplin is challenging us with this transition to see the problem of gay couples' citizenship rights not as a vague and hypothetical one, but through the lens of an actual individual struggling to secure his rights.

2. See the answer to Thinking Critically question 2 below—Toplin is characterizing the couple as normal, productive, and unthreatening to the basic American values of family and community.

3. Toplin brings up the fraud counterargument in paragraph 7, but responds cogently by arguing that the problem of defrauding immigration authorities is not a gay or straight one. The paragraph is important, however,

because anticipating one of her opponents' strongest and no doubt most popular arguments gives Toplin an edge and makes her entire essay read as more thoughtful and meticulous.

Thinking Critically

1. The arguments for extending citizenship are chiefly of convenience and encouraging the family unit—giving committed families in which one partner is from overseas the comfort and civil rights that domestically born couples have. The arguments against it are that it is easy to defraud, especially as relationships become more diaphanous, and that it admits lots of new citizens with access to our services. Some students may argue that the best way to control the number of citizens as entitlements increase is to continue to restrict new entrants, even those married to citizens. Indeed, some countries, like Kuwait, take this hard line on citizenship.

2. Toplin characterizes the couples as happy, functional, good citizens—carefully drawing her readers away from the ugly stereotypes of gay people that sometimes pervade the media and our national consciousness. She writes of Tan and Mercado, for instance, that "the family goes to church, the parents are involved in the school, and the kids get good grades." She also stresses that the couples are "tax-paying" and "law-abiding." This picture resembles our standard notion of a happy, productive family, and suggests that gay couples look only to expand this institution, not to corrupt it.

3. Toplin puts aside the well-worn argument over gay marriage and argues only for a modest, basic extension of rights. She lists other countries in which similar recognition already exists, but not all of these countries allow gay marriage. Her argument does not presume gay marriage should be legal, but students should recognize that reactions to Toplin's argument are likely to fall along the same lines as general feelings about gay rights, especially the right to marry.

In-Class Writing Activities

1. Students might guess correctly that immigration authorities must constantly struggle to tell phony relationships arranged for one partner to get a green card apart from sincere, committed ones, and that this is true of heterosexual as well as gay couples. It becomes even more of a problem, in fact, as the nature and variety of relationships change. Ask students to think up solutions that respect the different ways people show commitment but still reduces fraud and makes sure citizenship is extended neither too liberally nor too stingily.

2. Responses will vary widely, but look for recommendations that stress the importance of immigrants to the American workforce but also recognize the need to keep borders secure and reward legal immigration. Encourage students who are drawing a blank to look at both major parties' platforms on immigration, available on their Web sites.

Ira Berlin

Migrations Forced and Free

[*Smithsonian*, February 2010]

Vocabulary/Using a Dictionary

1. An *ideal* is an imaginary state of perfection, and *idealism* is the philosophical disposition that such a state is at least partially achievable. It is usually accompanied by political activity its practitioners believe will help make the world a better place. *Abolitionist idealism*, in turn, casts the efforts of the men and women who worked to abolish slavery in nineteenth-century America as striving for a more perfect future despite the opposition not only of slavery proponents but of cynics.

2. See the answer to In-Class Writing Activity question 2 below: "Collective consciousness" was a term coined by French sociologist Émile Durkheim to refer to the shared ideas and perceptions of a certain group that operate as a force in society.

3. *Disfranchisement* means the loss of an important civil right, especially the right to vote. One's *franchise* is often used to mean one's voting rights.

Responding to Words in Context

1. *Authorship* means being the creator of something, by analogy to writing it. Here Berlin means that the slaves did the work to create their own freedom.

2. Berlin uses *knot*, which here means a heavily congested crowd, to suggest visually a group of people huddled closely together.

3. *Rooted* means "coming from," as a tree comes out of its roots, but the word has further implications and significance here because of the context of our ancestry (or "roots").

Discussing Main Point and Meaning

1. A migration is a movement, particularly of a large group of people—like an ethnic group—from one geographical location to another. The "forced" migration in Berlin's title refers to the triangle trade and slavery; the Africans and Caribbean Americans who have come since slavery, Berlin implies, have had a relatively more "free" migratory experience.

2. Berlin is referring to slavery, and the ensuing segregation and discrimination particular to the Southern United States. Other black people, including those from the Caribbean, have no doubt faced adversity, but they tend not to share in this special history, according to Berlin.

3. Berlin was impressed by how little notionally "black" people understood about the heritage of slavery and discrimination when that her-

itage was not directly linked to their own. He suggests the conversation weighed on his mind so much partially because it occurred in the context of a discussion about the importance of black people in securing their own rights and future. But it led him to consider how important an understanding of one's own ancestral struggles is in confronting the struggles of the future.

Examining Sentences, Paragraphs, and Organization

1. The examples Berlin offers come from a wide variety of ethnic groups, not just blacks; this variety attempts to illustrate how important the celebration of ethnic identity is to all people everywhere.

2. Berlin begins with an anecdote that will illuminate his ultimate expositional point—that history is particularly important to African Americans who were "long denied a past." The anecdote is especially effective because the point is complicated, and best understood by witnessing people from outside the group whose cohesion Berlin is interested in discussing. After this anecdote, Berlin moves through a short history of African Americans and immigration, and how the two are related. He shows the transformation of Black America, giving a truncated history that supports his eventual argument, which he leaves the reader with in the final paragraph. Many students may find that this is an effective method, since he brings the reader into the article with an anecdote, provides ample support for his argument, and then leaves the reader with his final statement, that, as he puts it, "African-American history is, in the end, of one piece" (para. 18).

Thinking Critically

1. This question relies on a basic outline of the history of the Civil War—make sure to give some rudimentary background. Students should recognize the view that slaves were helpless in the physical battle over their emancipation, which was largely fought by white soldiers. Some may argue, however, that there were a number of well-known African American units in the Civil War, which played an outsize role in defeating the institution of slavery. Others might argue, as Berlin probably did on the radio show, that undergoing the horrible cruelty and oppression of slavery, and responding eloquently and peacefully through ambassadors like Frederick Douglass, hastened the end of the institution.

2. Some students will argue that *black* refers only to a color, whether the black person is from Africa, the Americas, or elsewhere. The other extreme view is that the descendants of African slaves are the only real "black" people in America. Ask students to think carefully about counterexamples. Are recent arrivals with dark skin, like the ones Berlin describes, who do not have the cultural memory of the legacy of slavery and discrimination other black people harbor, really part of the same racial equation? On the other hand, isn't a descendant of a recent African immigrant (like, say, Barack Obama) black?

3. Students will likely divide on celebrations like Black History Month—some seeing a ceremonial connection to heritage as an important part of that heritage in a diverse society, and others seeing these celebrations as divisive, arguing that America should celebrate only America. Prompt those advocating a more "race-blind" model to consider large-scale celebrations of their own legacy and tradition, and not only other groups'. Ask those who take the side of such celebrations, on the other hand, to acknowledge ways outsiders might feel alienated by them, and suggest ways of reconciling this feeling.

In-Class Writing Activities

1. Look for students to write not only about the larger group they come from (African, European, etc.) but the smaller subgroups and the specifics of their heritage as they've had it articulated to them. Ask them to consider not only how the vicissitudes of their origin stories have come to define them and the way they think about the world, but whether they feel connected to other people with similar origin stories today.

2. The "collective consciousness," especially as Berlin uses it, refers to the common ideas and principles that underlie the thinking of a group—whether everyone in society or, as used here, a particular ethnic group—such that it appears the group is almost of one mind. Point out that the term comes from sociology—it was coined by Émile Durkheim—but that Berlin is using it here as a measure of shared ideology. Students should divide in their writing between those who argue that individuals within a group, especially a group as large as "black people in mainland North America," are too unique and distinct to share such a consciousness, and those who believe that such a construct is useful or even accurate in describing the way people in groups think and draw their thinking from each other.

Discussing the Unit

Suggested Topic for Discussion

This unit requires students to consider a variety of perspectives on the border. Have them begin by thinking of what the border means—to an undocumented immigrant like Martinez, to an English-speaking activist like Rodríguez, and to Americans like Jacoby and Krikorian. What is the border, and what does it separate—physically as well as figuratively?

Preparing for Class Discussion

1. The twin cruces of the debate in this chapter are 1) how much immigrants add to or subtract from the lives of native-born Americans, and 2) what is the fairest and most humane way to treat recent arrivals. Jacoby and Krikorian, as well as Rodríguez to an extent, are preoccupied with the first question. Ask students which question is more important.

Can we, and should we, rightfully exclude people from our society even if we can say for sure they don't add economic value? Conversely, would a student who opposes immigration on philosophical grounds exclude immigrants even if it could be shown for sure that they do?

2. Conservatives tend to believe that the federal government should be weak—except in matters of the military and border protection. Notice that liberals and conservatives make a similar switch when it comes to international wars: Traditional defenders of smaller government often advocate for more spending on war in Iraq and Afghanistan. Discuss the origin of this apparent contradiction with students: Is it cultural, geographical, or does it not imply an actual contradiction at all?

From Discussion to Writing

1. All of the first four essays in this chapter advance, in some way, an image of a "typical" immigrant. Students should elaborate on those images where they're not as clear. Where is the immigrant from, and what is his or her family and work life like? How do these images relate to the conclusions the authors draw, or imply, about what we should do about our borders as a society? Compare the pictures of immigrants in Jacoby and Krikorian especially. As for the possible racism of such an image, consider with students whether a reductive picture of a member of a particular group can ever be useful in discussing that group as a whole. Think of other examples from outside this debate—of Native Americans, women, or "Wall Street bankers" to give a few examples.

2. Look for policies that address the central problems of the immigration debate: How can we be fair and humane to people trying to achieve a better life without overcrowding the country or diminishing the rule of law? Look for students to use Martinez's testimony about the actual event of crossing the border illegally, Jacoby's and Krikorian's agreement that immigrants come to the country for good, understandable reasons, or (perhaps on the other side of the debate) Toplin's description of the kinds of people waiting for legal citizenship, as evidence.

Topics for Cross-Cultural Discussion

1. Latin American immigrants are rarely claimed to be a threat to national security, but the 9/11 hijackers—some of whom came into the United States illegally through Canada—raise more immediate concerns on that front. Would students who could not stomach racial profiling of the kind Martinez and Ramírez describe perhaps condone it if lives were at stake? Should our immigration policy, in general, stress economic or security concerns, and how can the two be balanced?

2. Students will bring a number of examples to the table, but Western European countries like France and the Netherlands have seen the most acrimonious immigration debates in recent times. Isolate and identify the reasons: To give a few, these countries have traditionally had largely homogeneous populations where ethnic identity was a part of citizenship;

they are also especially secular societies, where very religious, and even fundamentalist, immigrants from the Middle East are seen as a particular threat to the culture and way of life.